Dedication

To Cliff Colby,
the Comma King

Thanks!

To Cliff Colby, for providing lots of guidance during the preparation of this sixth edition of my Mac OS VQS. Cliff helped me decide what topics should remain in this *Mac OS X: Visual QuickStart Guide* and which ones should be set aside for my upcoming *Mac OS X: Visual QuickPro Guide* for "power users." He churned through chapters quickly and remained remarkably calm throughout. This time, however, I think he removed all the commas he added for the previous edition. (I'm still trying to figure out Cliff's comma logic.)

To Victor Gavenda, for his technical editing skill. Victor pointed out a few different things about Mac OS X that I hadn't noticed and helped me figure out some of the undocumented features that were driving me bonkers.

To Nancy Ruenzel, Marjorie Baer, and the other powers-that-be at Peachpit Press, for continuing to put up with me, despite ever-more-frequent whining.

To Connie Jeung-Mills, for her sharp eyes and gentle layout editing. We make a great team!

To the rest of the folks at Peachpit Press—especially Gary-Paul, Mimi, Trish, Hannah, Paula, Zigi, Jimbo, and Keasley—for doing what they do so well. And an extra thanks to Gary-Paul, for designing a great new logo for me (see below).

To Apple Computer, Inc., for reinventing the world's best operating system.

And to Mike, for the usual reasons.

The Flying M

http://www.marialanger.com/

TABLE OF CONTENTS

Introduction to Mac OS X ix
Introduction ix
New Features in Mac OS X x

Chapter 1:   **Setting Up Mac OS X** 1
Setting Up Mac OS X 1
The Mac OS 9.1 Installer 2
Restarting Your Computer 7
The Mac OS Setup Assistant 8
The Mac OS X Installer 14

Chapter 2:   **Finder Basics** 25
The Finder & Desktop 25
The Mouse 26
Menus 28
The Keyboard 30
Icons 32
Windows 37
The Toolbar 43
The Dock 44
Sleeping, Restarting, & Shutting Down 45

Chapter 3:   **File Management** 49
File Management 49
Mac OS X Disk Organization 50
Pathnames 52
The Go Menu 53
Views 54
Cleaning Up & Arranging Icons 59
List Views 60

Icon Names 62

Folders 63

Moving & Copying Items 64

The Trash & Deleting Items 68

Storage Media 70

Mounting Disks 71

Ejecting Disks 72

Chapter 4:   **Advanced Finder Techniques** **73**

Advanced Finder Techniques 73

Finder Preferences 74

Customizing the Toolbar 76

Customizing the Dock 78

Outlines in List View 79

Aliases 80

Favorites 82

Recent Items 84

The Info Window 85

Chapter 5:   **Application Basics** **89**

Applications 89

Mac OS X Applications vs. Classic Applications 90

Multitasking & the Dock 91

Using Applications & Creating Documents 92

Standard Application Menus 94

The Application Menu 94

The File Menu 97

The Edit Menu 103

The Window Menu 104

The Help Menu 106

Dialogs 107

Using Classic Applications 110

Chapter 6:   **Using Mac OS Software** **115**

Mac OS Software 115

Address Book 117

Calculator 120

Chess 121

Clock 122

Preview 123

QuickTime Player *124*
Stickies *127*
Key Caps *130*

Chapter 7:   **Using TextEdit** **131**
TextEdit *131*
Launching & Quitting TextEdit *132*
Entering & Editing Text *134*
Basic Text Formatting *138*
Undoing & Redoing Actions *141*
Copy, Cut, & Paste *142*
Find & Replace *143*
Checking Spelling *145*
Saving & Opening Document Files *146*

Chapter 8:   **Printing** **149**
Printing *149*
Printer Drivers *150*
Print Center *151*
The Page Setup Dialog *154*
The Print Dialog *155*
Print Queues *162*
Troubleshooting Printing Problems *164*

Chapter 9:   **Connecting to the Internet** **165**
Connecting to the Internet *165*
TCP/IP, PPP, & Internet Connect *166*
Manually Setting Internet Configuration Options *167*
Network Preferences *168*
Internet Preferences *173*
Connecting to an ISP *176*
Internet Applications *177*
Mail *178*
Internet Explorer *181*

Chapter 10:   **Using Sherlock** **183**
Sherlock *183*
Channels *184*
Finding Files *185*
Searching the Internet *193*

Searching for People 195
Shopping Online 196
Saving Searches 197
Customizing Sherlock 198

Chapter 11: **Setting System Preferences** **201**
System Preferences 201
Date & Time 203
Dock 206
Energy Saver 207
General 208
Keyboard 209
Mouse 210
Screen Saver 211
Sound 213
Fonts 214

Chapter 12: **Getting Help** **215**
Getting Help 215
Help Tags 216
Apple Help 217
Application Help 220
Help & Troubleshooting Advice 221

Appendix A: **Menus & Keyboard Equivalents** **223**
Menus & Keyboard Equivalents 223

Appendix B: **Apple's Internet Tools** **227**
Internet Tools 227
iTools 228
iTunes 231
Apple's Tech Info Library 236

Index **237**

INTRODUCTION TO MAC OS X

Figure 1 The About This Mac window for Mac OS X.

Introduction

Mac OS X ("X" is pronounced "ten"; **Figure 1**) is the latest version of the computer operating system that put the phrase *graphic user interface* in everyone's vocabulary. With Mac OS, you can point, click, and drag to work with files, applications, and utilities. Because the same intuitive interface is utilized throughout the system, you'll find that a procedure that works in one program works in virtually all the others.

This Visual QuickStart Guide will help you learn Mac OS X by providing step-by-step instructions, plenty of illustrations, and a generous helping of tips. On these pages, you'll find everything you need to know to get up and running quickly with Mac OS X—and more!

This book was designed for page flipping. Use the thumb tabs, index, or table of contents to find the topics for which you need help. If you're brand new to Mac OS, however, I recommend that you begin by reading at least the first two chapters. In them, you'll find basic information about techniques you'll use every day with your computer.

If you're interested in information about new Mac OS X features, be sure to browse through this **Introduction**. It'll give you a good idea of what you can expect to see on your computer.

New Features in Mac OS X

Mac OS X is a major revision to the Macintosh operating system. Not only does it add and update features, but in many cases, it completely changes the way tasks are done. With a slick new look called "Aqua" (**Figure 2**) and with preemptive multitasking and protected memory that make the computer work more quickly and reliably, Mac OS X is like a breath of fresh air for Macintosh users.

Here's a look at some of the new and revised features you can expect to find in Mac OS X.

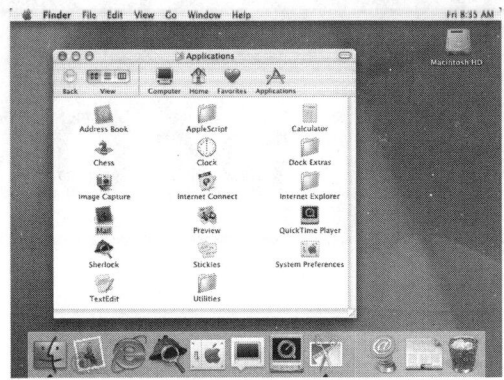

Figure 2 A look at the new Aqua interface.

✔ Tip

■ Many of these features are covered in this book. Others are covered in this book's sequel, *Mac OS X: Visual QuickPro Guide*.

Installer Changes

◆ The Mac OS X installer automatically launches when you start from the Mac OS X install CD.

◆ The installer offers fewer customization features for installation.

◆ The Mac OS X Setup Assistant, which runs automatically after the installer restarts the computer, has a new look and offers several new options.

System Changes

◆ System extensions and control panels no longer exist.

◆ By default, Mac OS X is set up for multiple users, making it possible for several people to set up personalized work environments on the same computer without the danger of accessing, changing, or deleting another user's files.

◆ A new Log Out command enables you to end your work session without shutting down the computer.

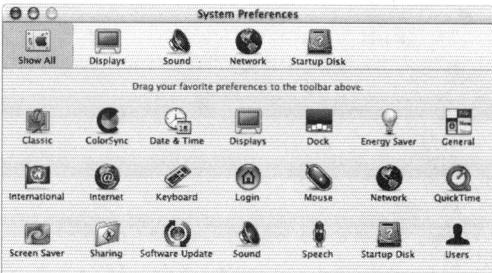

Figure 3 The new System Preferences application enables you to set many systemwide options.

Figure 4 A window in column view.

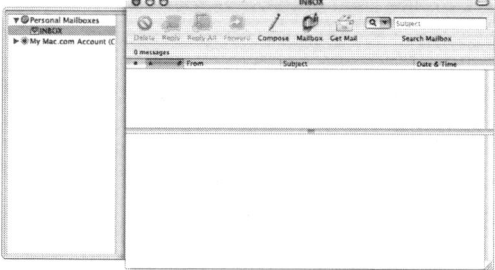

Figure 5 The new Mail application utilizes the drawer interface.

◆ A new System Preferences application (**Figure 3**) enables you to set options for the way the computer works.

◆ The default system font has been changed to Lucida Grande.

◆ Finder icons have a new "photo-illustrative" look (**Figure 2**).

◆ A new, customizable Dock (**Figure 2**) enables you to launch and switch to applications.

◆ Icons for applications in the Dock can have a different appearance when the application is running or performing a specific task.

Window Changes

◆ Finder windows offer a new column view (**Figure 4**). Button view is no longer available.

◆ Pop-up windows and spring-loaded folders are no longer supported.

◆ Window controls have been changed (**Figure 4**). The left end of a window's title bar now includes Close, Minimize, and Zoom buttons.

◆ *Drawers* (**Figure 5**) are subwindows that slide out the side of a window to offer more options.

◆ Document windows for different applications each reside on their own layer, making it possible for them to be intermingled. (This differs from previous versions of Mac OS which required all document windows for an application to be grouped together.)

◆ You can often activate items on an inactive window or dialog with a single click rather than clicking first to activate the window, then clicking again to activate the item.

NEW FEATURES IN MAC OS X

Menu Changes

◆ Menus are now translucent so you can see underlying windows right through them.

◆ Sticky menus no longer disappear after a certain amount of time. When you click a menu's title, the menu appears and stays visible until you either click a command or click elsewhere onscreen.

◆ The Apple menu, which is no longer customizable, includes commands that work in all applications (**Figure 6**).

◆ A number of commands have been moved to the revised Apple menu (**Figure 6**) and new Finder menu (**Figure 7**). There are also new commands and new keyboard equivalents throughout the Finder.

◆ A new Go menu (**Figure 8**) makes it quick and easy to open windows for specific locations, including favorite and recent folders.

Dialog Changes

◆ Dialogs can now appear as *sheets* that slide down from a window's title bar and remain part of the window (**Figure 9**). You can switch to another document or application when a dialog sheet is displayed.

◆ The Open and Save Location dialogs have been revised.

◆ The Save Location dialog can appear either collapsed (**Figure 10**) or expanded (**Figure 11**).

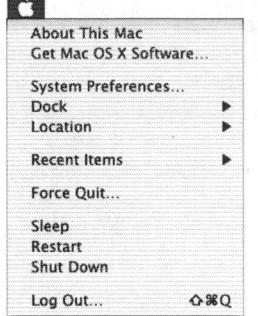

Figure 6
The revised
Apple menu.

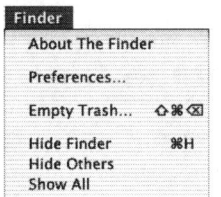

Figure 7
The new Finder
application menu.

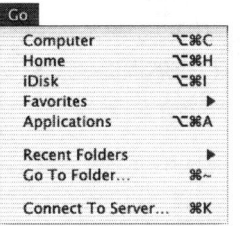

Figure 8
The new
Go menu.

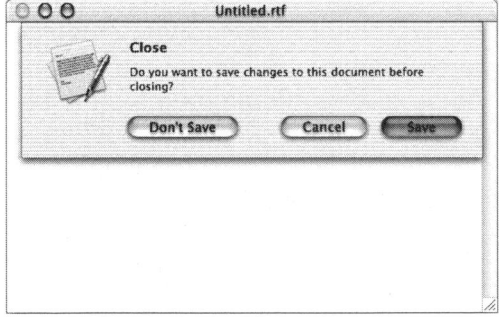

Figure 9 A dialog sheet is attached to a window.

Figure 10 The Save Location dialog box collapsed to show only the bare essentials...

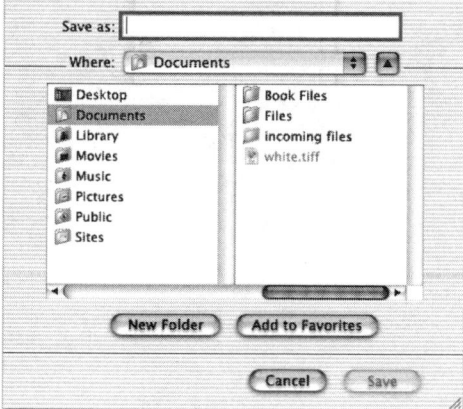

Figure 11 ...and expanded to show everything you need to save a file.

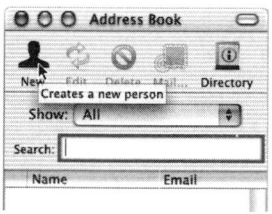

Figure 12
Help Tags replace Balloon Help.

Application Changes

◆ Applications that are not Mac OS X compatible run in the *Classic environment*, which utilizes Mac OS 9.1

◆ The list of applications and utilities that come with Mac OS has undergone extensive changes to add and remove many programs.

Help Changes

◆ Balloon Help has been replaced with Help Tags (**Figure 12**).

◆ The Help Viewer offers more options for searching and following links.

◆ Guide Help is no longer available.

NEW FEATURES IN MAC OS X

SETTING UP MAC OS X

Setting Up Mac OS X

Before you can use Mac OS X, you must install it on your computer and configure it to work the way you need it to. The steps you need to complete to do this depend on the software currently installed in your computer.

1. If Mac OS 9.0.4 or earlier is installed on your computer, use the Mac OS 9.1 installer to update to Mac OS 9.1. Then:

   ▲ Restart your computer.

   ▲ Use the Mac OS Setup Assistant to configure Mac OS 9.1.

2. Use the Mac OS X installer to install Mac OS X. Then:

   ▲ Restart your computer.

   ▲ Use the Mac OS Setup Assistant to configure Mac OS X.

This chapter explains how to complete all of these steps, so you can properly install and configure Mac OS X and the Classic environment on your computer.

✔ Tips

■ If Mac OS 9.1 is already installed on your computer, you can skip the first step and go right to the Mac OS X installation and configuration process.

■ Mac OS 9.1 is required to run Classic environment applications, so you'll install that first. The Classic environment is discussed in **Chapter 5**.

The Mac OS 9.1 Installer

Mac OS 9.1 comes with an installer application that makes software installation easy. Simply launch the installer and follow the instructions that appear on screen to select a destination disk, learn more about the software, agree to a license agreement, and select the Mac OS 9.1 components you want installed. The installer builds the System and Finder files for your computer and copies the software you specified to your hard disk.

The Mac OS 9.1 installer can perform two types of installations:

◆ **Standard Installation** lets you select the Mac OS 9.1 components you want installed. The installer copies all standard parts of each selected component to your hard disk.

◆ **Customized Installation** lets you select the Mac OS 9.1 components you want installed and then lets you select the individual parts of each component to be installed.

The first part of this chapter explains how to use the Mac OS 9.1 installer to perform both a standard and a customized installation.

✔ Tips

■ The installation instructions in this chapter assume you know basic Mac OS techniques, such as pointing, clicking, double-clicking, dragging, and selecting items from a menu. If you're brand new to the Mac and don't know any of these techniques, skip ahead to **Chapter 2**, which discusses Mac OS basics.

■ A standard installation of Mac OS 9.1 includes the following components: Mac OS 9.1, Internet Access, Remote Access, Personal Web Sharing, Text-to-Speech, Mac OS Runtime for Java, ColorSync, and English Speech Recognition.

Figure 1 To launch the Mac OS 9.1 installer, double-click this icon.

Figure 2 The Mac OS 9.1 installer's Welcome window appears when you launch it.

■ You can click the Go Back button at any time during installation to change options in a previous window.

■ You can press (Return) or (Enter) to "click" a default button—a button with a dark border around it—such as the Continue button in **Figure 2**.

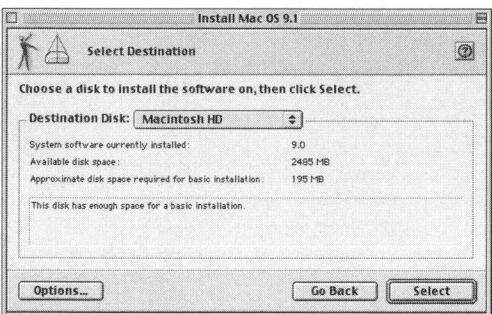

Figure 3 Use the Select Destination window to select the disk on which to install Mac OS 9.1.

Figure 4 Choose a disk from the Destination Disk pop-up menu.

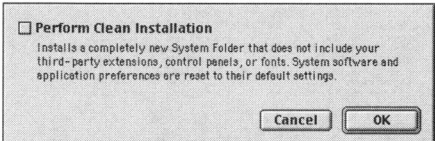

Figure 5 Turn on the Perform Clean Installation check box to create a brand new System Folder for Mac OS 9.1.

✔ Tips

■ Only those hard disks and removable high-capacity media (such as Zip and Jaz disks) that appear on your Desktop are listed in the Destination Disk pop-up menu (**Figure 4**).

■ A status area beneath the Destination Disk pop-up menu indicates the version of Mac OS that is installed on the disk, as well as the available disk space and the amount of disk space required for a basic installation (**Figure 3**).

To launch the installer

1. Start your computer from the Mac OS 9.1 CD-ROM disc.

or

Start your computer the usual way and insert the Mac OS 9.1 CD-ROM disc.

2. Locate and double-click the Mac OS Install icon (**Figure 1**).

3. After a moment, the installer's Welcome window appears (**Figure 2**). Click Continue.

✔ Tip

■ To start your computer from the Mac OS 9.1 CD-ROM disc, insert the disc, choose Special > Restart, and hold down [C] until the "Welcome to Mac OS" message appears. This is the recommended way to start your computer when installing OS software.

To select a destination disk

1. In the installer's Select Destination window (**Figure 3**), use the Destination Disk pop-up menu (**Figure 4**) to select the disk on which you want to install Mac OS 9.1.

2. Click Select.

■ To create a brand new System Folder for Mac OS 9.1, click the Options button. Turn on the Perform Clean Installation check box in the dialog that appears (**Figure 5**). The old System Folder is renamed "Previous System Folder," and you should delete it after you move non-Apple control panels, extensions, and preferences files to their proper locations in the new System Folder.

SELECTING A DESTINATION DISK

To read important information about Mac OS 9.1

1. Read the contents of the installer's Important Information window (**Figure 6**). Click the down arrow on the vertical scroll bar to scroll through the entire document.

2. When you have finished reading the information, click Continue.

✔ Tip

- Read the information in this window carefully! It provides important, late-breaking news about installing Mac OS, including compatibility information and special instructions not included in this book.

To read and agree to the Software License Agreement

1. If desired, choose a language from the pop-up menu at the top-right of the Software License Agreement window (**Figure 7**).

2. Read the contents of the window. Click the down arrow on the vertical scroll bar to scroll through the entire document.

3. When you have finished reading the agreement, click Continue.

4. A dialog appears, informing you that you must agree to the terms of the agreement you just read to continue (**Figure 8**). Click Agree.

✔ Tip

- If you click Disagree in step 4, the installer returns you to its Welcome window (**Figure 2**).

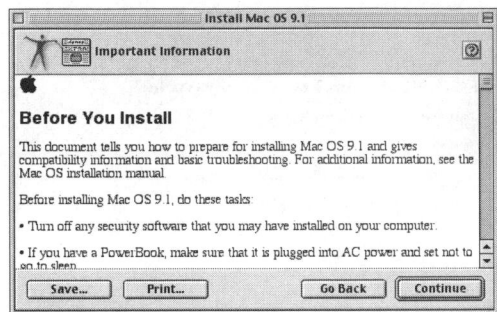

Figure 6 The Important Information window contains late-breaking news about installing Mac OS 9.1.

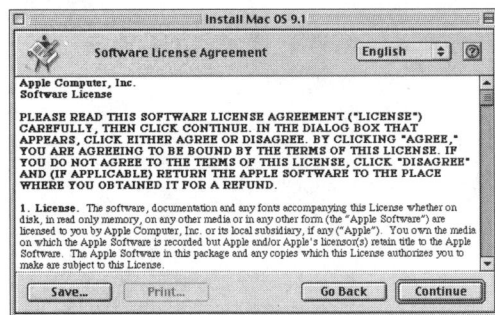

Figure 7 The Software License Agreement tells you exactly what you're allowed to do with Mac OS 9.1 software.

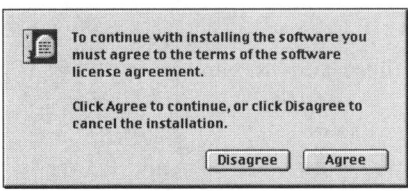

Figure 8 To complete the installation of Mac OS 9.1, you must click Agree in this dialog.

Figure 9 Use the Install Software window to select the Mac OS components you want to install.

Figure 10 Use the Custom Installation and Removal window to select Mac OS 9.1 components for a custom installation.

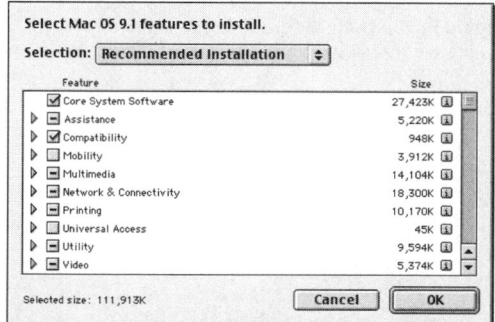

Figure 11 Windows like these enable you to select the parts of a specific component that you want to install.

To customize an installation

1. In the Install Software window (**Figure 9**), click the Customize button. The window changes to the Custom Installation and Removal window (**Figure 10**), which displays a list of software components.

2. Toggle the check box settings to turn on only those for the components you want to install. Be sure to click the down arrow at the bottom of the vertical scroll bar to view all the options.

3. If desired, choose an installation mode from the pop-up menu beside each checked component.

   ▲ **Recommended Installation** installs the recommended parts of the component for your computer.

   ▲ **Customized Installation** displays a dialog similar to the one in **Figure 11**. Use this option to specify which parts of the component should be installed, and click OK.

✔ Tips

- If you change your mind about making a custom installation, click the Don't Customize button (**Figure 10**) to go back to the Install Software window (**Figure 9**).

- To successfully use the Customized Installation option, you must be familiar with all parts of each component you want installed. This is a feature designed for Mac OS experts. If used improperly, it can cause erratic system behavior.

- You can click the triangle to the left of an item (**Figure 11**) to display individual items within it (**Figure 12**).

- You can click the info icon (or "i" button) to the right of an item to learn more about it (**Figure 13**). Click OK to dismiss the information dialog.

To set other installation options

1. Click the Options button in the Install Software or Custom Installation and Removal window to display a dialog like the one in **Figure 14**.

2. To prevent the installer from attempting to update the hard disk driver of the destination disk, turn off the Update Apple Hard Disk Driver check box.

3. To prevent the installer from creating an installation log file, turn off the Create Installation Report check box.

4. Click OK.

✔ Tips

- As shown in **Figure 14**, both of these options are enabled by default. If you're not sure how to set these options, leave them both turned on.

- If you're not sure what to do in step 3, leave the check box turned on. The Mac OS 9.1 installer can only update the driver on an Apple-branded hard disk—one that comes with a Macintosh computer. It cannot affect a hard disk made by another manufacturer. If the installer cannot update your disk's driver, it will display a message saying so and provide additional information about updating your driver.

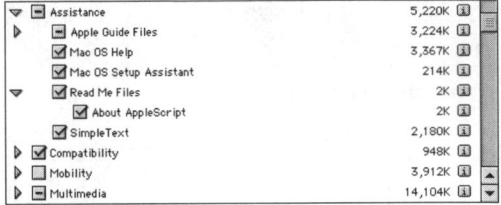

Figure 12 Clicking the triangle to the left of an item displays individual items within it.

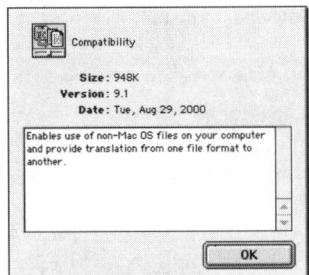

Figure 13 When you click an item's "i" button, a window full of information about the item appears.

Figure 14 You can use this dialog to set two additional installation options.

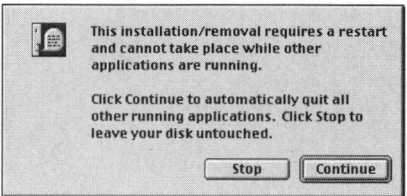

Figure 15 A dialog like this may appear after you click the Start button.

Figure 16 The Mac OS 9.1 installer displays a progress window as it works.

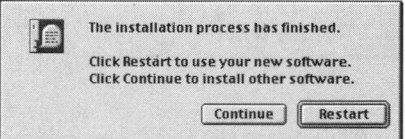

Figure 17 A dialog like this appears when the installation is complete.

Figure 18
To restart your computer, choose Restart from the Special menu.

To complete the installation

1. In the Install Software window (**Figure 9**) or Custom Installation and Removal window (**Figure 10**), click the Start button.

2. A dialog like the one in **Figure 15** may appear, informing you that other applications cannot be running during the install process and that you will have to restart your computer when it's finished. Click Continue.

3. The installer performs some maintenance tasks, then begins installing the software you selected. A progress window like the one in **Figure 16** appears to show you how it's doing.

4. When the installation is complete, a dialog like the one in **Figure 17** appears. Click Restart.

Restarting Your Computer

To configure and use your newly installed Mac OS 9.1 software, you must restart your computer. This loads the new software into the computer's RAM and, if necessary, launches the Mac OS Setup Assistant.

To restart your computer

If you are not prompted to restart your computer at the conclusion of the installation process (**Figure 17**), choose Special > Restart (**Figure 18**).

✔ Tip

- Do not restart your computer by turning off power and then turning it back on! This can cause file corruption.

The Mac OS Setup Assistant

When you restart your computer after installing Mac OS 9.1, the Mac OS Setup Assistant automatically appears (**Figure 19**). This program uses a simple question and answer process to get information about you and the way you use your computer. The information you provide is automatically entered into the appropriate control panels to configure Mac OS 9.1.

✔ Tips

- ■ Your computer may automatically rebuild the Desktop file for attached disks when you restart after installing Mac OS 9.1. If so, a dialog like the one in **Figure 20** appears. Do not stop this process. When it is finished, the dialog will automatically disappear.

- ■ If the Mac OS Setup Assistant does not automatically appear at startup, you can launch it by opening the Mac OS Setup Assistant icon in the Assistants folder on your hard disk.

To use the Mac OS Setup Assistant

1. Read the information in each Mac OS Setup Assistant window. Enter information or make selections when prompted.

2. Click the right arrow button to continue.

   or

   Click the left arrow button to go back and make changes in previous windows.

✔ Tip

- ■ The next few pages explain exactly how to enter information in each window that appears.

Figure 19 The Mac OS Setup Assistant offers an easy way to configure Mac OS 9.1.

Figure 20 When you first start your computer after installing Mac OS 9.1, it may automatically rebuild the invisible Desktop files on attached disks.

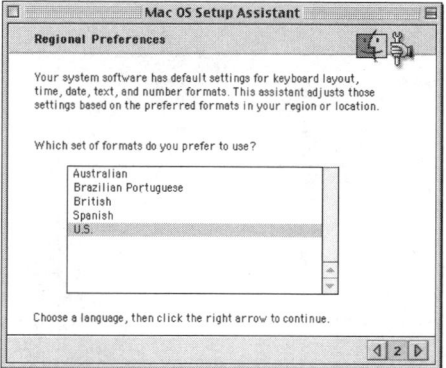

Figure 21 Use the Regional Preferences window to select your language version.

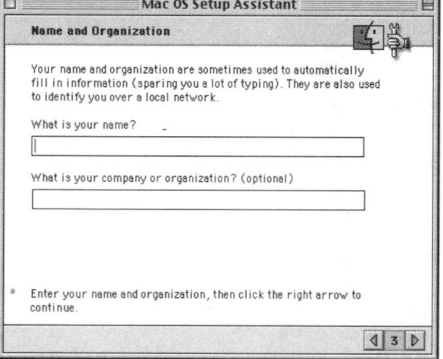

Figure 22 Enter your name and organization in these edit boxes.

To select regional preferences

1. If you haven't already done so, click the right arrow button in the Introduction window of the Mac OS Setup Assistant (**Figure 19**).

2. Read the information in the Regional Preferences window (**Figure 21**) to learn how Mac OS 9.1 uses your language version.

3. Click the language you prefer to select it.

4. Click the right arrow button.

✔ Tip

■ The languages that appear in this dialog will vary depending on the language supported by your copy of Mac OS 9.1.

To enter your name & organization

1. Read the information in the Name and Organization window (**Figure 22**) to learn how Mac OS 9.1 uses your name and company.

2. Enter your name in the What is your name? edit box.

3. Press (Tab) or click in the What is your company or organization? edit box to position the blinking insertion point.

4. Enter the name of your company or organization.

5. Click the right arrow button.

✔ Tip

■ You must enter a name in the What is your name? box. You may, however, leave the What is your company or organization? box empty if desired.

To set the time & date

1. Read the information in the Time and Date window of the Mac OS Setup Assistant (**Figure 23**) to learn how Mac OS 9.1 uses the time and date.

2. If daylight savings time is currently in effect, select the Yes radio button by clicking it.

3. If the time in the What time is it? box is not correct, change it. To do this, click an incorrect number in the time sequence to select it (**Figure 24**) and either type in the correct number or click the up or down arrow button beside the time until the correct number appears.

4. If the date in the What is today's date? box is not correct, change it. To do this, click an incorrect number in the date sequence to select it and either type in the correct number or click the up or down arrow button beside the date until the correct number appears.

5. Click the right arrow button.

✔ Tip

■ The time and date, which are tracked by your computer's internal clock, may already be correct. If so, no changes will be necessary.

To select your geographic location

1. Read the information in the Geographic Location window of the Mac OS Setup Assistant (**Figure 25**) to learn how Mac OS 9.1 uses your location.

2. Click the up or down arrow on the scroll bar until the name of a city in your time zone (preferably near you) appears. Click it once to select it.

3. Click the right arrow button.

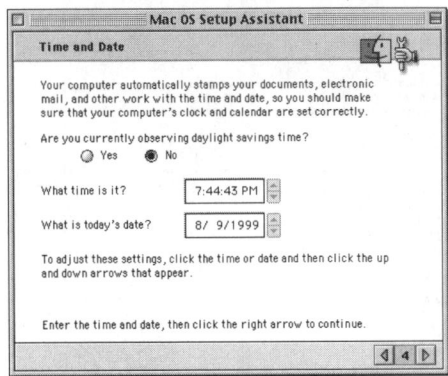

Figure 23 Use the Time and Date window to check and, if necessary, change the time or date.

Figure 24 To change the time (or date), click an incorrect number in the sequence to select it and then click the up or down arrow until the right number appears.

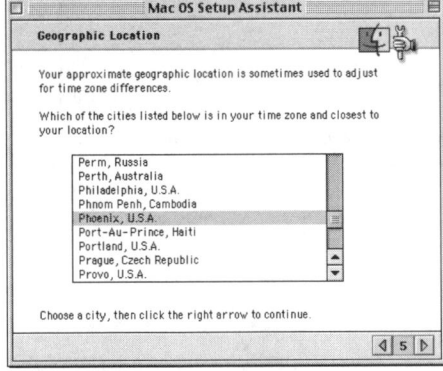

Figure 25 The Geographic Location window lists cities all over the world—including one near you.

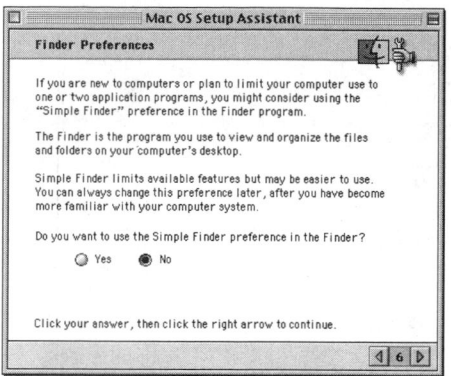

Figure 26 Use the Finder Preferences window to turn Simple Finder on or off.

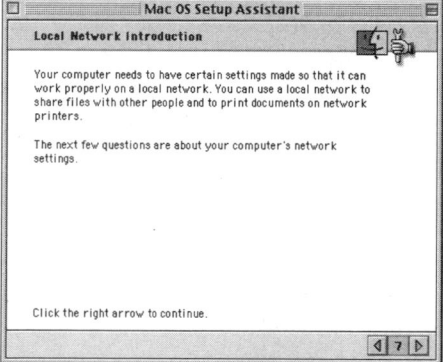

Figure 27 The Local Network Introduction window tells you a little about networks.

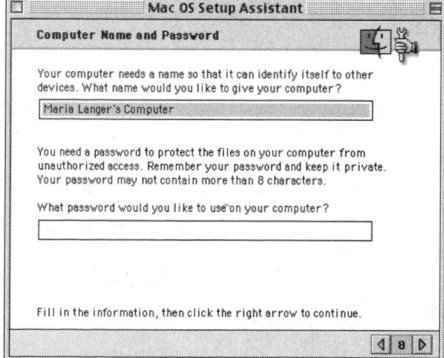

Figure 28 Use this window to enter a name for your computer and a password to protect your files from unauthorized network users.

To set Finder preferences

1. Read the information in the Finder Preferences window of the Mac OS Setup Assistant (**Figure 26**) to learn about the difference between the standard Finder and Simple Finder.

2. If you want fewer menu commands in the Finder, click the Yes radio button to select it.

3. Click the right arrow button.

To set network options

1. Read the information in the Local Network Introduction window of the Mac OS Setup Assistant (**Figure 27**) to learn more about networks.

2. Click the right arrow button.

3. Read the information in the Computer Name and Password window (**Figure 28**) to learn how Mac OS uses your computer's name and password.

4. To change the default name that the Mac OS Setup Assistant has assigned to your computer, type it in the top edit box. (The name should be selected as shown in **Figure 28** so it is not necessary to click in the box first; simply type to overwrite the contents of the edit box.) Then press (Tab) or click in the bottom edit box to position the insertion point there.

   or

   To accept the default name that the Mac OS Setup Assistant has assigned to your computer, just press (Tab) or click in the bottom edit box to position the insertion point there.

5. In the bottom edit box, enter a password you want to use to protect your computer from unauthorized access by other network users.

Continued on next page...

USING THE MAC OS SETUP ASSISTANT

Continued from previous page.

6. Click the right arrow button.

7. Wait while the Mac OS Setup Assistant validates the computer name and password.

8. Read the information in the Shared Folder window (**Figure 29**) to learn what a shared folder is and how it is used.

9. If you do not want a shared folder on the network, select the No radio button by clicking it. Then skip to step 11.

10. To change the default name that the Mac OS Setup Assistant has assigned to your shared folder, type it in the edit box. (The name should be selected as shown in **Figure 29**, so it is not necessary to click in the box first; simply type to overwrite the contents of the box.)

11. Click the right arrow button.

✔ Tips

■ You must go through these steps even if your computer is not connected to a network.

■ You must provide both a name and password for your computer.

Figure 29 Use this window to set up a shared folder—if you want one.

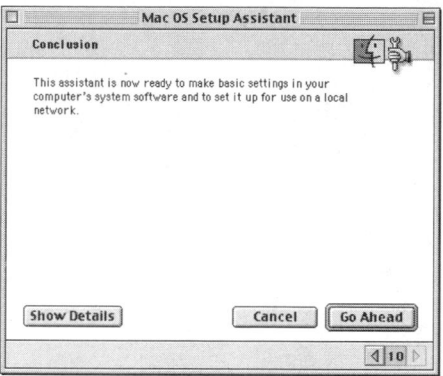

Figure 30 When the Mac OS Setup Assistant is finished asking for information, it displays this window.

Figure 31 The Conclusion window also indicates the configuration progress.

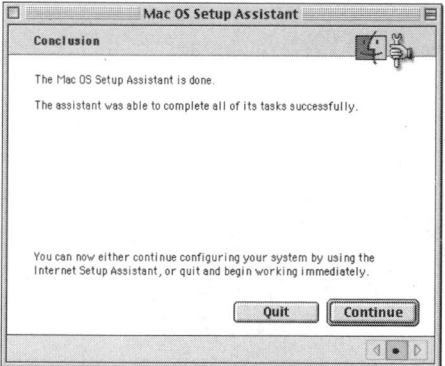

Figure 32 Finally, the Conclusion window tells you when the configuration is done.

To complete the setup process

1. Click the Go Ahead button in the Conclusion window of the Mac OS Setup Assistant (**Figure 30**).

2. Wait while the Mac OS Setup Assistant configures your system. The Conclusion window changes to indicate the configuration progress (**Figure 31**). When the configuration is complete, the Conclusion window tells you that the Mac OS Setup Assistant is done (**Figure 32**).

3. To stop configuring your computer, click the Quit button.

   or

   To go on to the Internet Setup Assistant, click the Continue button.

✔ Tips

- To check your settings one last time before they're written to your computer's configuration files, click the Show Details button (**Figure 30**). The Conclusion window changes to list all configuration options you entered or selected.

- If you have not installed the Internet Access component of Mac OS 9.1, the Continue button in the Conclusion window (**Figure 32**) will not appear.

- The Internet Setup Assistant is not covered in this book. You can find complete instructions for using it, excerpted from *Mac OS 9.1: Visual QuickStart Guide* on the companion Web site to this book: http://www.flyingmproductions.com/macosxvqs/

The Mac OS X Installer

Mac OS X's installer application handles all aspects of a Mac OS X installation. Simply start your computer from the Mac OS Installer CD-ROM and follow the instructions that appear on screen to install Mac OS X, restart your computer, and configure Mac OS X for your use.

The remaining pages in this chapter explain how to install and configure Mac OS X. Unfortunately, since it is currently impossible to take screen shots of the Mac OS X install procedure, this part of the chapter won't be very "visual." But if you follow along closely, you'll get all the information you need to complete the installation and configuration process without problems.

✔ Tips

■ The installation instructions in this chapter assume you know basic Mac OS techniques, such as pointing, clicking, double-clicking, dragging, and selecting items from a menu. If you're brand new to the Mac and don't know any of these techniques, skip ahead to **Chapter 2**, which discusses Mac OS basics.

■ You can click the Go Back button at any time during installation to change options in a previous window.

■ If screen shots become available for these steps, they will be posted in PDF format on the companion Web site for this book, http://www.flyingmproductions.com/macosxvqs/. Check in occasionally to see whether this or other new information is available.

To launch the Mac OS X installer

1. Start your computer from the Mac OS X CD-ROM disc.

2. Wait while Mac OS X and the installer load. (This could take several minutes.)

3. In the Select Language window that appears, select the radio button for the primary language you want to use with the installer and Mac OS X.

4. Click Continue.

✔ Tip

■ To start your computer from the Mac OS X CD-ROM disc, insert the disc, choose Special > Restart, and hold down ⒞ until the "Welcome to Mac OS" message appears. This is the recommended way to start your computer when installing OS software.

LAUNCHING THE MAC OS X INSTALLER

To read important information about the installer & Mac OS X

1. Read the information in the Introduction ("Welcome to the Mac OS X Installer") window.

2. Click Continue.

3. Read the information in the Read Me ("Important Information") window.

4. Click Continue.

5. Read the information in the License ("Software License Agreement") window.

6. Click Continue.

7. Click the Agree button in the dialog sheet that appears.

✔ Tips

■ Read the information in this window carefully! It provides important, late-breaking news about installing Mac OS, including compatibility information and special instructions not included in this book.

■ If necessary, in step 5 you can use the pop-up menu to select a different language for the license agreement.

■ In step 7, if you click the Disagree button, you will not be able to install Mac OS X.

To select a destination disk

1. In the Select Destination ("Select a Destination") window, click to select the icon for the disk on which you want to install Mac OS X. A green arrow appears on the disk icon.

2. Click Continue.

✔ Tips

■ A note beneath the disk icons indicates how much space is available on each disk. You can see how much space a Mac OS X installation takes by looking at the bottom of the window. Make sure the disk you select has enough space for the installation.

■ Although the Mac OS X Install CD will appear as an icon in the window, you cannot select it.

■ If you turn on the Erase destination check box, you will erase all data on the destination disk. You will then have to reinstall Mac OS 9.1 as discussed earlier in this chapter.

To complete the installation

1. In the Installation Type ("Easy Install") window, click Install.

2. Wait while Mac OS X installs. A status window tells you what the installer is doing and may indicate how much longer the installation will take.

3. When the installer is finished, it restarts the computer and displays the first screen of the setup application.

✔ Tip

■ The Customize button in the Installation Type window enables you to customize your Mac OS X installation. This option is provided for "Power Users" and should only be utilized if you have a complete understanding of Mac OS X components and features.

SELECTING A DESTINATION, INSTALLING

To start the Mac OS X configuration

1. In the Welcome window that appears after your computer restarts, select the name of the country you're in.

2. Click Continue.

3. In the Personalize Your Settings window, select a keyboard layout.

4. Click Continue.

5. In the Registration Information window, fill in the form. You can press [Tab] to move from one field to another.

6. Click Continue.

7. In the A Few More Questions window, use the pop-up menus and radio buttons to answer a few marketing questions.

8. Click Continue.

9. Read the information in the Thank You window.

10. Click Continue.

11. In the Create Your Account window, fill in the form to enter account information.

12. Click Continue.

13. Continue following instructions on the next page.

✔ Tips

- If your country is not listed in step 1, turn on the Show All check box to display more options. (If your country still isn't listed, you may be the only one in that country with a Macintosh!)

- In step 3, you can turn on the Show All check box to show additional keyboard layouts.

- In step 5, you can learn more about Apple's privacy policy by clicking the Privacy button. When you're finished reading the information in the dialog sheet that appears, click OK to dismiss it and return to the Registration Information window.

- When you enter your password in step 11, it displays as bullet characters. That's why you enter it twice: so you're sure you entered what you thought you did the first time.

- Remember the password you enter in step 11! If you forget your password, you may not be able to use your computer. It's a good idea to use the Password Hint field to enter a hint that makes your password impossible to forget.

To set up Mac OS X to use your existing Internet service

1. In the Get Internet Ready window, select the radio button for I'll use my existing Internet service.

2. Click Continue.

3. In the How Do You Connect window, select the radio button for your connection method. Your options are Telephone modem, Local area network (LAN), and Cable modem, DSL (Digital Subscriber Line).

4. Click Continue.

5. Follow the instructions in one of the next three sections for your connection method.

✔ Tip

■ You can get all of the information you need for setup from your ISP or network administrator.

To set up a telephone modem connection

1. In the Set up existing service window to enter information about your ISP connection.

2. Click Continue.

3. In the Setting up your modem window, select your modem connection port and make and model.

4. Click Continue.

5. Skip ahead to the section titled "To set up iTools."

To set up a local area network connection

1. The Your Local Area Network window may appear to tell you that your network configuration has been obtained from a DHCP server.

   ▲ If you want to use this information, select Yes and click Continue. You can then skip ahead to the section titled "To set up iTools."

   ▲ If this window does not appear or you don't want to use this information, select No, change the configuration and click Continue.

2. In the Your Internet Connection window, select an option from the TCP/IP Connection Type pop-up menu. The option you select will determine what fields appear beneath it.

3. Enter IP address, subnet mask, router address, DNS hosts, domain name, and proxy server information as required.

4. Click Continue.

5. Skip ahead to the section titled "To set up iTools."

To set up a cable modem or DSL connection

1. In the Your Internet Connection window, select an option from the TCP/IP Connection Type pop-up menu. The option you select will determine what fields appear beneath it.

2. Enter IP address, subnet mask, router address, DNS hosts, domain name, and proxy server information as required.

3. Click Continue.

4. Skip ahead to the section titled "To set up iTools."

To skip Internet setup

1. In the Get Internet Ready window, select the radio button for I'm not ready to connect to the Internet.

2. Click Continue.

3. In the dialog sheet that appears, click Yes to confirm that you don't want to setup an Internet connection.

4. In the Register With Apple window, select one of the options:

   ▲ **Register Now** enables you to use your modem to send registration information to Apple. Click Continue.

   ▲ **Register Later** enables you to skip registration for now. Click Continue and skip ahead to the section titled "To set the time zone."

5. In the Your Phone Service window, enter your telephone number and provide other information as requested.

6. Click Continue.

7. In the Setting up your modem window, select your modem connection port and make and model.

8. Click Continue.

9. Continue following instructions in the section titled "To set up iTools."

SKIPPING INTERNET SETUP

To set up iTools

1. In the Get iTools window, select one of the options:

   ▲ **I'd like to create my iTools account** enables you to create a new iTools account. Click continue and follow step 2.

   ▲ **I'm already using iTools** enables you to enter your iTools user name and password. After entering this information, click Continue and skip ahead to to the section titled "To send registration information."

   ▲ **I'm not ready for iTools** enables you to skip the iTools setup. Click Continue and skip ahead to the section titled "To send registration information."

2. In the Your iTools Account window, fill in the form with the requested information, including a user name, password, and birthday.

3. Click Continue.

4. Continue following instructions in the next section (if they apply).

✔ Tip

■ **Appendix B** provides more information about iTools.

To send registration information

1. If the Now you're ready to connect window appears, click Continue to send your registration to Apple via modem or network connection.

2. Continue following instructions in the next section (if they apply).

To set up an e-mail account

1. If the Set Up Mail window appears, use it to enter information about your e-mail account.

2. Click Continue.

✔ Tip

- If the Set Up Mail window identifies your iTools mac.com e-mail account and you want to add another account, select the Add my existing e-mail acccount radio button. Then enter information for your account.

To set the time zone, date, & time

1. If the Select Time Zone window appears, click on the map to indicate your time zone.

2. If necessary, choose an option from the pop-up menu to specify the exact time zone by name.

3. Click Continue.

4. If the Set Your Date and Time window appears, use it to set your computer's date and time:

   ▲ To set the date, click on today's date on the calendar. (You may have to use the arrow keys beside the name of the month and the year number to set the appropriate month and year first.)

   ▲ To set the time, click on the time digits you want to change and type a new entry. Repeat this process to enter the current time, then click Save.

5. Click Continue.

6. In the final window that appears, click Go.

✔ Tips

- The Set Your Date and Time window will only appear if Mac OS X cannot connect to the Internet to retrieve date and time information from a time server.

- In step 4, you can also change the time by dragging the clock's hands and clicking Save when the time is correct.

FINDER BASICS

The Finder & Desktop

The *Finder* is a program that is part of Mac OS. It launches automatically when you start your computer.

The Finder provides a graphic user interface called the *desktop* (**Figure 1**) that you can use to open, copy, delete, list, organize, and perform other operations on computer files.

This chapter provides important instructions for using the Finder and items that appear on the Mac OS X desktop. It's important that you understand how to use these basic Finder techniques, since you'll use them again and again every time you work with your computer.

✔ Tips

- You never have to manually launch the Finder; it always starts automatically.

- Under normal circumstances, you cannot quit the Finder.

- If you're new to Mac OS, don't skip this chapter. It provides the basic information you'll need to use your computer successfully.

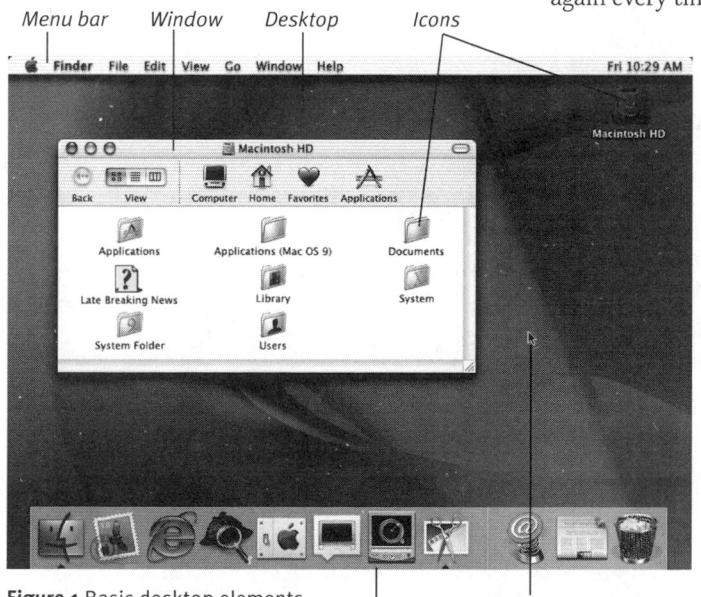

Figure 1 Basic desktop elements.

The Mouse

Mac OS, like most graphic user interface systems, uses the mouse as an input device. There are several basic mouse techniques you must know to use your computer:

◆ **Point** to a specific item on screen.

◆ **Click** an item to select it.

◆ **Double-click** an item to open it.

◆ **Press** an item to activate it.

◆ **Drag** to move an item or select multiple items.

✔ Tips

■ Some computers use either a trackball or a trackpad instead of a mouse.

■ You can customize the way the mouse works with the Mouse pane of System Preferences, which is discussed in **Chapter 11**.

To point

1. Move the mouse on the work surface or mouse pad.

   or

   Use your fingertips to move the ball of the trackball.

   or

   Move the tip of *one* finger (usually your forefinger) on the surface of the trackpad.

   The mouse pointer, which usually looks like an arrow (**Figure 2**), moves on your computer screen.

2. When the tip of the mouse pointer's arrow is on the item to which you want to point (**Figure 3**), stop moving it.

✔ Tip

■ The tip of the mouse pointer is its "business end."

 Figure 2 The mouse pointer usually looks like an arrow pointer when you are working in the Finder.

Applications **Figure 3** Move the mouse pointer so the arrow's tip is on the item to which you want to point.

Figure 4
Click to select
an icon...

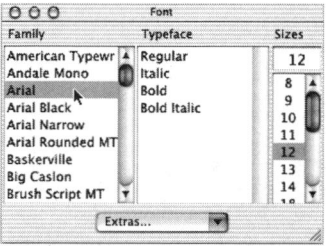

Figure 5 ...or an item in a list.

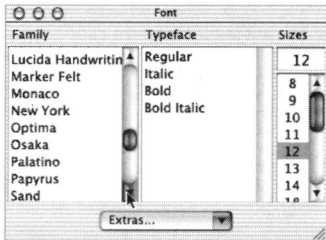

Figure 6 Press a scroll bar arrow to
activate it.

Figure 7
Drag to move items
such as folders.

To click

1. Point to the item you want to click.

2. Press (and release) the mouse button once.
    The item you clicked becomes selected
    (**Figures 4** and **5**).

To double-click

1. Point to the item you want to double-click.

2. Press (and release) the mouse button twice
    quickly. The item you double-clicked opens.

✔ Tip

■   It is vital that you keep the mouse pointer
    still while double-clicking. If you move the
    mouse pointer during the double-click
    process, you may move the item instead of
    double-clicking it.

To press

1. Point to the item you want to press.

2. Press and hold the mouse button without
    moving the mouse. The item you are
    pressing is activated (**Figure 6**).

✔ Tip

■   The press technique is often used when
    working with scroll bars, as shown in
    Figure 6, where pressing is the same as
    clicking repeatedly.

To drag

1. Point to the item you want to drag.

2. Press the mouse button down.

3. While holding the mouse button down,
    move the mouse pointer. The item you are
    dragging moves (**Figure 7**).

Menus

The Finder—and just about every other Mac OS-compatible program—offers menus full of options. There are four types of menus in Mac OS X:

◆ A **pull-down menu** appears on the menu bar at the top of the screen (**Figure 8**).

◆ A **submenu** appears when a menu option with a right-pointing triangle is selected (**Figure 9**).

◆ A **pop-up menu**, which displays a pair of triangles (or double arrow), appears within a window (**Figures 10** and **11**).

◆ A **contextual menu** appears when you hold down Control while clicking an item (**Figure 12**).

✔ Tips

■ A menu option followed by an ellipsis (...) (**Figure 8**) will display a dialog when chosen. Dialogs are discussed in detail in **Chapter 5**.

■ A menu option that is dimmed or gray (**Figure 8**) cannot be chosen. The commands that are available vary depending on what is selected on the desktop or in a window.

■ A menu option preceded by a check mark (**Figure 9**) is selected, or "turned on."

■ A menu option followed by a series of keyboard characters (**Figure 8**) has a keyboard equivalent. Keyboard equivalents are discussed later in this chapter.

■ Contextual menus only display options that apply to the item to which you are pointing.

■ In Mac OS X, menus are translucent. Although this makes them look cool on screen, it certainly makes an author's job tough when it comes time to illustrate them on paper.

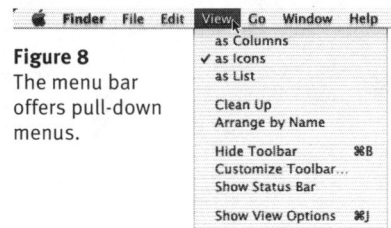

Figure 8
The menu bar offers pull-down menus.

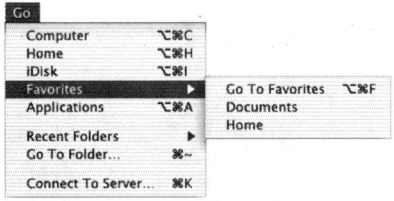

Figure 9 A submenu appears when you select a menu option with a right-pointing triangle beside it.

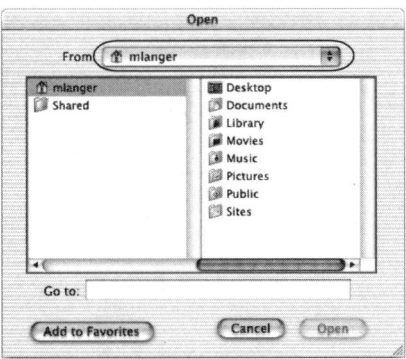

Figure 10 Pop-up menus can appear within dialogs.

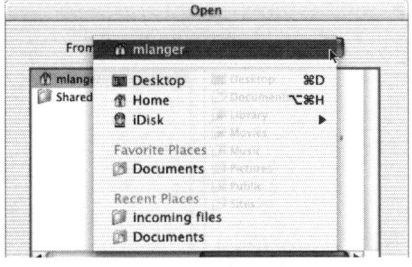

Figure 11 To display a pop-up menu, click it.

Figure 12
A contextual menu appears when you hold down Control while clicking.

Figure 13 Point to the menu name.

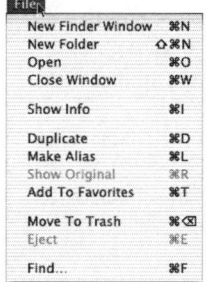

Figure 14
Click (or press) to display the menu.

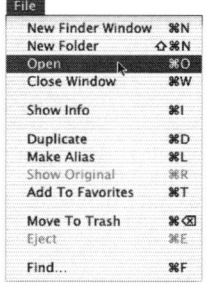

Figure 15
Click (or drag) to select the menu option you want.

Users

Figure 16
Hold down (Control) while pointing to an item.

Figure 17
A contextual menu appears when you click.

Figure 18
Click (or drag) to select the option you want.

To use a menu

1. Point to the name of the menu (**Figure 13**).

2. Click. The menu opens, displaying its options (**Figure 14**).

3. Point to the menu option you want (**Figure 15**).

4. Click to choose the selected option. The menu disappears.

✔ Tips

- Mac OS X's menus are "sticky menus"— each menu opens and stays open when you click its name.

- To close a menu without choosing an option, click outside the menu.

- This book uses the following notation to indicate menu commands: *Menu Name > Submenu Name* (if necessary) *> Command Name*. For example, the instructions for choosing the Documents command from the Favorites submenu under the Go menu (**Figure 9**) would be: "choose Go > Favorites > Documents."

To use a contextual menu

1. Point to the item on which you want to act.

2. Press and hold down (Control). A tiny contextual menu icon appears beside the mouse pointer (**Figure 16**).

3. Click. A contextual menu appears at the item (**Figure 17**).

4. Click the menu option you want (**Figure 18**).

The Keyboard

The keyboard offers another way to communicate with your computer. In addition to typing text and numbers, you can also use it to choose menu commands.

There are three types of keys on a Mac OS keyboard:

◆ **Character keys**, such as letters, numbers, and symbols, are for entering information. Some character keys have special functions, as listed in **Table 1**.

◆ **Modifier keys** alter the meaning of a character key being pressed or the meaning of a mouse action. Modifier keys are listed in **Table 2**.

◆ **Function keys** perform specific functions in Mac OS or an application. Dedicated function keys, which always do the same thing, are listed in **Table 3**. Function keys labeled [F1] through [F15] on the keyboard can be assigned specific functions by applications.

✔ Tips

■ [⌘ ⌘] is called the Command key (not the Apple key).

■ Contextual menus are discussed on the previous page.

Table 1

Special Character Keys	
KEY	FUNCTION
[Enter]	Enters information or "clicks" a default button.
[Return]	Begins a new paragraph or line or "clicks" a default button.
[Tab]	Advances to the next tab stop or the next item in a sequence.
[Delete]	Deletes a selection or the character to the left of the insertion point.
[Del]	Deletes a selection or the character to the right of the insertion point.
[Clear]	Deletes a selection.
[Esc]	"Clicks" a Cancel button or ends the operation that is currently in progress.

Table 2

Modifier Keys	
KEY	FUNCTION
[Shift]	Produces uppercase characters or symbols. Also works with the mouse to extend selections and to restrain movement in graphic applications.
[Option]	Produces special symbols.
[⌘ ⌘]	Accesses menu commands via keyboard equivalents.
[Control]	Modifies the functions of other keys and displays contextual menus.

Table 3

Dedicated Function Keys	
KEY	FUNCTION
[Help]	Displays onscreen help.
[Home]	Scroll to the beginning.
[End]	Scroll to the end.
[Page Up]	Scroll up one page.
[Page Down]	Scroll down one page.
[←][→][↑][↓]	Move the insertion point or change the selection.

To use a keyboard equivalent

1. Hold down the modifier key(s) in the sequence. This is usually ⌃⌘ but can be Option, Control, or Shift.

2. Press the letter, number, or symbol key in the sequence.

For example, to choose the Open command, which can be found under the File menu (**Figure 15**), hold down ⌃⌘ and press O.

✔ Tips

■ You can learn keyboard equivalents by observing the key sequences that appear to the right of some menu commands (**Figures 8** and **9**).

■ Some commands include more than one modifier key. You must hold all modifier keys down while pressing the letter, number, or symbol key for the keyboard equivalent.

■ You can find a list of all Finder keyboard equivalents in **Appendix A**.

■ Some applications refer to keyboard equivalents as *shortcut keys*.

Icons

Mac OS uses icons to graphically represent files and other items on the desktop, in the Dock, or within Finder windows:

◆ **Applications** (**Figure 19**) are programs you use to get work done. **Chapters 5** through **7** discuss working with applications.

◆ **Documents** (**Figure 20**) are the files created by applications. **Chapter 5** covers working with documents.

◆ **Folders** (**Figure 21**) are used to organize files. **Chapters 3** and **4** discuss using folders.

◆ **Disks** (**Figure 22**), including removable media, are used to store files. **Chapter 3** covers working with disks.

◆ The **Trash** (**Figure 23**), which is in the Dock, is for discarding items you no longer want and for ejecting removable media. The Trash is covered in **Chapter 3**.

✔ Tip

■ Icons can appear a number of different ways, depending on the view and view options chosen for a window. Windows are discussed later in this chapter; views are discussed in **Chapter 3**.

TextEdit **Preview** **Microsoft Word**

Figure 19 Application icons, including a Mac OS 9.1 application icon (Microsoft Word).

Letter.rtf **white.tiff Brochure Wizard**

Figure 20 Document icons, including a TextEdit document, a Preview document, and a generic document.

System **Applications** **My Stuff**

Figure 21 Folder icons.

Macintosh HD **Microsoft Office 2001** **Sirocco II**

Figure 22 Three different disk icons: hard disk, CD-ROM disc, and networked disk.

Figure 23 The three faces of the Trash icon in the Dock: empty, full, and while dragging removable media.

ICONS

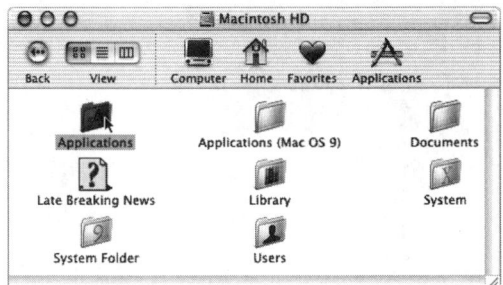

Figure 24 To select an icon, click it.

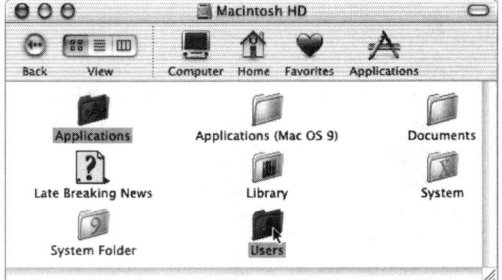

Figure 25 Hold down (Shift) while clicking other icons to add them to a multiple selection.

To select an icon

Click the icon that you want to select. The icon darkens and its name becomes highlighted (**Figure 24**).

✔ Tip

- You can also select an icon in an active window by pressing the keyboard key for the first letter of the icon's name or by pressing (Tab), (Shift)(Tab), (←), (→), (↑), or (↓) until the icon is selected.

To deselect an icon

Click anywhere in the window or on the Desktop other than on the selected icon.

✔ Tips

- If you select one icon and then click another icon, the originally selected icon is deselected and the icon you clicked becomes selected instead.

- Windows are discussed later in this chapter.

To select multiple icons by clicking

1. Click the first icon that you want to select.

2. Hold down (Shift) and click another icon that you want to select (**Figure 25**).

3. Repeat step 2 until all icons that you want to select have been selected.

✔ Tip

- Icons that are part of a multiple selection must be in the same window. Windows are discussed later in this chapter.

SELECTING & DESELECTING ICONS

To select multiple icons by dragging

1. Position the mouse pointer slightly above and to the left of the first icon in the group that you want to select (**Figure 26**).

2. Press the mouse button down, and drag diagonally across the icons you want to select. A shaded box appears to indicate the selection area, and the items within it become selected (**Figure 27**).

3. When all the icons that you want to select are included in the selection area, release the mouse button (**Figure 28**).

✔ Tip

■ To select multiple icons by dragging, the icons must be adjacent.

To select all icons in a window

Choose Edit > Select All (**Figure 29**), or press ⌃⌘A.

All icons in the active window are selected.

✔ Tip

■ Activating windows is covered later in this chapter.

To deselect one icon in a multiple selection

Hold down (Shift) while clicking the icon that you want to deselect. That icon is deselected while the others remain selected.

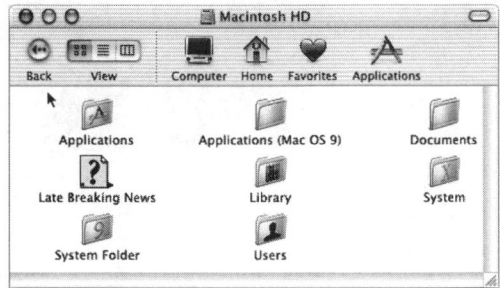

Figure 26 Position the mouse pointer above and to the left of the first icon that you want to select.

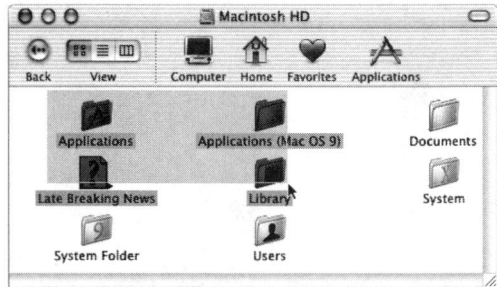

Figure 27 Drag to draw a shaded selection box around the icons that you want to select.

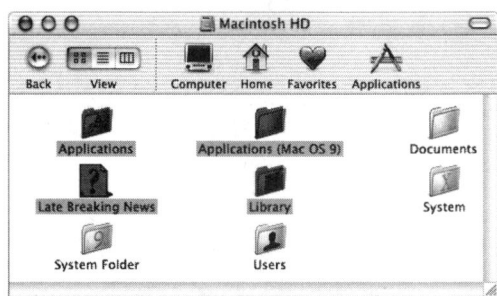

Figure 28 Release the mouse button to complete the selection.

Figure 29 Choose Select All from the Edit menu.

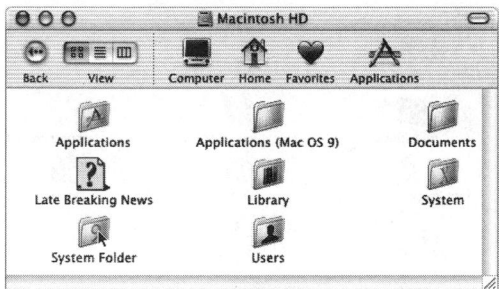

Figure 30 Point to the icon that you want to move.

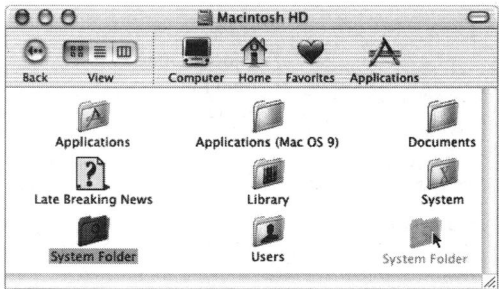

Figure 31 Drag the icon to the new location.

Figure 32 When you release the mouse button, the icon moves.

To move an icon

1. Position the mouse pointer on the icon that you want to move (**Figure 30**).

2. Press the mouse button down, and drag the icon to the new location. As you drag, a shadowy image of the icon moves with the mouse pointer (**Figure 31**).

3. Release the mouse button when the icon is in the desired position. The icon moves (**Figure 32**).

✔ Tips

■ You cannot drag to reposition icons within windows set to list or column view. Views are discussed in **Chapter 3**.

■ You move icons to rearrange them in a window or on the Desktop, or to copy or move the items they represent to another folder or disk. Copying and moving items is discussed in **Chapter 3**.

■ You can also move multiple icons at once. Simply select the icons first, then position the mouse pointer on one of the selected icons and follow steps 2 and 3 above. All selected icons move together.

MOVING ICONS

To open an icon

1. Select the icon you want to open (**Figure 33**).

2. Choose File > Open (**Figure 34**), or press
   ⌘O.

or

Double-click the icon that you want to open.

✔ Tips

- Only one click is necessary when opening an item in a Finder window toolbar or the Dock. The toolbar and Dock are covered in detail later in this chapter.

- What happens when you open an icon depends on the type of icon you open. For example:

  ▲ Opening a folder icon displays the contents of the folder in the same Finder window (**Figure 35**). Windows are discussed next.

  ▲ Opening an application icon launches the application so that you can work with it. Working with applications is covered in **Chapters 5** through **7**.

  ▲ Opening a document icon launches the application that created that document and displays the document so you can view or edit it. Working with documents is covered in **Chapter 5**.

  ▲ Opening the Trash displays items that will be deleted when you empty the Trash. Using and emptying the Trash is discussed in **Chapter 3**.

- To open a folder or disk in a new Finder window, hold down ⌘ while opening it.

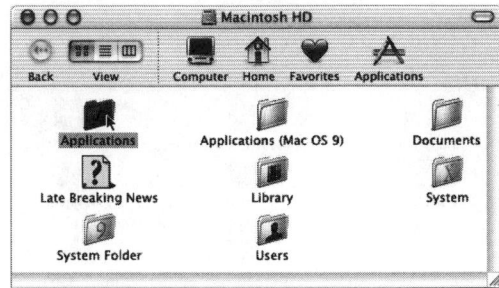

Figure 33 Select the icon.

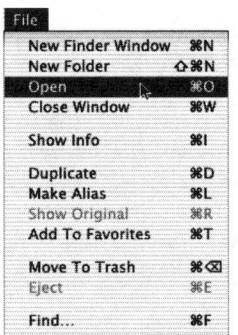

Figure 34 Choose Open from the File menu.

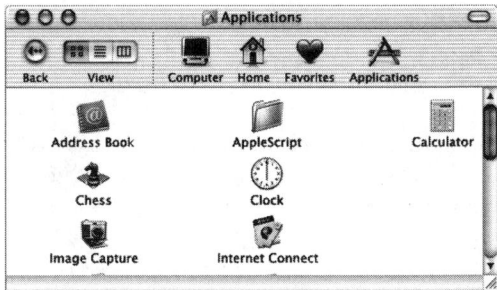

Figure 35 Opening a folder icon opens a window that displays the contents of the folder.

OPENING ICONS

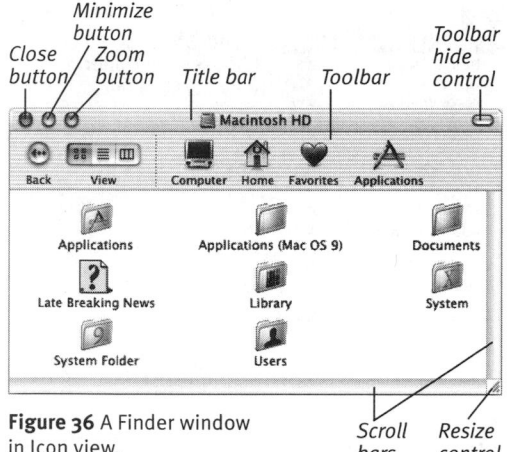

Figure 36 A Finder window in Icon view.

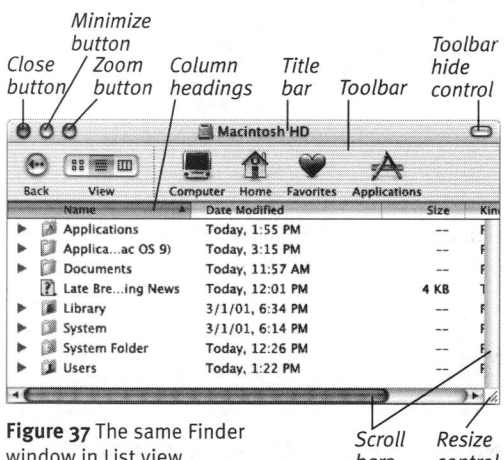

Figure 37 The same Finder window in List view.

Windows

Mac OS makes extensive use of windows for displaying icons and other information in the Finder and documents in other applications. **Figures 36** and **37** show two different views of a Finder window.

Each window includes a variety of controls you can use to manipulate it:

◆ The **title bar** displays the window's icon and name and can be used to move the window. (You can also move a window by dragging any of its edges.)

◆ The **close button** closes the window.

◆ The **minimize button** collapses the window to an icon in the Dock.

◆ The **zoom button** toggles the window's size between full size and a custom size.

◆ The **resize control** enables you to set a custom size for the window.

◆ **Scroll bars** scroll the contents of the window.

◆ **Column headings** (in list view only) display the names of the columns and let you quickly sort by a column. (The selected column heading is the column by which the list is sorted.)

✔ Tips

■ The Finder's three window views are discussed in **Chapter 3**.

■ In Mac OS X, when you open a folder or disk icon, its contents appear in the currently active window. This differs from previous versions of Mac OS, which opened folders and disks into new Finder windows.

WINDOWS

To open a new Finder window

Choose File > New Finder Window (**Figure 38**), or press ⌃ ⌘ N. A new top-level window appears (**Figure 39**).

✔ Tip

■ The top-level window is discussed in **Chapter 3**.

To open a folder or disk in a new Finder window

Hold down ⌃ ⌘ while opening a folder or disk icon. A new window containing the contents of the folder or disk appears.

✔ Tip

■ Opening folders and disks is explained earlier in this chapter.

To close a window

Click the window's close button (**Figures 36** and **37**).

or

Choose File > Close Window (**Figure 40**), or press ⌃ ⌘ W.

To close all open windows

Hold down Option while clicking the active window's close button (**Figures 36** and **37**).

or

Hold down Option while choosing File > Close All (**Figure 41**), or press ⌃ ⌘ Option W.

✔ Tip

■ The Close Window/Close All commands (**Figures 40** and **41**) are examples of *dynamic menu items*—pressing a modifier key (in this case, Option), changes the menu command from Close Window (**Figure 40**) to Close All (**Figure 41**).

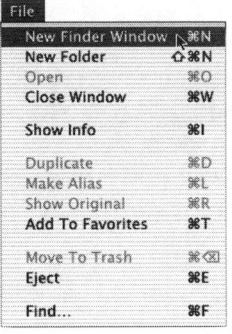

Figure 38
Choose New Finder Window from the File menu.

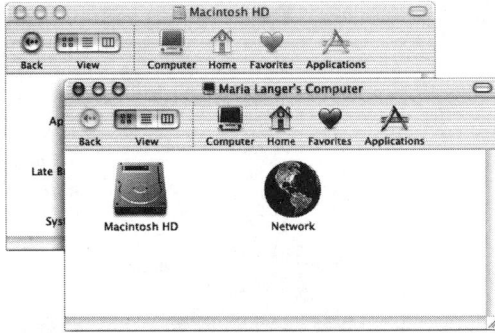

Figure 39 The active window's title bar includes color and appears atop all other windows.

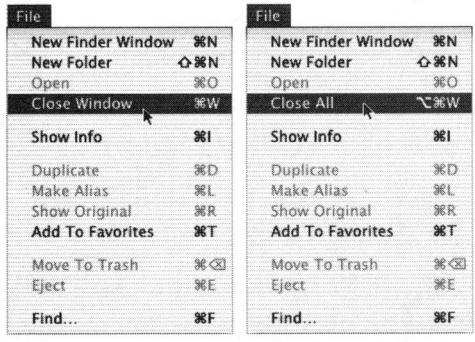

Figure 40 Choose Close Window from the File menu...

Figure 41 ...or hold down Option and choose Close Window from the File menu.

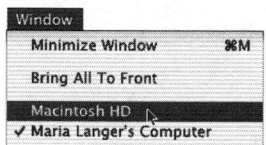

Figure 42 The Window menu lists all open Finder windows.

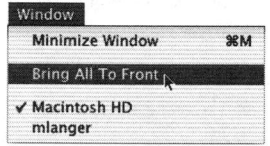

Figure 43 The Bring All To Front command brings all Finder windows to the top.

To activate a window

Click anywhere in or on the window.

or

Choose the name of the window you want to activate from the Window menu (**Figure 42**).

✔ Tips

■ It's important to make sure that the window you want to work with is open and active *before* using commands that work on the active window—such as Close Window, Select All, and View menu options.

■ You can distinguish between active and inactive windows by the appearance of their title bars; the active window's title bar includes color (**Figure 39**). In addition, a check mark appears beside the active window's name in the Window menu (**Figure 42**).

■ When two or more windows overlap, the active window will always be on top of the stack (**Figure 39**).

To bring all Finder windows to the top

Choose Window > Bring All To Front (**Figure 43**). All open Finder windows that are not minimized become the top windows.

✔ Tip

■ In Mac OS X, Finder windows can be intermingled with other application's windows. The Bring All To Front command gathers the windows together in the top layers. You may find this command useful when working with many windows from several different applications.

To move a window

1. Position the mouse pointer on the window's title bar (**Figure 44**).

or

Position the mouse pointer on the border of the window.

2. Press the mouse button and drag the window to a new location. As you drag, the window moves along with your mouse pointer (**Figure 45**).

3. When the outline of the window is in the desired position, release the mouse button.

To resize a window

1. Position the mouse pointer on the window's resize control (**Figure 46**).

2. Press the mouse button and drag. As you drag, the resize control moves with the mouse pointer, changing the size and shape of the window (**Figure 47**).

3. When the window is the desired size, release the mouse button.

✔ Tips

■ The larger a window is, the more you can see inside it.

■ By resizing and repositioning windows, you can see inside more than one window at a time. This comes in handy when moving or copying the icons for files and folders from one window to another. Moving and copying files and folders is covered in **Chapter 3**.

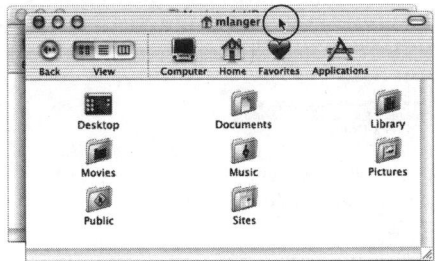

Figure 44 Position the mouse pointer on the title bar.

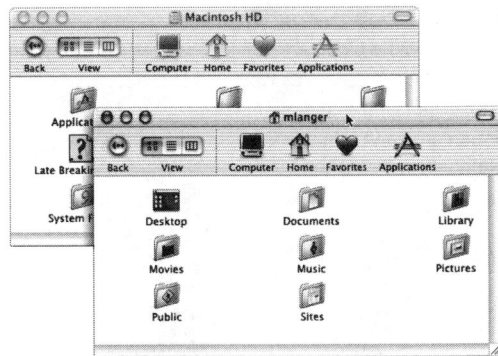

Figure 45 As you drag, the window moves.

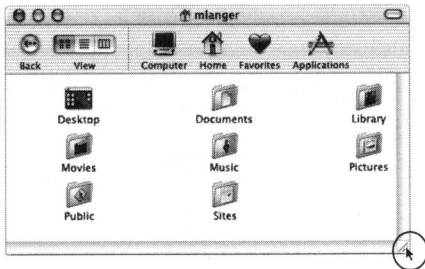

Figure 46 Position the mouse pointer on the resize control.

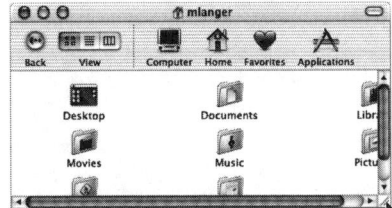

Figure 47 As you drag, the window's size and shape changes.

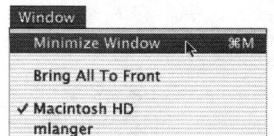

Figure 48
The Minimize Window command minimizes the active window.

Figure 49 Minimized windows shrink down into icons in the Dock.

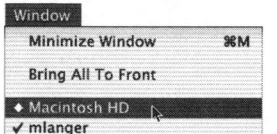

Figure 50
A diamond beside a window name indicates that the window has been minimized.

To minimize a window

Click the window's minimize button (**Figures 36** and **37**).

or

Choose Window > Minimize Window (**Figure 48**), or press ⌃ ⌘ M.

or

Double-click the window's title bar.

The window shrinks into an icon and slips into the Dock at the bottom of the screen (**Figure 49**).

To redisplay a minimized window

Click the window's icon in the Dock (**Figure 49**).

or

Choose the window's name from the Window menu (**Figure 50**).

To zoom a window

Click the window's zoom button (**Figures 36** and **37**).

Each time you click the zoom button, the window's size toggles between two sizes:

◆ **Standard state** size is the largest possible size that would accommodate the window's contents (**Figure 46**).

◆ **User state** size, which is the size you specify with the resize control (**Figure 47**).

MINIMIZING & ZOOMING WINDOWS

To scroll a window's contents

Click one of the scroll bar arrows (**Figure 51**) as follows:

◆ To scroll the window's contents up, click the down arrow on the vertical scroll bar.

◆ To scroll the window's contents down, click the up arrow on the vertical scroll bar.

◆ To scroll the window's contents to the left, click the right arrow on the horizontal scroll bar.

◆ To scroll the window's contents to the right, click the left arrow on the horizontal scroll bar.

✔ Tips

■ If you have trouble remembering which scroll arrow to click, think of it this way:

▲ Click down to see down.

▲ Click up to see up.

▲ Click right to see right.

▲ Click left to see left.

■ You can also scroll a window's contents by either clicking in the scroll track on either side of the scroller or by dragging the scroller to a new position on the scroll bar. Both of these techniques enable you to scroll a window's contents more quickly.

■ If all of a window's contents are displayed, you will not be able to scroll the window. A window that cannot be scrolled will have flat or empty looking scroll bars (**Figure 46**).

■ The scrollers in Mac OS X are *proportional*— this means that the more of a window's contents you see, the more space the scroller will take up in its scroll bar.

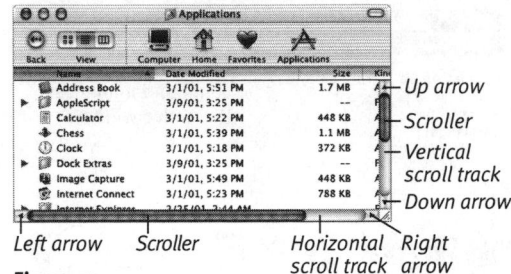

Figure 51
Scroll bars components.

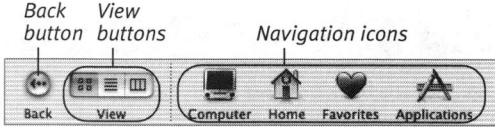

Back button *View buttons*   *Navigation icons*

Figure 52 The toolbar.

Figure 53 When the window is narrow, some toolbar buttons may be hidden.

Figure 54 Click the double arrow to display a menu of hidden buttons.

Toolbar hide control

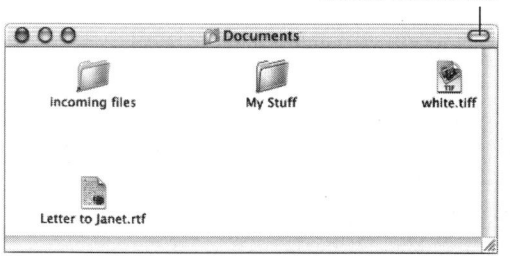

Figure 55 The toolbar hide control button can hide the toolbar...

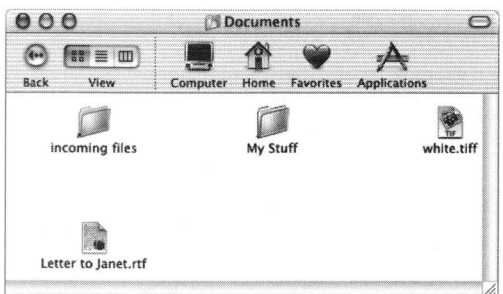

Figure 56 ...or display it.

The Toolbar

The Toolbar (**Figure 52**), which is new in Mac OS X, offers navigation tools and view buttons within Finder windows:

◆ Back button displays the previous window's contents.

◆ View buttons enable you to change the window's view.

◆ Navigation icons open specific Finder windows.

✔ Tips

■ The toolbar can be customized to show the items you use most; **Chapter 4** explains how.

■ Views are covered in detail in **Chapter 4**; file management and navigation is discussed in **Chapter 3**.

■ If the window is not wide enough to show all toolbar buttons, a double arrow appears on the right side of the toolbar (**Figure 53**). Click the arrow to display a menu of missing buttons (**Figure 54**) and select the button you want.

To hide or display the toolbar

Click the toolbar hide control button (**Figure 55**).

If the toolbar is displayed, it disappears (**Figure 55**); if the toolbar is not displayed, it appears (**Figure 56**).

To use a toolbar button

Click the button once.

The Dock

The Dock (**Figure 57**), which is new in Mac OS X, offers easy access to often-used applications and documents, as well as minimized windows.

Figure 57 The Dock displays often-used applications and documents.

✔ Tip

■ The Dock can be customized; **Chapter 11** explains how.

To identify items in the Dock

Point to the item. The name of the item appears above the Dock (**Figure 58**).

Figure 58 Point to an icon to see what it represents.

To identify open items in the Dock

Look at the Dock. A triangle appears beneath each open item.

To open an item in the Dock

Click the icon for the item you want to open. One of four things happens:

Figure 59 An item's icon bounces while it is being opened.

◆ If the icon is for an open application, the application becomes the active application.

◆ If the icon is for an application that is not open, the application opens. While it opens, the icon in the Dock bounces (**Figure 59**) so you know something is happening.

◆ If the icon is for a minimized window, the window is displayed.

◆ If the icon is for a document that is not open, the application that created the document opens (if necessary) and the document opens.

✔ Tip

■ Using applications and opening documents is discussed in greater detail in **Chapter 5**; minimizing and displaying windows is discussed earlier in this chapter.

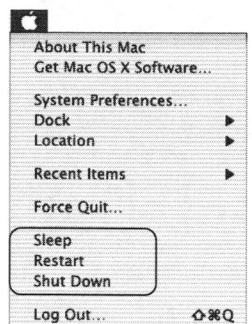

Figure 60
Three commands under the Apple menu let you change the work state of your computer.

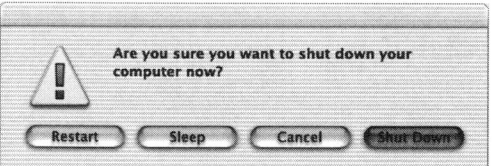

Figure 61 Pressing the Power key on some Mac OS computers displays a dialog like this one.

Sleeping, Restarting, & Shutting Down

The Apple menu (**Figure 60**) offers several options that change the work state of your computer:

◆ **Sleep** puts the computer into a state where it uses very little power. The screen goes blank and the hard disk may stop spinning.

◆ **Restart** instructs the computer to shut down and immediately start back up.

◆ **Shut Down** closes all open documents and programs, clears memory, and cuts power to the computer.

✔ Tips

■ You can view a dialog with buttons for Restart, Sleep, and Shut Down commands (**Figure 61**) by pressing the Power key on the keyboard. This feature, however, does not work with all Mac OS-computer models.

■ The Energy Saver pane of System Preferences, which is discussed in **Chapter 11**, can automatically put a computer to sleep or shut it down after a specific period of inactivity.

■ Do *not* restart or shut down a computer by simply flicking off the power switch. Doing so prevents the computer from properly closing files, which may result in file corruption and related problems.

To put your computer to sleep

Choose Apple menu > Sleep (**Figure 60**).

or

1. Press the Power key.

2. In the dialog that appears (**Figure 61**), click Sleep.

✔ Tips

■ Not all computers support sleep mode. If your computer does not support sleep mode, the Sleep command will not appear on the Apple menu.

■ When you put your computer to sleep, everything in memory is preserved. When you wake the computer, you can quickly continue working where you left off.

■ Sleep mode is an effective way to conserve the battery life of a PowerBook or iBook without turning it off.

To wake a sleeping computer

Press any keyboard key. Expect to wait from 10 to 30 seconds for the computer to fully wake.

✔ Tips

■ It's much quicker to wake a sleeping computer than to restart a computer that has been shut down.

■ On some computer models, pressing Caps Lock or certain other keys may not wake the computer. When in doubt, press a letter key—they always work.

To restart your computer

Choose Apple menu > Restart (**Figure 60**).

or

1. Press the Power key.

2. In the dialog that appears (**Figure 61**), click Restart.

✔ Tip

■ Restarting the computer clears memory and reloads all system files.

To shut down your computer

Choose Apple menu > Shut Down (**Figure 60**).

or

1. Press the Power key.

2. In the dialog that appears (**Figure 61**), click Shut Down or press Return or Enter.

✔ Tip

■ On most computers, the Shut Down command will cut power to the computer as part of the shut down process. If it doesn't, a dialog will appear on screen, telling you it's safe to turn off your computer. You can then use the power switch to cut power to the computer.

FILE MANAGEMENT

File Management

In Mac OS, you use the Finder to organize and manage your files.

- ◆ View the contents of your disks in windows in a variety of ways.

- ◆ Automatically sort items by name, kind, creation date, or other criteria in ascending or descending order.

- ◆ Rename items.

- ◆ Create folders to store related items.

- ◆ Move items stored on disk to organize them so they're easy to find and back up.

- ◆ Copy items to other disks to back them up or share them with others.

- ◆ Delete items you no longer need.

- ◆ Mount and eject disks.

✔ Tip

- ■ If you're brand new to Mac OS, be sure to read the information in **Chapter 2** before working with this chapter. That chapter contains information and instructions about techniques that are used throughout this chapter.

Mac OS X Disk Organization

Like previous versions of Mac OS and most other computer operating systems, Mac OS X uses a hierarchical filing system (HFS) to organize and store files, including system files, applications, and documents.

The top level of the filing system is the computer level. You can view the computer level window (**Figure 1**) by clicking the Computer icon in the toolbar of any Finder window. This level shows the computer's internal hard disk, any other disks the computer has access to, and the Network icon.

The next level down is the computer's hard disk level. You can view this level by opening the hard disk icon in the computer level window (**Figure 1**) or on the desktop. While the contents of your hard disk may differ from what's shown in **Figure 2**, some elements should be the same:

◆ **Applications** contains Mac OS X applications.

◆ **Applications (Mac OS 9)** contains applications that run under the Classic environment.

◆ **System** contains the Mac OS X system files.

◆ **System Folder** contains the Mac OS 9.1 system files for running the Classic environment.

◆ **Documents** contains documents you saved on your hard disk before upgrading to Mac OS X.

◆ **Users** (**Figure 3**) contains individual folders for each of the computer's users, as well as a Shared Items folder.

Figure 1 The top level of your computer shows all mounted disks and a Network icon.

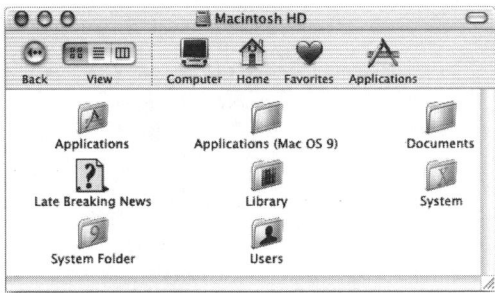

Figure 2 A typical hard disk window might look like this.

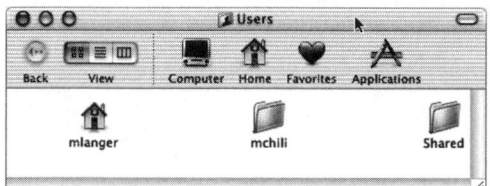

Figure 3 The Users folder contains a home folder for each user, as well as a Shared folder.

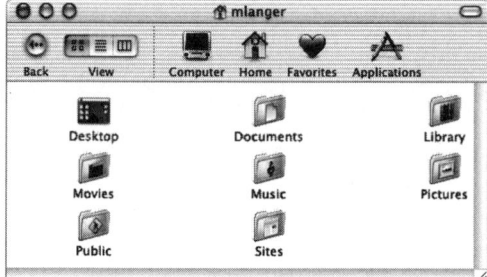

Figure 4 Your home folder is preconfigured with folders for storing a variety of item types.

By default, a Mac OS X hard disk is organized for multiple users. Each users has his or her own "home" folder, which is stored in the Users folder (**Figure 3**). You can view the items inside your home folder by opening the house icon with your name on it inside the Users folder (**Figure 3**) or by clicking the Home icon in the toolbar of any Finder window. Your home folder is preconfigured with folders for all kinds of items you may want to store on disk (**Figure 4**).

✔ Tips

- Applications and the Classic environment are discussed in greater detail in **Chapter 5**.

- When you install new applications on your computer, you should install Mac OS X compatible applications in the Applications folder and Mac OS 9 applications in the Applications (Mac OS 9) folder.

- If you upgraded from a previous version of Mac OS to Mac OS X, you may want to move the contents of the Documents folder on your hard disk (**Figure 2**) to the Documents folder inside your home folder (**Figure 4**) to keep your documents together and easier to find.

- Unless you are an administrator, you cannot open any other user's home folder.

- If you place an item in the Shared folder inside the Users folder (**Figure 3**), it can be opened by anyone who uses the computer.

- Sharing computers and networking is beyond the scope of this book. For more information about these advanced topics, consult this book's sequel, *Mac OS X: Visual QuickPro Guide*.

MAC OS X DISK ORGANIZATION

Pathnames

A *path* or *pathname* is a kind of address for a file on disk. It includes the name of the disk on which the file resides, the names of the folders the file is stored within, and the name of the file itself. For example, the pathname for a file named *Letter.rtf* in the Documents folder of the mlanger folder shown in **Figure 4** would be: Macintosh HD/Users/mlanger/Documents/Letter.rtf

When entering a pathname from a specific folder, you don't have to enter the entire pathname. Instead, enter the path as it relates to the current folder. For example, the path to the above-mentioned file from the mlanger folder would be: /Documents/Letter.rtf

To indicate a previous or parent folder, use a tilde (~) character. So the path to the file from the Movies folder inside the mlanger folder would be: ~mlanger/Documents/Letter.rtf

Don't worry if this sounds confusing to you. You don't really need to know it to use Mac OS X. It's just a good idea to be familiar with the concept of pathnames in case you run across it while working with your computer.

✔ Tip

- As discussed in **Chapter 5**, Mac OS X's Open dialogs support pathnames in the Go to field. If you decide to take advantage of this feature, use the guidelines above for entering pathnames.

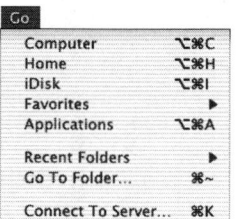

Figure 5
The Go menu.

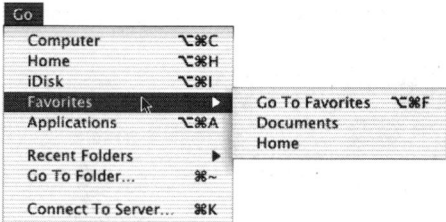

Figure 6 The Favorites submenu on the Go menu lists your favorite locations.

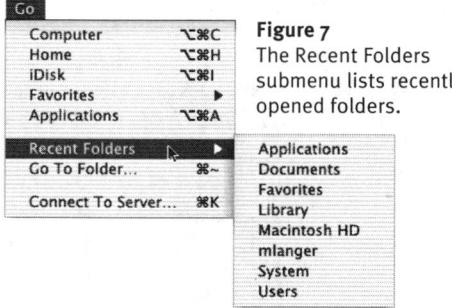

Figure 7
The Recent Folders submenu lists recently opened folders.

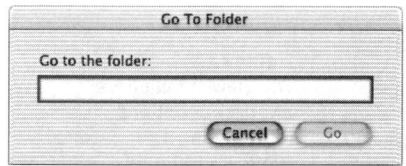

Figure 8 Use the Go To Folder dialog to enter the pathname of the folder you want to open.

The Go Menu

The Go menu (**Figure 5**) offers a quick and easy way to open specific locations on your computer:

◆ **Computer** (Option ⌘ C) opens the top level window for your computer (**Figure 1**).

◆ **Home** (Option ⌘ H) opens your home folder (**Figure 4**).

◆ **iDisk** offers access to folders stored on Apple's Web site via the Internet and iDisk.

◆ **Favorites** displays a submenu of favorite locations (**Figure 6**).

◆ **Applications** (Option ⌘ A) opens the Applications folder.

◆ **Recent Folders** displays a submenu of recently opened folders (**Figure 7**).

◆ **Go To Folder** (Option ⌘ ~) displays a dialog that you can use to enter the pathname of the folder you want to open (**Figure 8**). Enter the pathname and click Go to open that folder.

✔ Tip

■ iDisk is discussed in **Appendix B**, favorites are covered in **Chapter 4**, pathnames are discussed on the previous page.

To open a Go menu item

Choose the item's name from the Go menu (**Figure 5**) or one of its submenus (**Figures 6** and **7**).

Views

A Finder window's contents can be displayed using three different views:

◆ **Icons** displays the window's contents as small or large icons (**Figure 9**).

◆ **List** displays the window's contents as a sorted list (**Figure 10**).

◆ **Columns** displays the window's contents with a two-column format that shows the currently selected folder and the items within it (**Figure 11**).

In addition to setting the view of a window, you can set view options to fine tune the view.

To change a window's view

1. If necessary, activate the window whose view you want to change.

2. Choose the view option you want from the View menu (**Figure 12**).

   or

   Click the toolbar's view button for the view you want (**Figure 13**).

   The view of the window changes.

✔ Tips

■ Commands on the View menu (**Figure 12**) work on the active window only.

■ A check mark appears on the View menu beside the name of the view currently applied to the active window (**Figure 12**).

■ You can set the view for each window individually.

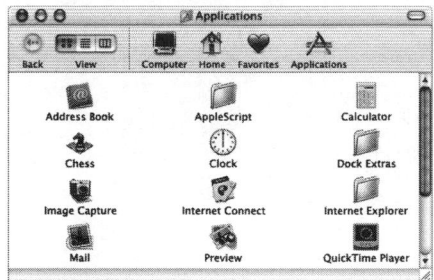

Figure 9 You can display a window's contents as icons,...

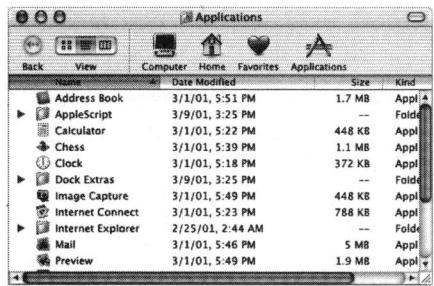

Figure 10 ...as a list,...

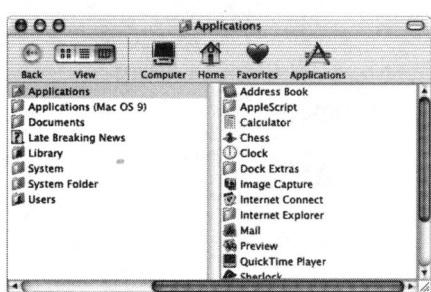

Figure 11 ...or as columns.

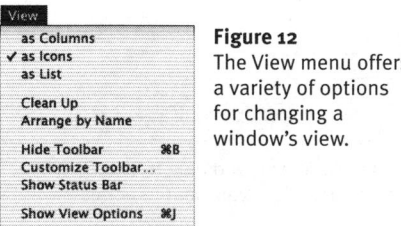

Figure 12 The View menu offers a variety of options for changing a window's view.

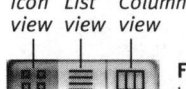

Icon view   List view   Column view

Figure 13 The view buttons in the toolbar.

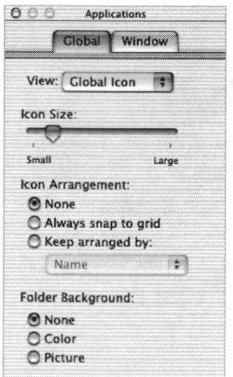

Figure 14
Use this palette to set options for the default icon view throughout Mac OS X.

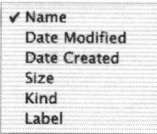

Figure 15
Use this pop-up menu to specify the arrangement order for icons.

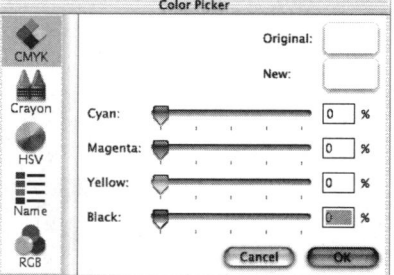

Figure 16 The Color Picker window offers buttons and sliders for selecting a color.

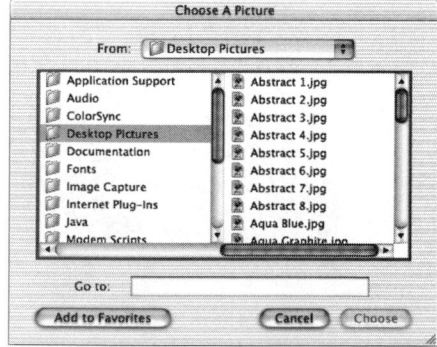

Figure 17 The Choose A Picture dialog.

To set global icon view options

1. Choose View > Show View Options (**Figure 13**), or press ⌃ ⌘ J.

2. In the view options palette that appears, click the Global tab and choose Global Icon from the pop-up menu (**Figure 14**).

3. Use the slider to set the Icon Size. Dragging the slider to the left makes the icon size smaller; dragging it to the right makes the icon size larger.

4. Select an Icon Arrangement option:

   ▲ **None** removes any automatic icon arrangement.

   ▲ **Always snap to grid** forces icons to snap to an invisible grid within the window.

   ▲ **Keep arranged by** automatically arranges icons in a certain order. If you select this option, choose a sort order from the pop-up menu beneath it (**Figure 15**).

5. Select a Folder Background option:

   ▲ **None** removes any window background.

   ▲ **Color** enables you to select a background color for the window. If you select this option, click the color well that appears beside it, use the Color Picker that appears (**Figure 16**) to select a color, and click OK.

   ▲ **Picture** enables you to set a background picture for the window. If you select this option, click the Select button that appears beside it, use the Choose A Picture dialog that appears (**Figure 17**) to locate and select a background picture, and click Choose.

Continued on next page...

SETTING GLOBAL ICON VIEW OPTIONS

Continued from previous page.

6. When you're finished setting options in the view options palette, click its close button to dismiss it.

✔ Tips

■ When you set global icon view options, your settings affect all icon view windows that do not have custom settings.

■ Working with dialogs is discussed in **Chapter 5**.

■ Background pictures fill the window's background behind the icons (**Figure 18**).

To set icon view options for a specific window

1. Open and activate the window you want to set options for, and if necessary, set it to icon view.

2. Choose View > Show View Options (**Figure 12**), or press ⌃⌘J.

3. In the view options palette that appears, click the Window tab (**Figure 19**).

4. If necessary, turn off the Use Global View Preferences check box.

5. Follow steps 3 through 6 in the previous section to set options for the view and close the view options palette.

✔ Tip

■ To set current window options the same as global options, turn on the Use Global View Preferences check box.

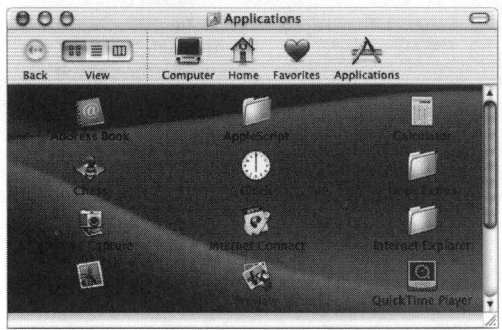

Figure 18 A window background picture can certainly make a window look...interesting.

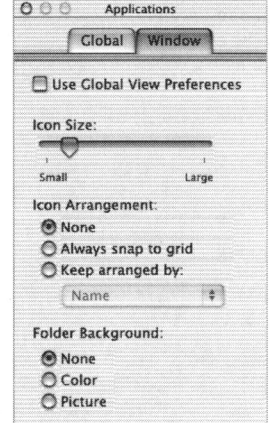

Figure 19
Use this palette to set icon view options for a the active window.

Figure 20
Use this palette to set options for the default list view throughout Mac OS X.

To set global list view options

1. Choose View > Show View Options (**Figure 12**), or press ⌃ ⌘ J.

2. In the view options palette that appears, click the Global tab and choose Global List from the pop-up menu (**Figure 20**).

3. Select the columns you want to appear in list view by turning Show Columns check boxes on or off:

   ▲ **Date Modified** is the date and time an item was last changed.

   ▲ **Date Created** is the date and time an item was first created.

   ▲ **Size** is the amount of disk space the item occupies.

   ▲ **Kind** is the type of item. I tell you about types of icons in **Chapter 2**.

   ▲ **Label** is the label assigned to the item.

   ▲ **Version** is the item's version number.

   ▲ **Comments** is the information you entered in the comments field of the Info window. I tell you about the Info window in **Chapter 4**.

4. To display the date in relative terms (that is, using the words "today" and "yesterday"), turn on the Use relative dates check box.

5. To display the total disk space occupied by the contents of folders in the list, turn on the Calculate folder sizes check box.

6. Select an Icon Size option by clicking the radio button beneath the size you want.

7. When you're finished setting options in the view options palette, click its close button to dismiss it.

✔ Tip

■ Turning on the Calculate folder sizes check box in step 4 could slow down the opening of list view windows.

To set list view options for a specific window

1. Open and activate the window you want to set options for, and if necessary, set it to list view.

2. Choose View > Show View Options (**Figure 12**), or press ⌃ ⌘ J.

3. In the view options palette that appears, click the Window tab (**Figure 21**).

4. If necessary, turn off the Use Global View Preferences check box.

5. Follow steps 3 through 7 in the previous section to set options for the view and close the view options palette.

✔ Tip

■ To set current window options the same as global options, turn on the Use Global View Preferences check box.

To display the status bar

Choose View > Show Status Bar (**Figure 12**).

The status bar appears above the window's contents (**Figure 22**).

✔ Tips

■ As shown in **Figure 22**, the status bar shows the number of items in the window and the total amount of space available on the disk.

■ The status bar can be displayed in any window view.

To hide the status bar

Choose View > Hide Status Bar (**Figure 23**).

The status bar disappears.

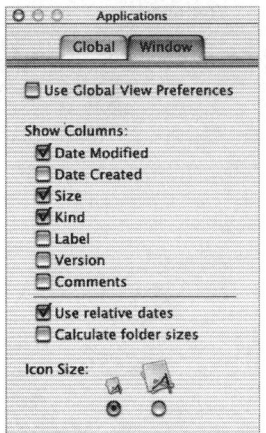

Figure 21
Use this palette to set list view options for a the active window.

Figure 22 The status bar shows how many items are in the window and how much space is left on disk.

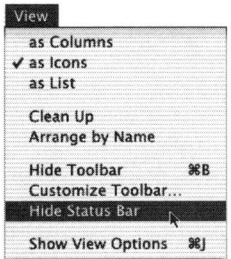

Figure 23
To hide the status bar, choose Hide Status Bar from the View menu.

SETTING A WINDOW'S LIST VIEW OPTIONS

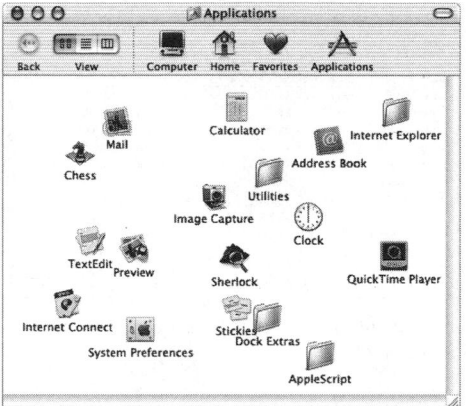

Figure 24 Start with a messy window like this one...

Figure 25 ...and use the Clean Up command to put the icons in place...

Figure 26 ...or the Arrange by Name command to put them in alphabetical order by name.

Cleaning Up & Arranging Icons

Even if you're not a neat freak, you'll like the automatic clean-up and arrangement features that are part of the Finder.

◆ **Clean Up** neatly arranges icons or buttons in the window's invisible grid.

◆ **Arrange by Name** sorts the icons and arranges them alphabetically by name.

To clean up a window

1. Activate the window that you want to clean up (**Figure 24**).

2. Choose View > Clean Up (**Figure 12**). The icons move into empty slots in the window's invisible grid (**Figure 25**).

✔ Tip

■ You can specify that the window's contents should automatically be snapped to the grid in the view options palette, which is covered earlier in this chapter.

To arrange a window's contents

1. Activate the window whose contents you want to arrange (**Figure 25**).

2. Choose View > Arrange by Name (**Figure 12**). The icons are arranged alphabetically (**Figure 26**).

✔ Tip

■ You can specify a default arrangement order for the window in the view options palette, which is covered earlier in this chapter.

List Views

In addition to setting view options as discussed earlier in this chapter, a list view window can be modified in the following ways:

◆ Sort by any column in ascending or descending order.

◆ Change the width of columns.

◆ Change the order in which columns appear.

To sort a window's contents

Click the column heading for the column by which you want to sort (**Figure 27**). The list is sorted by that column (**Figure 28**).

✔ Tips

■ You can always identify the column by which a list is sorted because its column heading is colored (**Figures 27** and **28**).

■ To properly sort folders in a window sorted by size, you should turn on the Calculate folder sizes check box in the window's view options (**Figure 21**). Otherwise, a folder has no size and is sorted to the top or bottom of the list.

To reverse the sort order of a window's contents

Click the column heading again. The sort order reverses (**Figure 29**).

✔ Tip

■ You can easily see the sort direction by looking at the arrow in the sort column. When it points up, the items are sorted in ascending order; when it points down, the items are sorted in ascending order. You can see this in **Figures 28** and **29**.

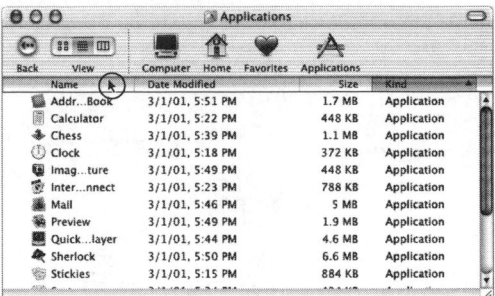

Figure 27 Point to the heading for the column by which you want to sort.

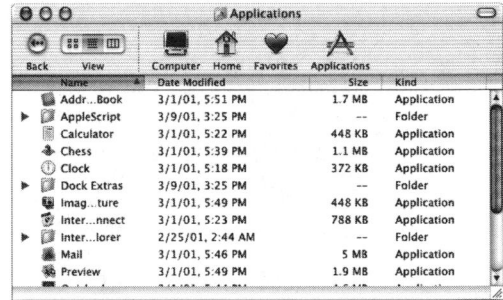

Figure 28 The list view is sorted by the column you clicked.

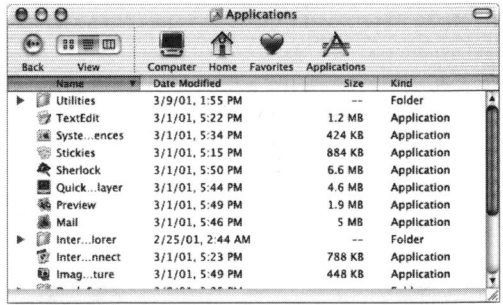

Figure 29 Clicking the column heading again reverses the sort order.

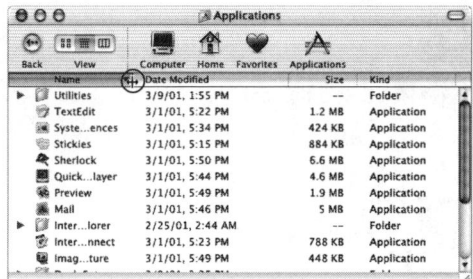

Figure 30 Position the mouse pointer between two column headings.

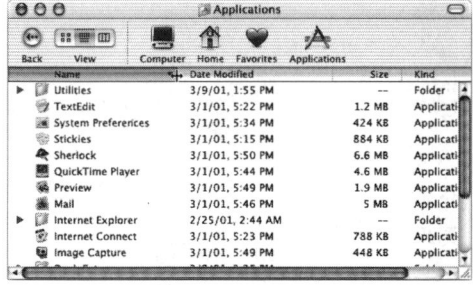

Figure 31 As you drag, the column's width changes.

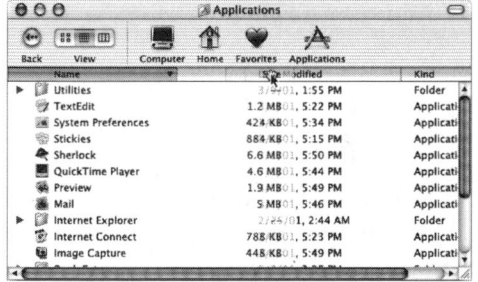

Figure 32 Drag a column on top of the column where you want to move it.

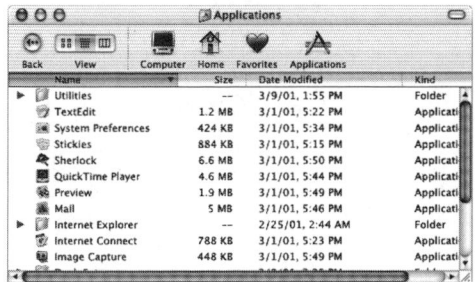

Figure 33 When you release the mouse button, the column moves.

To change a column's width

1. Position the mouse pointer on the line between the heading for the column whose width you want to change and the column to its right. The mouse pointer turns into a vertical bar with two arrows (**Figure 30**).

2. Press the mouse button down and drag as follows:

   ▲ To make the column narrower, drag to the left (**Figure 31**).

   ▲ To make the column wider, drag to the right.

3. When the column is displayed at the desired width, release the mouse button.

✔ Tip

■ If you make a column too narrow to display all of its contents, information may be truncated or condensed.

To change a column's position

1. Position the mouse pointer on the heading for the column you want to move.

2. Press the mouse button down and drag as follows:

   ▲ To move the column to the left, drag to the left (**Figure 32**).

   ▲ To move the column to the right, drag to the right.

   As you drag, the other columns shift to make room for the column you're dragging.

3. When the column is in the desired position, release the mouse button. The column changes its position (**Figure 33**).

✔ Tip

■ You cannot change the position of the Name column.

Icon Names

Mac OS is very flexible when it comes to names for files, folders, and disks.

- ◆ A file or folder name can be up to 255 characters long. A disk name can be up to 27 characters long.

- ◆ A name can contain any character except a colon (:).

This makes it easy to give your files, folders, and disks names that make sense to you.

✔ Tips

- ■ Normally, you name documents when you save them. Saving documents is covered in **Chapter 5**.

- ■ A lengthy file name may appear truncated (or shortened) when displayed in windows and lists.

- ■ No two documents in the same window can have the same name.

- ■ Disks are covered later in this chapter.

To rename an icon

1. Point to the name of the icon (**Figure 34**), and click. After a brief pause, a box appears around the name and the name becomes selected (**Figure 35**).

2. Type the new name. The text you type automatically overwrites the selected text (**Figure 36**).

3. Press Return or Enter, or click anywhere else. The icon is renamed (**Figure 37**).

✔ Tips

- ■ Not all icons can be renamed. If the edit box does not appear around an icon name (**Figure 35**), that icon cannot be renamed.

- ■ You can also rename an icon in the Info window, which is covered in **Chapter 4**.

Figure 34
Select the icon.

Figure 35
When you click, an edit box appears around the name.

Figure 36
Type a new name for the icon.

Figure 37
When you press Return, the name changes.

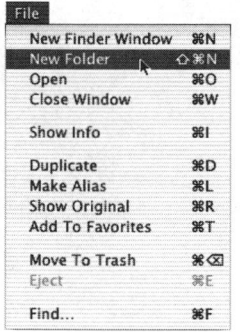

Figure 38
Choose New Folder from the File menu.

Figure 39
A new folder appears.

Figure 40
Enter a name for the folder while the edit box appears around it.

Folders

Mac OS uses folders to organize files and other folders on disk. You can create a folder, give it a name that makes sense to you, and move files and other folders into it. It's a lot like organizing paper files and folders in a file cabinet.

✔ Tips

- ■ A folder can contain any number of files and other folders.

- ■ It's a very good idea to use folders to organize the files on your hard disk. Imagine a file cabinet without file folders—that's how your hard disk would appear if you never used folders to keep your files tidy.

To create a folder

1. Choose File > New Folder (**Figure 38**), or press [Shift][⌃][⌘][N].

   A new untitled folder (**Figure 39**) appears in the active window.

2. While the edit box appears around the new folder's name (**Figure 39**), type a name for it (**Figure 40**) and press [Return].

✔ Tips

- ■ You can rename a folder the same way you rename any other icon. Renaming icons is discussed on the previous page.

- ■ Working with windows is discussed in **Chapter 2**.

CREATING FOLDERS

Moving & Copying Items

In addition to moving icons around within a window or on the desktop, which I discuss in **Chapter 2**, you can move or copy items to other locations on the same disk or to other disks by dragging them:

◆ When you drag an item to a location on the same disk, the item is moved to that location.

◆ When you drag an item to a location on another disk, the item is copied to that location.

◆ When you hold down (Option) while dragging an item to a location on the same disk, the item is copied to that location.

The next few pages provide instructions for all of these techniques, as well as instructions for duplicating items.

✔ Tips

■ You can move or copy more than one item at a time. Begin by selecting all of the items that you want to move or copy, then drag any one of them to the destination. All items will be moved or copied.

■ You can continue working with the Finder— even start more copy jobs—while a copy job is in progress.

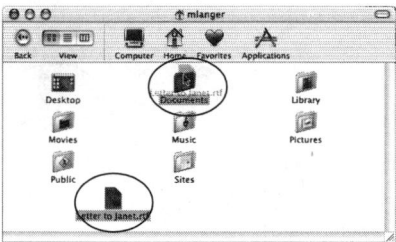

Figure 41 Drag the icon onto the icon for the folder to which you want to move it...

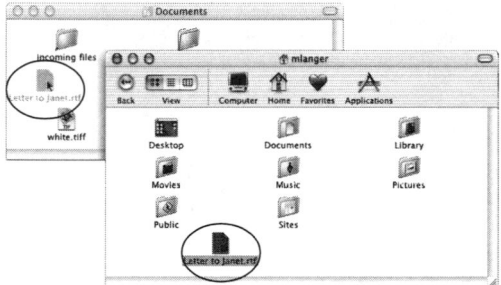

Figure 42 ...or drag the icon into the window in which you want to move it.

To move an item to another location on the same disk

1. Drag the icon for the item that you want to move as follows:

   ▲ To move the item into a specific folder on the disk, drag the icon to the icon for the folder. The icon becomes selected when the mouse pointer moves over it (**Figure 41**).

   ▲ To move the item into a specific window on the disk, drag the icon into the window (**Figure 42**).

2. Release the mouse button. The item moves.

✔ Tip

■ If the destination location is on another disk, the item you drag will be copied rather than moved. You can always delete the original after the copy is made. Deleting items is discussed later in this chapter.

To copy an item to another disk

1. Drag the icon for the item that you want to copy as follows:

   ▲ To copy the item to the top (or *root*) level of a disk, drag the icon to the icon for the destination disk (**Figure 43**).

   ▲ To copy the item into a folder on the disk, drag the icon to the icon for the folder on the destination disk (**Figure 44**).

   ▲ To copy the item into a specific window on the disk, drag the icon into the window (**Figure 45**).

   When the item you are dragging moves on top of the destination location, a plus sign appears beside the mouse pointer. If the destination is an icon, the icon becomes selected.

2. Release the mouse button. A Copy status window like the one in **Figure 46** appears. When it disappears, the copy operation is complete.

✔ Tip

■ You cannot copy items to a disk that is write protected. I tell you about write-protecting disks later in this chapter.

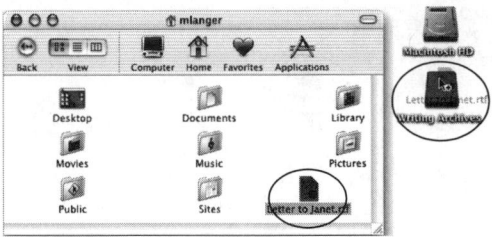

Figure 43 Drag the icon to the destination disk's icon...

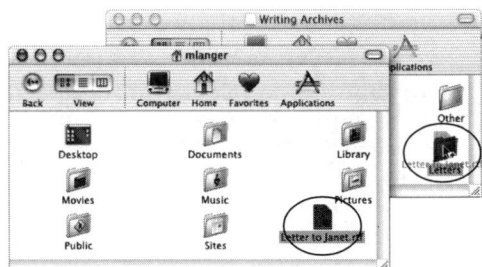

Figure 44 ...or to a folder icon in a window on the destination disk.

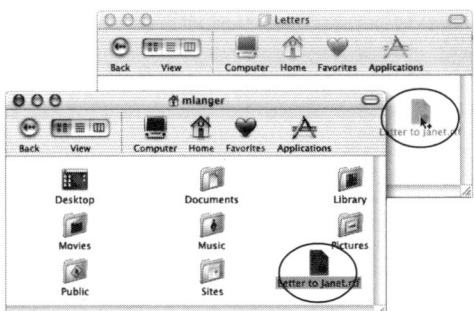

Figure 45 ...or to an open window on the destination disk...

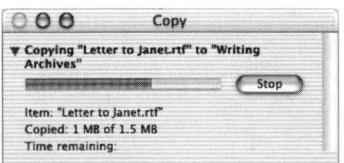

Figure 46 A window like this indicates copy progress.

COPYING ITEMS TO ANOTHER DISK

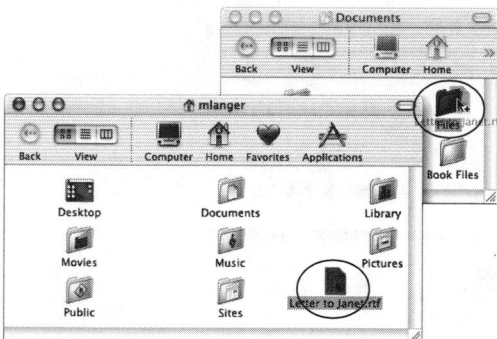

Figure 47 Hold down (Option) while dragging the item onto a folder...

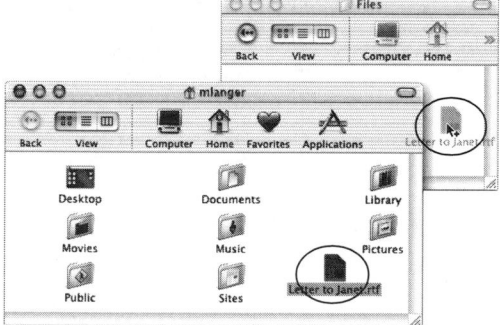

Figure 48 ...or into a window on the same disk.

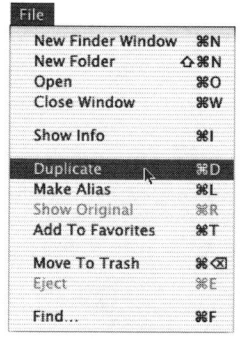

Figure 49
Choose Duplicate
from the File menu.

Figure 50
A duplicate appears
beneath the original.

To copy an item to another location on the same disk

1. Hold down (Option) while dragging the icon for the item that you want to copy onto a folder icon (**Figure 47**) or into a window (**Figure 48**).

   When the mouse pointer on the item you are dragging moves on top of the destination location a plus sign appears beside it. If the destination is an icon, the icon becomes highlighted.

2. Release the mouse button. A Copy status window like the one in **Figure 46** appears. When it disappears, the copy operation is complete.

✔ Tip

- When copying an item to a new location on the same disk, you *must* hold down (Option). If you don't, the item will be moved rather than copied.

To duplicate an item

1. Select the item that you want to duplicate.

2. Choose File > Duplicate (**Figure 49**), or press (⌘ ⌘ D).

or

Hold down (Option) while dragging the item that you want to duplicate to a different location in the same window.

A copy of the item you duplicated appears beside the original. The word *copy* appears at the end of the file name (**Figure 50**).

The Trash & Deleting Items

The Trash is a special place on your hard disk where you place items you want to delete. Items in the Trash remain there until you empty the Trash, which permanently deletes them. In Mac OS X, the Trash appears as an icon in the Dock.

To move an item to the Trash

1. Drag the icon for the item you want to delete to the Trash icon in the Dock.

2. When the mouse pointer moves over the Trash icon, the Trash icon becomes selected (**Figure 51**). Release the mouse button.

or

1. Select the item that you want to delete.

2. Choose File > Move To Trash (**Figure 52**), or press ⌃ ⌘ Delete.

✔ Tips

- The Trash icon's appearance indicates its status:

  ▲ If the Trash is empty, the Trash icon looks like an empty wire basket.

  ▲ If the Trash is not empty, the Trash icon looks like a wire basket with crumpled papers in it (**Figure 53**).

- You can delete more than one item at a time. Begin by selecting all the items you want to delete, then drag any one of them to the Trash. All items will be moved to the Trash.

- Moving a disk icon to the Trash does not delete or erase it. Instead, it ejects, or *unmounts*, it. Working with disks is covered a little later in this chapter.

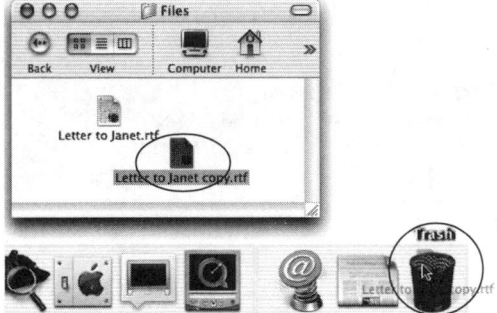

Figure 51 To move an item to the Trash, drag it there...

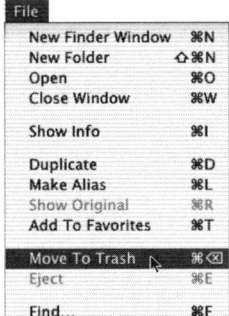

Figure 52
...or select the item and choose Move To Trash from the File menu.

Figure 53
When an item has been moved to the Trash, the Trash icon looks full.

Figure 54 Opening the Trash displays the Trash window.

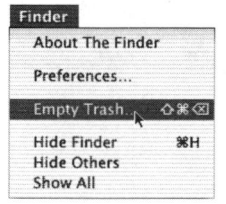

Figure 55
Choose Empty Trash from the Finder menu.

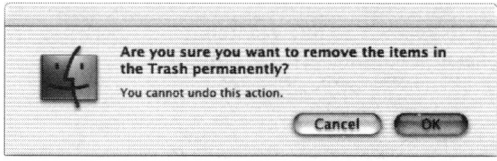

Figure 56 The Trash warning dialog asks you to confirm that you really do want to delete the items in the Trash.

To move an item out of the Trash

1. Click the Trash icon in the Dock to open the Trash window (**Figure 54**).

2. Drag the item from the Trash window to the Desktop or to another window on your hard disk.

To empty the Trash

1. Choose Finder > Empty Trash (**Figure 55**), or press Shift ⌃ ⌘ Delete.

2. A Trash warning dialog like the one in **Figure 56** appears. Click OK to permanently remove all items that are in the Trash.

MOVING ITEMS FROM & EMPTYING THE TRASH

Storage Media

A Mac OS-compatible computer can read data from or write data to a wide range of storage media, including:

◆ **Hard disks**—high capacity magnetic media.

◆ **Floppy disks or diskettes**—low capacity, removable magnetic media.

◆ **CD-ROM, CD-R, and DVD discs**—high capacity, removable optical media.

◆ **Zip, Jaz, or other disks or cartridges**—high capacity, removable magnetic media.

To use storage media, it must be:

◆ **Mounted**—inserted, attached, or otherwise accessible to your computer.

◆ **Formatted** or **initialized**—specially prepared for use with your computer.

All of these things are covered in this section.

✔ Tips

■ Don't confuse storage media with memory. The term *memory* usually refers to the amount of RAM in your computer, not disk space. RAM is discussed in **Chapter 5**.

■ At a minimum, all new Mac OS computers include a hard disk and CD-ROM disc drives.

■ Disk and other storage media drives can be internal (inside your computer) or external (attached to your computer by a cable).

■ Some external storage devices must be properly connected and turned on *before* you start your computer or your computer may not recognize the device.

■ Disk storage media capacity is specified in terms of bytes, kilobytes, megabytes, and gigabytes (**Table 1**).

■ You can tell how much space is available on a disk by checking the status bar in any of the disk's windows (**Figure 57**).

Table 1

Terminology for Storage Media Capacity		
TERM	**ABBREVIATION**	**SIZE**
byte	byte	1 character
kilobyte	KB	1,024 bytes
megabyte	MB	1,024 KB
gigabyte	GB	1,024 MB

Figure 57 A write-protected icon appears in the status bar of CD-ROM discs and other write-protected media.

■ If a disk is *write-protected* or *locked*, files cannot be saved or copied to it. To write protect a floppy disk, move the plastic tab on the back of the disk so it exposes the square hole beneath it. To unlock a disk, move the plastic tab on the back of the disk so it covers the square hole.

■ You cannot write data to a CD-ROM. But if your Mac has a CD-Recordable (CD-R) drive, you can use special software to create or burn your own CDs.

■ All windows for a write-protected or locked disk display a pencil with a line through it in the upper left corner of the status bar (**Figure 57**).

■ Displaying the status bar is explained earlier in this chapter.

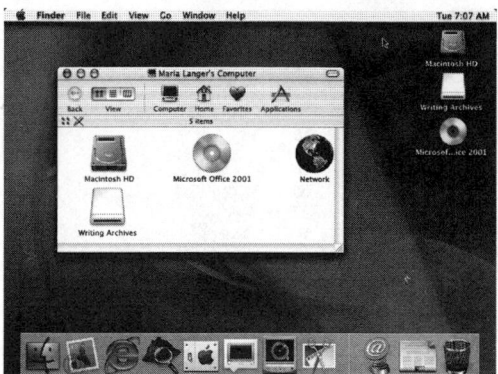

Figure 58 Here's a desktop with a hard disk, Zip disk, and CD-ROM disc mounted.

Mounting Disks

You *mount* a disk by inserting it in the disk drive so it appears on the Mac OS desktop.

✔ Tips

- You must mount a disk to use it.

- To learn how to mount disks that are not specifically covered in this book, consult the documentation that came with the disk drive.

- Mounted disks appear on the desktop as well as in the top-level window for your computer (**Figure 58**).

To mount a CD or DVD disc

1. Follow the manufacturer's instructions to open the CD or DVD disc tray or eject the CD or DVD caddy.

2. Place the CD or DVD disc in the tray or caddy, label side up.

3. Gently push the tray or caddy into the drive. After a moment, the disc icon appears on the desktop (**Figure 58**).

✔ Tip

- If your CD or DVD drive does not use a disc tray or caddy, consult its documentation for specific instructions.

To mount a Zip or Jaz disk

Insert the disk in the Zip or Jaz drive, label side up, metal side in. After a moment, the disk icon appears on the Desktop (**Figure 58**).

To mount a floppy disk

Insert the disk in the floppy disk drive, label side up, metal side in. The disk's icon appears on the desktop.

MOUNTING DISKS

Ejecting Disks

When you eject a disk, the disk is physically removed from the disk drive and its icon disappears from the desktop.

✔ Tip

■ When the disk's icon disappears from the desktop, it is said to be *unmounted*.

To eject a disk

1. Click the disk's icon once to select it.

2. Choose File > Eject (**Figure 59**), or press ⌃ ⌘ E .

or

1. Drag the disk's icon to the Trash (**Figure 60**). As you drag, the Trash icon turns into a rectangle with a triangle on top (**Figure 61**).

2. When the mouse pointer moves over the Trash icon, it becomes selected (**Figure 60**). Release the mouse button.

✔ Tip

■ If you try to eject a disk that contains one or more files that are in use by your computer, a dialog like the one in **Figure 62** appears. Click OK or press Return or Enter to dismiss the dialog, then quit the open application. You should then be able to eject the disk. Working with applications is covered in **Chapter 5**.

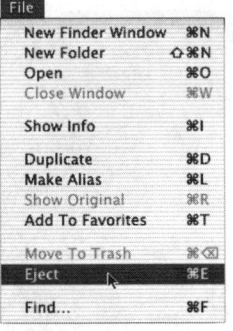

Figure 59
Select the disk, and then choose Eject from the File menu...

Figure 60
...or drag the disk icon to the Trash.

Figure 61
When you drag a disk icon, the Trash icon transforms into an icon like this.

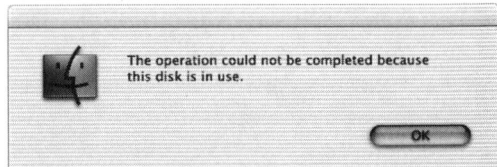

Figure 62 A dialog like this appears if you try to eject a disk that contains open files.

ADVANCED FINDER TECHNIQUES

Advanced Finder Techniques

In addition to the basic Finder and file management techniques covered in **Chapters 2** and **3**, Mac OS X offers more advanced techniques you can use to customize the Finder, work with windows, and manage files:

◆ Customize the desktop and Finder windows.

◆ Customize the toolbar to add buttons for the items you use most.

◆ Customize the Dock to add applications and documents you access often.

◆ Use hierarchical outlines in list view windows.

◆ Use aliases to make frequently used files easier to access without moving them.

◆ Create and organize favorite items.

◆ Use the Info window to learn more about an item or set options for it.

✔ Tips

■ If you're brand new to Mac OS, be sure to read the information in **Chapters 2** and **3** before working with this chapter. Those chapters contain information and instructions about techniques that are used throughout this chapter.

■ This chapter is especially useful for experienced Mac OS users since it goes beyond the basics with new or advanced Mac OS features.

Finder Preferences

The Finder Preferences window enables you to customize several aspects of the desktop and Finder windows.

✔ Tip

- More Mac OS X customization features are covered in **Chapter 11**.

To set Finder Preferences

1. Choose Finder > Preferences (**Figure 1**) to display the Finder Preferences window (**Figure 2**).

2. To set the desktop picture, click the Select Picture button. The Choose A Picture dialog appears (**Figure 3**). Locate and select the desktop picture you want to use, and click Choose. Your change takes effect immediately.

3. To change the size of icons that appear on the desktop, drag the Icon Size slider. Dragging to the left makes the icons smaller; dragging to the right makes them larger.

4. Choose an Icon Arrangement option:

   ▲ **None** enables you to place icons anywhere you like on the desktop.

   ▲ **Always snap to grid** forces icons on the desktop to move into locations on an invisible grid. This keeps things neater but restricts where icons can appear.

5. To show all mounted disks on the desktop, turn on the Show disks on the Desktop check box.

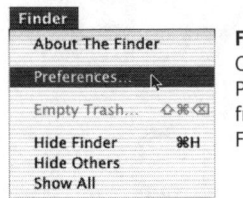

Figure 1
Choose Preferences from the Finder menu.

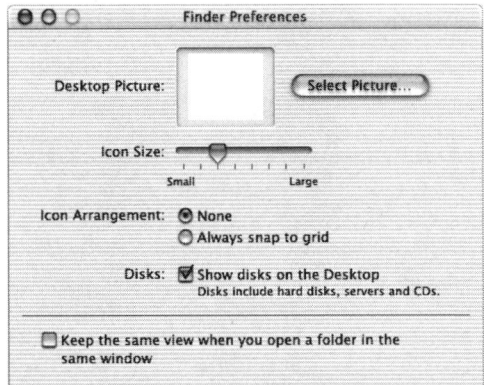

Figure 2 The Finder Preferences window offers options for customizing the desktop and Finder windows.

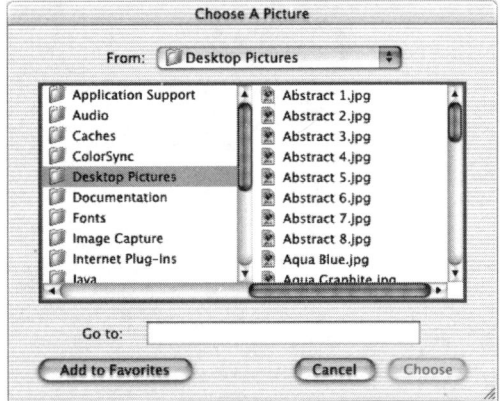

Figure 3 Use the Choose A Picture dialog to select a desktop picture.

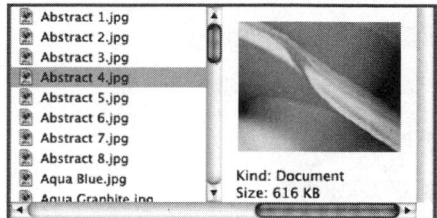

Figure 4 When you select the name of a desktop picture file, a preview of it appears in the right side of the Choose a Picture window.

6. To retain the view settings of a window for each folder you open in the same window, turn on the check box labeled Keep the same view when you open a folder in the same window.

7. Click the Finder Preferences window's close button to dismiss it and save your settings.

✔ Tips

■ A desktop picture is a graphic file that appears beneath all windows and icons.

■ As shown in **Figure 3**, the Choose A Picture dialog should automatically display the contents of the Desktop Pictures folder that is installed with Mac OS X. When you select a picture file, a preview of the picture appears in the dialog (**Figure 4**).

■ Changing the icon size in the Finder Preferences window does not change the size of icons in Finder windows. To change the size of icons in Finder windows, use the view options palette, which is discussed in **Chapter 3**.

■ Disks and mounting disks are discussed in **Chapter 3**.

Customizing the Toolbar

The toolbar, which is discussed in **Chapter 2**, can be customized to include buttons and icons for a variety of commands and items.

✔ Tip

■ When you customize the toolbar, your changes affect the toolbar in all windows in which the toolbar is displayed.

To customize the toolbar

1. With any Finder window open, choose View > Customize Toolbar (**Figure 5**). Toolbar customization options appear in the current window (**Figure 6**).

2. To add an item to the toolbar, drag it from the center part of the window to the position you want it to occupy in the toolbar (**Figure 7**). When you release the mouse button, the item appears (**Figure 8**).

3. To remove an item from the toolbar, drag it from the toolbar into the center part of the window (**Figure 9**). When you release the mouse button, the item disappears (**Figure 10**).

4. To rearrange the order of items on the toolbar, drag them into the desired position (**Figure 11**). When you release the mouse button, the items are rearranged (**Figure 12**).

5. To specify how items should appear on the toolbar, choose an options from the Show pop-up menu at the bottom of the window (**Figure 13**).

6. When you are finished making changes, click Done to hide the toolbar customization options and return to your view of the window.

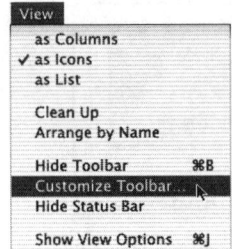

Figure 5
Choose Customize Toolbar from the View menu.

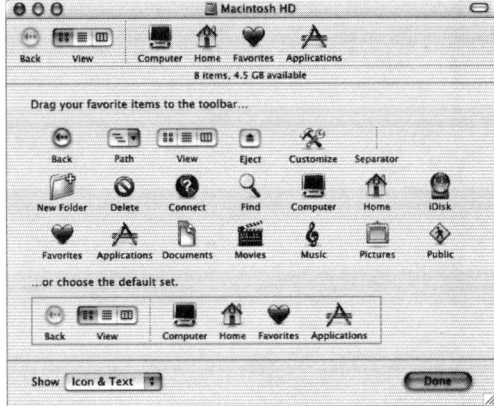

Figure 6 Toolbar customization options appear in the currently open window.

Figure 7 To add an item, drag it from the center part of the window to the toolbar.

Figure 8 When you release the mouse button, the item is added.

CUSTOMIZING THE TOOLBAR

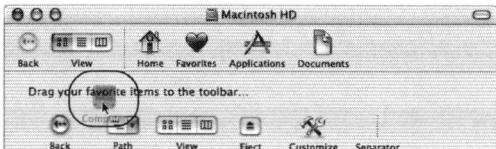

Figure 9 To remove an item, drag it from the toolbar into the center part of the window.

Figure 10 When you release the mouse button, the item is removed.

Figure 11 To rearrange toolbar items, drag them around the toolbar.

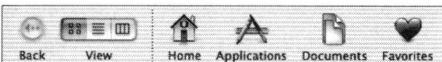

Figure 12 When you release the mouse button, the items are rearranged.

Figure 13
Show pop-up
menu options.

To restore the toolbar to its default settings

1. With any Finder window open, choose View > Customize Toolbar (**Figure 5**). Toolbar customization options appear in the window (**Figure 6**).

2. Drag the group of items in a box near the bottom of the window to the toolbar (**Figure 14**). When you release the mouse button, the toolbar's default items appear (**Figure 6**).

3. Click Done to hide the toolbar customization options and return to your view of the window.

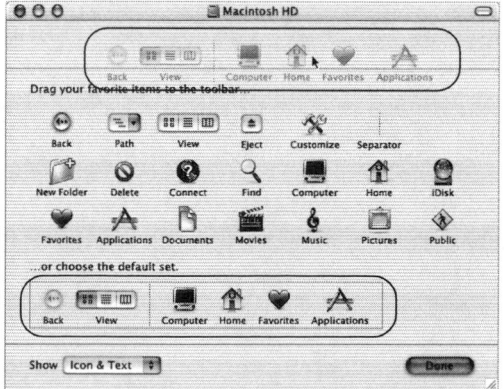

Figure 14 Drag the default set of icons to the toolbar.

Customizing the Dock

The Dock, which is discussed in **Chapter 2**, can be customized to include icons for specific documents and applications that you use often. This makes them quick and easy to open any time you need them.

✔ Tips

- If you used the customizable Apple menu in previous versions of Mac OS, you may want to customize the Dock to include the items you previously included on the Apple menu.

- The discussion of System Preferences in **Chapter 11** includes additional customization options for the Dock.

Figure 15 Drag an icon from the window to the Dock.

To add an icon to the Dock

1. Open the window containing the icon you want to add to the Dock.

2. Drag the icon from the window to the Dock (**Figure 15**). When you release the mouse button, the icon appears (**Figure 16**).

Figure 16 The Icon appears in the Dock.

✔ Tip

- Dragging an icon to the Dock does not remove it from its original location.

To remove an icon from the Dock

Drag the item from the Dock to the desktop (**Figure 17**). When you release the mouse button, the icon disappears in a puff of "smoke" and no longer appears in the Dock (**Figure 18**).

Figure 17 Drag an icon off the Dock.

✔ Tips

- Removing an icon from the Dock does not delete it from disk.

- If you try to remove an icon for an application that is running, the icon will not disappear from the Dock until you quit the application.

Figure 18 The icon is removed from the Dock.

Click a right-pointing triangle to expand the outline.

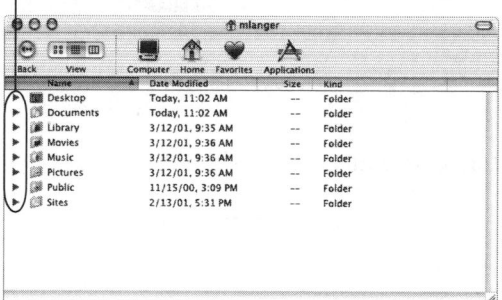

Figure 19 Right-pointing triangles indicate collapsed outlines.

Click a down-pointing triangle to collapse an outline.

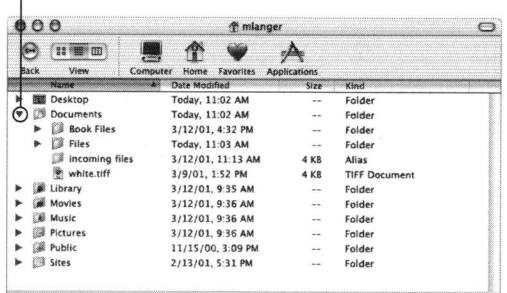

Figure 20 Folder contents can be displayed as an outline...

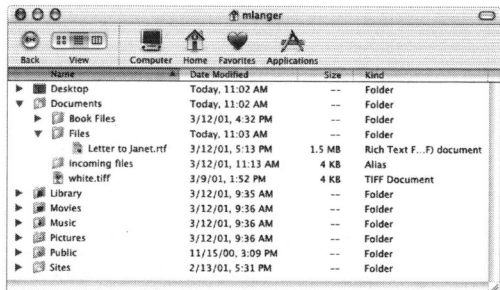

Figure 21 ...that can show several levels.

Outlines in List View

Windows displayed in list view have a feature not found in icon or column views: They can display the contents of folders within the window as an outline (**Figures 20** and **21**).

✔ Tip

- Views are discussed in detail in **Chapters 2** and **3**.

To display a folder's contents

Click the right-pointing triangle beside the folder (**Figure 19**).

or

Click the folder once to select it, and press ⌃ ⌘ →.

The items within that folder are listed below it, slightly indented (**Figure 20**).

✔ Tip

- As shown in **Figure 21**, you can use this technique to display multiple levels of folders in the same window.

To hide a folder's contents

Click the down-pointing triangle beside the folder (**Figure 20**).

or

Click the folder once to select it, and press ⌃ ⌘ ←.

The outline collapses to hide the items in the folder (**Figure 19**).

WORKING WITH LIST VIEW OUTLINES

Aliases

An *alias* is a pointer to an item. You can make an alias of an item and place it anywhere on your computer. Then, when you need to open the item, just open its alias.

✔ Tips

- It's important to remember that an alias is not a copy of the item—it's a pointer. If you delete the original item, the alias will not open.

- You can use the Fix Alias dialog (**Figure 44**) to reassign an original to an alias, as explained later in this chapter.

- By putting aliases of frequently used items together where you can quickly access them—such as on the desktop—you make the items more accessible without actually moving them.

- The Favorites and Recent Items features work with aliases. These features are discussed a little later in this chapter.

- You can name an alias anything you like, as long as you follow the file naming guidelines discussed in **Chapter 3**. An alias's name does not need to include the word *alias*.

- The icon for an alias looks very much like the icon for the original item but is slightly lighter in appearance and includes a tiny arrow (**Figure 22**).

- You can move, copy, rename, open, and delete an alias just like any other file.

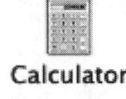

Calculator

Calculator alias

Figure 22
The icon for an alias looks like the original item's icon but includes an arrow.

ALIASES

Figure 23
To create an alias, begin by selecting the item for which you want to make an alias.

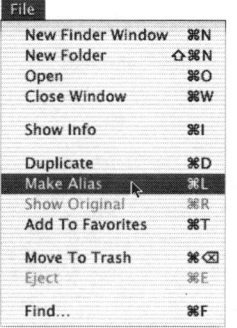

Figure 24
Choose Make Alias from the File menu.

Figure 25
The alias appears right beneath the original.

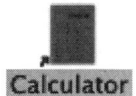

Figure 26
Select the alias's icon.

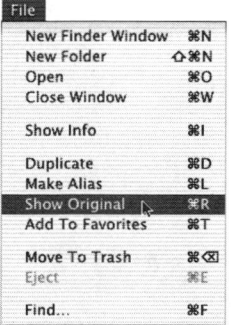

Figure 27
Choose Show Original from the File menu.

To create an alias

1. Select the item you want to make an alias for (**Figure 23**).

2. Choose File > Make Alias (**Figure 24**), or press ⌃ ⌘ L.

   The alias appears right beneath the original item (**Figure 25**).

or

Hold down ⌃ ⌘ Option and drag the item for which you want to make an alias to a new location. The alias appears in the destination location.

✔ Tip

■ An alias's name is selected right after it is created (**Figure 25**). If desired, you can immediately type in a new name to replace the default name.

To find an alias's original file

1. Select the alias's icon (**Figure 26**).

2. Choose File > Show Original (**Figure 27**), or press ⌃ ⌘ R.

   The original item appears selected in the window in which it resides on disk (**Figure 28**).

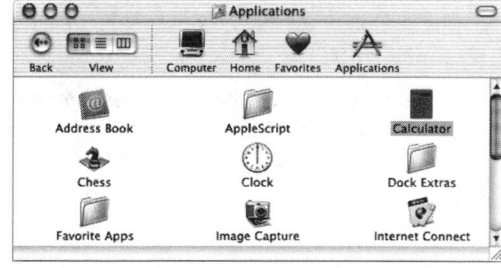

Figure 28 The original item appears selected in its window.

WORKING WITH ALIASES

Favorites

Favorites enables you to add frequently used documents, applications, and other items to the Favorites submenu on the Go menu (**Figure 29**). This makes these items quick and easy to access.

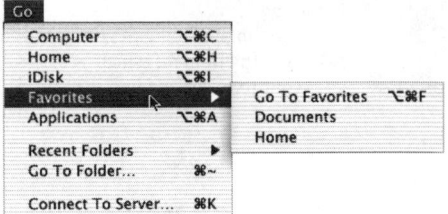

Figure 29 Favorites are listed on the Favorites submenu on the Go menu.

✔ Tips

- Favorites also appear in the Open and Save Location dialogs. The Open and Save Location dialogs are covered in **Chapter 5**.

- The favorites feature works with aliases, which is discussed on the previous two pages.

- Your favorite item aliases are stored in the Favorites folder in the Library folder inside your home folder. You can learn more about your home folder in **Chapter 3**.

- The Mac OS X installer creates favorites for two items (**Figure 29**):

  - ▲ **Documents** is an alias to your Documents folder, which is the default location for storing documents.

  - ▲ **Home** is an alias to your home folder.

Figure 30 Select the item that you want to add as a favorite item.

To add a favorite item

1. In the Finder, select the icon for the item that you want to add as a favorite item (**Figure 30**).

2. Choose File > Add To Favorites (**Figure 31**), or press ⌘ ⌘ T.

   The item is added to the Favorites submenu on the Go menu (**Figure 32**).

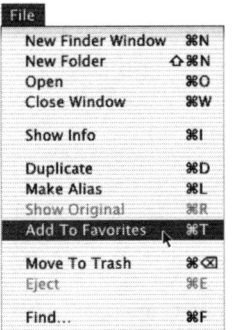

Figure 31 Choose Add To Favorites from the File menu.

✔ Tip

- You can also add a currently selected folder to favorites by clicking the Add to Favorites button in the Open or expanded Save Location (**Figure 33**) dialogs. These dialogs are covered in **Chapter 5**.

Figure 32 The item is added to the Favorites submenu on the Go menu.

ADDING FAVORITES

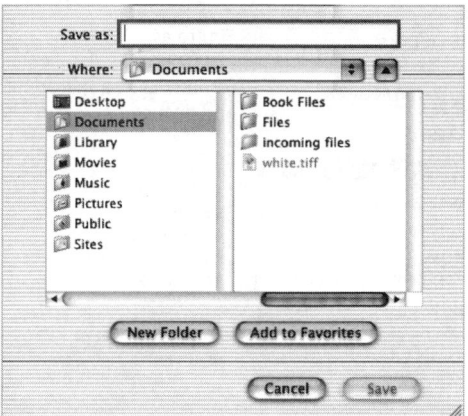

Figure 33 You can click the Add to Favorites button in a Save Location dialog like this one to add the currently selected folder to your favorite items.

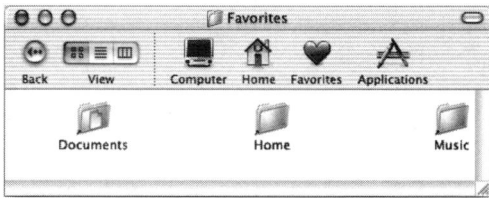

Figure 34 The Favorites folder contains icons for all your favorite items.

To use a favorite item

From the Favorites submenu on the Go menu (**Figures 29** and **32**), choose the item you want to open.

To remove a favorite

1. Click the Favorites button in the toolbar of any Finder window.

   or

   Choose Go > Favorites > Go To Favorites (**Figures 29** and **32**).

   The Favorites folder window opens (**Figure 34**).

2. Drag the item that you want to remove out of the window.

3. Close the Favorites folder window.

   The item is removed from the Favorites submenu.

USING & REMOVING FAVORITES

Recent Items

Recent items are recently opened applications and documents. Mac OS automatically tracks the things you open and creates submenus of the most recently opened items in each category, making it quick and easy to open them again.

To open recent items

To open a recently used item, choose its name from the Recent Items submenu under the Apple menu (**Figure 35**).

✔ Tips

■ The favorites feature works with aliases, which is discussed earlier in this chapter.

■ Working with applications and documents is discussed in **Chapter 5**.

To clear the Recent Items submenu

Choose Apple > Recent Items > Clear Recent Items (**Figure 35**).

✔ Tip

■ Clearing the Recent Items submenu does not delete any application or document files.

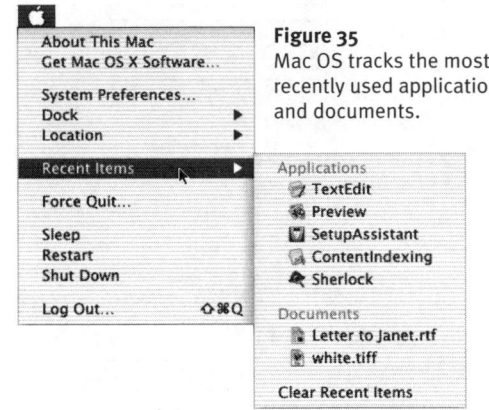

Figure 35
Mac OS tracks the most recently used applications and documents.

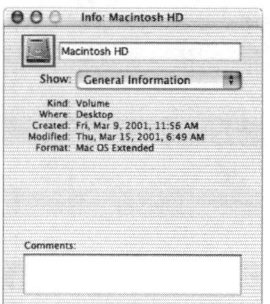

Figure 36
The Info window
for a hard disk.

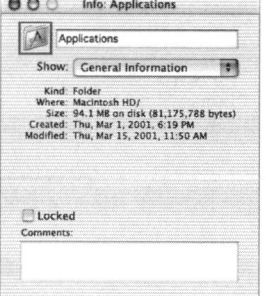

Figure 37
The Info window
for a folder.

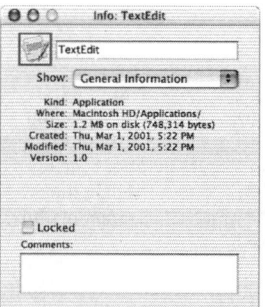

Figure 38
The Info window
for an application.

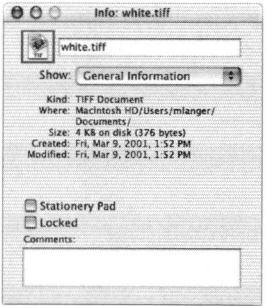

Figure 39
The Info window
for a document.

The Info Window

You can learn more about an item by opening its Info window (**Figures 36** through **39**). Depending on the type of icon (disk, folder, application, document, alias, etc.), the General Information in the Info window will provide some or all of the following information:

◆ **Icon** that appears in the Finder.

◆ **Name** of the item.

◆ **Kind** or type of item.

◆ **Where** item is on disk.

◆ **Size** of item or contents (folders and files only).

◆ **Created** date and time.

◆ **Modified** date and time.

◆ **Format** of item (disks only).

◆ **Version** number or copyright date (files only).

◆ **Original** location on disk (aliases only).

◆ **Stationery Pad** check box to convert the file into a stationery format file (documents only).

◆ **Locked** check box to prevent the file from being deleted or overwritten (folders and files only).

◆ **Comments** entered by users (like you).

✔ Tip

■ Other types of information available for a disk, folder, or file—including Application, Application Files, Preview, and Privileges—are of an advanced nature and are not discussed in this book. You can learn more about this information and about stationery pads in *Mac OS X: Visual QuickPro Guide*, the sequel to this book.

To open the Info window

1. Select the item for which you want to open the Info window (**Figure 40**).

2. Choose File > Show Info (**Figure 41**), or press ⌃ ⌘ I.

   The Info window for that item appears (**Figure 37**).

✔ Tip

■ When the Info window is open, clicking a different icon displays the information for that icon.

To change an item's name

1. In the Info window, drag the mouse pointer over the item's name to select it.

2. Type in the new name. What you type replaces the selected text.

✔ Tip

■ You can change the name of an item only if its name appears within a box (**Figures 36** through **39**). If there is no box around the item's name, you cannot rename it.

To enter comments in the Info window

1. Open the Info window for the item for which you want to enter comments.

2. Click in the Comments box to position the blinking insertion point there.

3. Type your comments (**Figure 42**).

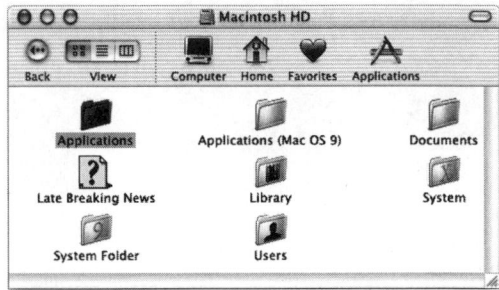

Figure 40 Select the item for which you want to open the Info window.

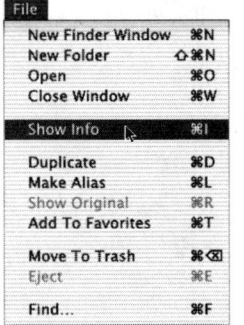

Figure 41
Choose Show Info from the File menu.

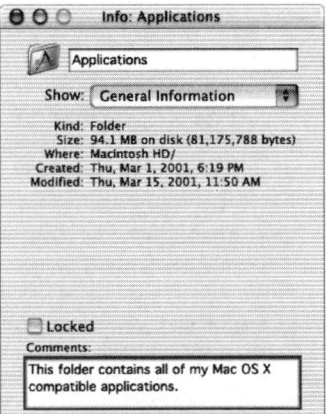

Figure 42
You can enter information about the item in the Comments box.

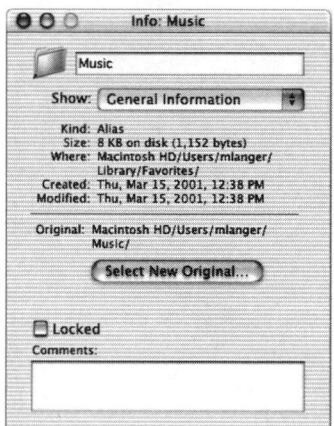

Figure 43
You can click the Select New Original button in the Info window for an alias to assign a new original to the alias.

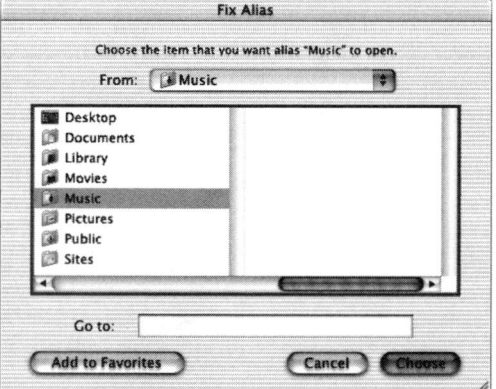

Figure 44 Use the Fix Alias dialog to locate and choose a new original for an alias.

To lock an application or document

1. Open the Info window for the item you want to lock (**Figures 37** through **39** and **42**).

2. Turn on the Locked check box.

✔ Tip

- Locked items cannot be deleted or over-written. They can, however, be moved.

To select a new original item for an alias

1. In the Info window for the alias (**Figure 43**), click the Select New Original button.

2. Use the Fix Alias dialog that appears (**Figure 44**) to locate and select the item that you want to use as the original for the alias.

3. Click Choose. The item you selected is assigned to the alias.

✔ Tip

- The Fix Alias dialog is similar to an Open dialog, which is covered in **Chapter 5**.

To close the Info window

Click the Info window's close button.

or

1. Activate the Info window.

2. Choose File > Close Window, or press ⌘ W.

✔ Tip

- Closing the Info window saves all changes you made to its contents.

WORKING WITH THE INFO WINDOW

APPLICATION BASICS

5

Applications

Applications, which are also known as *programs*, are software packages you use to get work done. Here are some examples:

- ◆ **Word processors**, such as TextEdit and Microsoft Word, are used to write letters, reports, and other text-based documents.

- ◆ **Spreadsheets**, such as Microsoft Excel, have built-in calculation features that are useful for creating number-based documents such as worksheets and charts.

- ◆ **Databases**, such as FileMaker Pro, are used to organize related information, such as the names and addresses of customers or the artists and titles in a record collection.

- ◆ **Graphics** and **presentation** programs, such as Adobe Photoshop, Macromedia FreeHand, and Microsoft PowerPoint, are used to create illustrations, animations, and presentations.

- ◆ **Communications** programs, such as Internet Connect, Microsoft Internet Explorer, and America Online, are used to connect to other computers, including online services and the Internet.

- ◆ **Integrated** software, such as AppleWorks, combines "lite" versions of most other types of software into one cost-effective package.

- ◆ **Utility** software, such as Disk Utility and StuffIt Expander, performs tasks to manage computer files or keep your computer in good working order.

✔ Tips

- ■ Your Mac OS-compatible computer comes with some application software, some of which is discussed throughout this book.

- ■ Make sure the software you buy is Mac OS-compatible.

Mac OS X Applications vs. Classic Applications

Mac OS X supports two types of Mac OS applications:

◆ **Mac OS X applications** are those written specifically for Mac OS X. These programs take advantage of many of the new features of Mac OS X and use its new interface for menus, commands, and onscreen display. You can usually identify Mac OS X applications by the "Made for Mac OS X" label on them.

◆ **Classic applications** are those written for Mac OS 9.x and earlier but not rewritten for Mac OS X. These programs must be run in the Classic environment, which utilizes Mac OS 9.1.

You don't have to do anything special to run a Classic application. Mac OS X will automatically launch the Classic environment when it needs to.

✔ Tips

■ All of the applications that come with Mac OS X are Mac OS X applications.

■ If you upgraded to Mac OS X from a previous version of Mac OS, all of the applications that were on your computer before the upgrade are probably Classic applications.

■ Whenever possible, you should use Mac OS X applications. You'll find that applications run better and faster under Mac OS X than in the Classic environment.

■ Classic applications are covered in greater detail near the end of this chapter.

■ The hard disk window should include two applications folders, as shown in **Figure 1**: Applications and Applications (Mac OS 9).

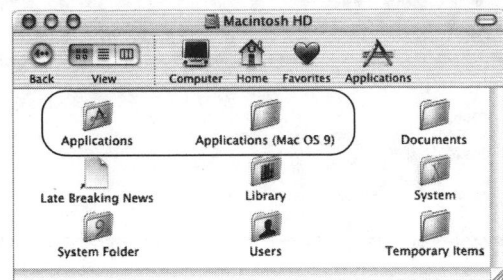

Figure 1 A typical Mac OS X setup includes two Applications folders.

Figure 2 A tiny triangle appears beneath each open application. Click an icon to make its application active.

Multitasking & the Dock

Mac OS uses a form of *multitasking*, which makes it possible for more than one application to be open at the same time. Only one application, however, can be *active*. You must make an application active to work with it.

Since Mac OS X features *preemptive multitasking*, if one application freezes up or bombs, your computer won't freeze up. You can continue using the other applications that are running. Mac OS 8 and 9 use *cooperative multitasking*.

As discussed in **Chapter 2**, you can identify open applications by looking at the Dock; a tiny triangle appears beneath each application that is running (**Figure 2**). You can also use the Dock to switch from one open application to another; simply click on the application's icon in the Dock to make the application active and bring its windows to the foreground on the screen.

✔ Tips

- One application that is always open is Finder, which I cover in detail in **Chapters 2** through **4**.

- The active application is the one whose name appears at the top of the application menu—the menu to the right of the Apple menu—on the menu bar. The application menu is covered in more detail a little later in this chapter.

- Another way to activate an application is to click any of its windows. This brings the window to the foreground onscreen and makes the application active.

Using Applications & Creating Documents

You use an application by opening, or *launching*, it. It loads into the computer's memory. Its menu bar replaces the Finder's menu bar and offers commands that can be used only with that application. It may also display a document window and tools specific to that program.

Most applications create *documents*—files written in a format understood by the application. When you save documents, they remain on disk so you can open, edit, print, or just view them at a later date.

For example, you may use Microsoft Word to write a letter. When you save the letter, it becomes a Word document file that includes all the text and formatting you put into the letter, written in a format that Microsoft Word can understand.

Your computer keeps track of applications and documents. It automatically associates documents with the applications that created them. That's how your computer is able to open a document with the correct application when you open the document from the Finder.

✔ Tips

- You can launch an application by opening a document that it created.

- A document created by an application that is not installed on your computer is sometimes referred to as an *orphan* document since no *parent* application is available. An orphan document usually has a generic document icon (**Figure 3**).

Figure 3

Ducati.jpg An orphan document often has a generic document icon like this one.

Figure 4

Select the icon for the application that you want to open.

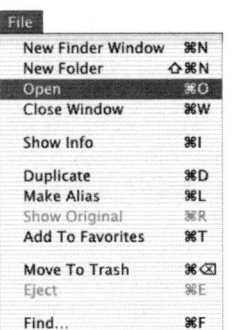

Figure 5

Choose Open from the File menu.

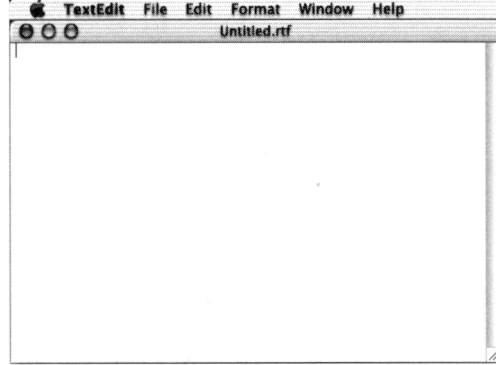

Figure 6 When you launch TextEdit by opening its application icon, it displays an empty document window.

Figure 7 Select the icon for the document that you want to open.

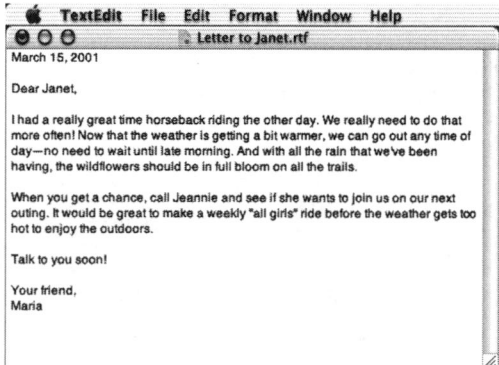

Figure 8 When you launch TextEdit by opening one of its documents, it displays the document.

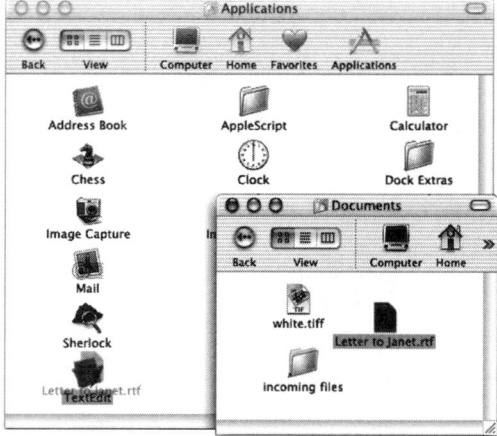

Figure 9 Drag the icon for the document you want to open onto the icon for the application you want to open it with.

To launch an application

Double-click the application's icon.

or

1. Select the application's icon (**Figure 4**).

2. Choose File > Open (**Figure 5**), or press ⌘O.

The application opens (**Figure 6**).

To launch an application & open a document at the same time

Double-click the icon for the document that you want to open.

or

1. Select the icon for the document that you want to open (**Figure 7**).

2. Choose File > Open (**Figure 5**), or press ⌘O.

If the application that created the document is not already running, it launches. The document appears in an active window (**Figure 8**).

To open a document with drag & drop

1. Drag the icon for the document that you want to open onto the icon for the application with which you want to open it.

2. When the application icon becomes selected (**Figure 9**), release the mouse button. The application launches and displays the document (**Figure 8**).

✔ Tips

- This is a good way to open a document with an application other than the one that created it.

- Not all applications can read all documents. Dragging a document icon onto the icon for an application that can't open it either won't launch the application or will display an error message.

LAUNCHING APPS & OPENING DOCS

Standard Application Menus

Apple's Human Interface Guidelines provide basic recommendations to software developers to ensure a certain amount of consistency from one application to another. Nowhere is this more obvious than in the standard menus that appear in most applications: the application menu, File, Edit, Window, and Help. You'll see these menus with the same kinds of commands over and over in most of the applications you use. This consistency makes it easier to learn Mac OS applications.

The next few pages provide a closer look at the standard menus you'll find in most applications.

✔ Tips

■ Finder, which is covered in **Chapters 2** through **4**, has standard menus similar to the ones discussed here.

■ The Finder rules regarding the ellipsis character and keyboard commands displayed on menus also apply to applications. **Chapter 2** explains these rules.

The Application Menu

The application menu is named for the application—for example, the TextEdit application menu (**Figure 10**) or the Address Book application menu (**Figure 11**). It includes commands for working with the entire application.

To learn about an application

1. From the application menu, choose About *application name* (**Figures 10** and **11**).

2. A window with version and other information appears (**Figure 12**). Read the information it contains.

3. When you're finished reading about the application, click the window's close button.

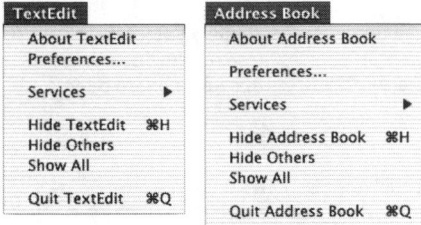

Figures 10 & 11
The TextEdit application menu (left) and the Address Book application menu (right).

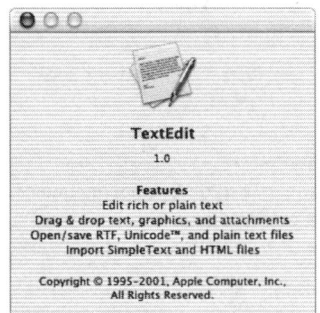

Figure 12
The about window for TextEdit provides its version number and other information.

LEARNING ABOUT APPLICATIONS

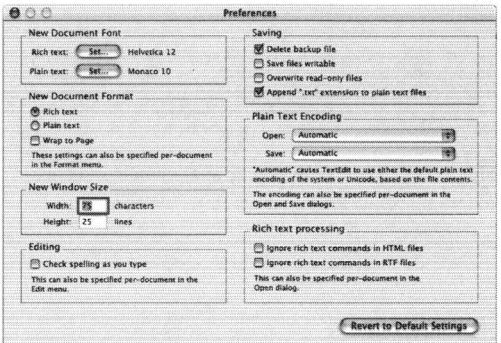

Figure 13 TextEdit's Preferences window offers a number of options you can set to customize the way TextEdit works.

To set application preferences

1. From the application menu, choose Preferences (**Figures 10** and **11**).

2. The application's Preferences window (**Figure 13**) or dialog appears. Set options as desired.

3. Click the window's close button.

   or

   Click the dialog's OK or Save button.

✔ Tip

- Preference options vary greatly from one application to another. To learn more about an application's preferences, check its documentation or online help.

To hide an application

From the application menu, choose Hide *application name* (**Figures 10** and **11**) or press ⌃ ⌘ H. All of the application's windows, as well as its menu bar, are hidden from view.

✔ Tip

- You cannot hide the active application if it is the only application that is open (Finder) or if all the other open applications are already hidden.

To hide all applications except the active one

From the application menu, choose Hide Others (**Figures 10** and **11**).

To display a hidden application

Click the application's icon (or any of its document icons) in the Dock (**Figure 2**).

To unhide all applications

From the Application menu, choose Show All (**Figures 10** and **11**).

To quit an application

1. From the application menu, choose Quit *application name* (**Figures 10** and **11**), or press ⌃⌘Q.

2. If unsaved documents are open, a Save Changes dialog sheet like the one in **Figure 14** appears for each unsaved document.

   ▲ Click Don't Save to quit without saving the document.

   ▲ Click Cancel or press Esc to return to the application without quitting.

   ▲ Click Save or press Return or Enter to save the document.

   The application closes all windows, saves preference files (if applicable), and quits.

✔ Tips

■ Closing all of an application's open windows is not the same as quitting. An application is still running until you quit it.

■ I tell you more about saving documents later in this chapter.

■ In Classic applications, the Quit command is on the File menu.

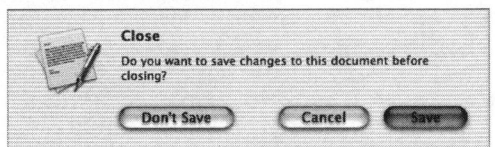

Figure 14 This Close dialog appears when you close a document that contains unsaved changes.

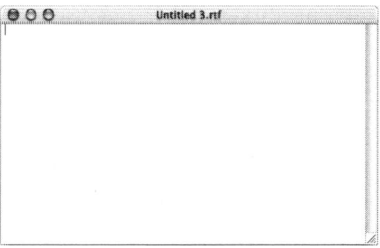

Figures 15, 16, & 17
The File menu in QuickTime Player (top left), TextEdit (bottom left), and Microsoft Internet Explorer (above).

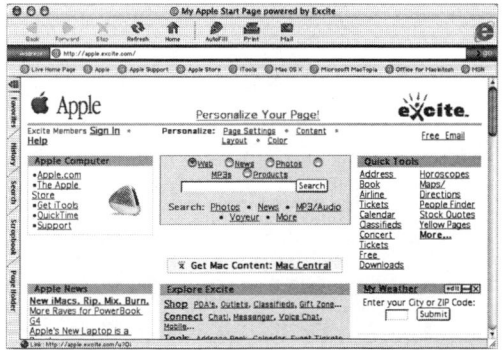

Figure 18 TextEdit's New command displays a new, untitled document window.

The File Menu

The File menu (**Figures 15**, **16**, and **17**) includes commands for working with files or documents. This section discusses the commands most often found under the File menu: New, Open, Close, and Save.

✔ Tip

- The Page Setup and Print commands are also found on the File menu. These commands are discussed in detail in **Chapter 8**.

To create a new document or window

Choose File > New (**Figure 16**).

or

Choose File > New Window (**Figure 17**).

or

Press ⌃ ⌘ N.

A new untitled document (**Figure 18**) or window (**Figure 19**) appears.

✔ Tip

- As shown in **Figures 15**, **16**, and **17**, the exact wording of the command for creating a new document or window varies depending on the application and what the command does. This command, however, is usually the first one on the File menu.

Figure 19 Explorer's New Window command opens a new Web browser window displaying the default Home page.

To open a file

1. Choose File > Open (**Figures 15**, **16**, and **17**) or press ⌃⌘O to display the Open dialog (**Figure 20**).

2. Use any combination of the following techniques to locate the document you want to open:

   ▲ Use the From pop-up menu (**Figure 21**) to select a specific location.

   ▲ Click one of the items in either list to view its contents in the list on the right side of the window. (The list containing the item you clicked shifts to the left if necessary.)

   ▲ Use the scroll bar at the bottom of the two lists to shift lists. Shifting lists to the right enables you to see your path from the root directory (usually your hard disk).

   ▲ In the Go to field, enter the path from the currently selected folder to the folder you want to open. (This is an advanced technique that requires you to know the exact location of a folder or file.)

3. When the name of the file you want to open appears in the list on the right side of the window, use one of the following techniques to open it:

   ▲ Click it to select it and then click Open or press Return or Enter.

   ▲ Double-click it.

✔ Tips

■ The exact wording of the Open command varies depending on the application and what you want to open. For example, the Open command on QuickTime Player's File menu (**Figure 15**) is Open Movie and the Open command on Explorer's File menu (**Figure 17**) is Open File.

Figure 20 A standard Open dialog.

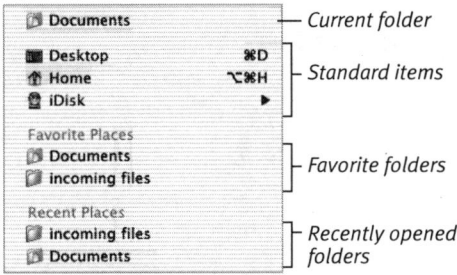

Figure 21 The From (and Where) pop-up menu includes several standard items, as well as your Favorite folders and up to five of the folders most recently accessed by the application.

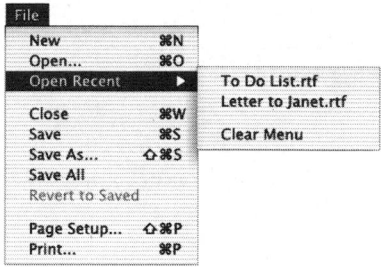

Figure 22 TextEdit's Open Recent submenu makes it easy to reopen a recently opened document.

Figure 23 When you select a file in the Open dialog, a preview or other information for the file appears. This example shows the Open dialog for Preview with a TIFF format file selected.

- The Open Recent command, which is available on the File menu of some applications (**Figure 16**), displays a submenu of recently opened items (**Figure 22**). Choose the item you want to open to open it again.

- The Open dialog (**Figure 20**) has many standard elements that appear in all Open dialogs.

- In step 2, you can make a selected folder into a favorite item by clicking the Add to Favorites button.

- In step 3, you can only select the files that the application can open; other files will either not appear in the list or will appear in gray (**Figure 20**). Some applications include a Show menu that enables you to display the types of files that appear in the Open dialog.

- In step 3, selecting a file's name in the Open dialog may display a preview or other information for the file on the right side of the dialog (**Figure 23**).

- Favorites are covered in **Chapter 4**; iDisk, which requires Internet access, is discussed in **Chapter 9** and **Appendix B**; and file paths are discussed in **Chapter 3**.

To close a window

1. Choose File > Close (**Figures 15**, **16**, and **17**), or press ⌃ ⌘ W.

2. If the window contains a document with changes that have not been saved, a Save Changes dialog sheet like the one in **Figure 14** appears.

    ▲ Click Don't Save to close the window without saving the document.

    ▲ Click Cancel or press Esc to keep the window open.

    ▲ Click Save or press Return or Enter to save the document.

To save a document for the first time

1. Choose File > Save (**Figure 16**) or press
   ⌃ ⌘ S.

   or

   Choose File > Save As (**Figures 16** and **17**).

   A Save dialog sheet appears (**Figure 24** or
   25).

2. Use the Where pop-up menu (**Figure 21**)
   to select a location in which to save the
   document.

   or

   If necessary, click the triangle beside the
   Where pop-up menu (**Figure 24**) to expand
   the dialog (**Figure 25**). Then use any
   combination of the following techniques
   to select a location in which to save the
   document:

   ▲ Click one of the items in either list to
     view its contents on the right side of
     the dialog. (The list containing the
     item you clicked shifts to the left if
     necessary.)

   ▲ Use the scroll bar at the bottom of the
     two lists to shift lists. Shifting lists to
     the right enables you to see your path
     from the root directory (usually your
     hard disk).

   ▲ Click the New Folder button to create a
     new folder inside the currently selected
     folder. Enter a name for the folder in
     the New Folder dialog that appears
     (**Figure 26**), and click Create.

3. When the name of the folder in which you
   want to save the document appears on the
   Where pop-up menu, enter a name for the
   document in the Save as field and click Save.

   The document is saved in the location you
   specified. The name of the file appears in the
   document window's title bar (**Figure 27**).

Figure 24 The Save dialog sheet can be collapsed
to offer fewer options...

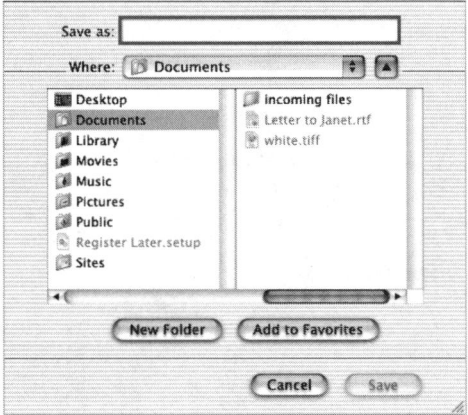

Figure 25 ...or expanded to offer more options.

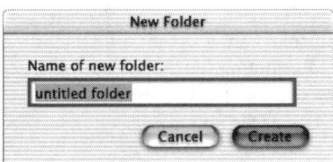

Figure 26 Use the New Folder dialog
to enter a name for a new folder.

Figure 27 The name of the newly saved file appears in
the window's title bar.

Close button

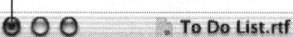

Figure 28 A bullet in the close button of a document window indicates that the document has unsaved changes.

✔ Tips

■ Not all applications enable you to save documents. The standard version of QuickTime Player, for example, does not include a Save command on its File menu (**Figure 15**).

■ The Save dialog (**Figure 24**) is also known as the Save Location dialog because it enables you to select a location in which to save a file.

■ In step 2, you can make a selected folder into a favorite item by clicking the Add to Favorites button.

■ Some applications automatically append a period and a three-character *extension* to a file's name when you save it (**Figure 28**). This extension is used primarily by Windows applications to identify the file type.

■ Favorites are covered in **Chapter 4**; iDisk, which requires Internet access, is discussed in **Chapter 9** and **Appendix B**; and file paths are discussed in **Chapter 3**.

To save changes to a document

Choose File > Save (**Figure 16**), or press ⌃ ⌘ S.

The document is saved in the same location with the same name, thus overwriting the existing version of the document with the new version.

✔ Tip

■ Mac OS X includes two ways to indicate whether a window contains unsaved changes:

▲ A bullet character appears in the close button on the title bar of a window with unsaved changes (**Figure 28**).

▲ A bullet character appears in the Window menu beside the name of a window with unsaved changes (**Figure 32**). The Window menu is discussed a little later in this chapter.

To save a document with a new name or in a new location

1. Choose File > Save As (**Figures 16** and **17**) to display the Save dialog sheet (**Figure 24** or **25**).

2. Follow steps 2 and 3 in the section titled "To save a document for the first time" to select a location, enter a name, and save the document.

✔ Tips

- Saving a document with a new name or in a new location creates a copy of the existing document. From that point forward, you work with the copy, not the original.

- If you use the Save dialog to save a document with the same name as a document in the selected location, a Replace Confirmation dialog like the one in **Figure 29** appears. You have two options:

  ▲ Click Cancel or press ⌷Esc⌷ to return to the Save dialog and either change the document's name or the save location.

  ▲ Click Replace or press ⌷Return⌷ or ⌷Enter⌷ to replace the document on disk with the current document.

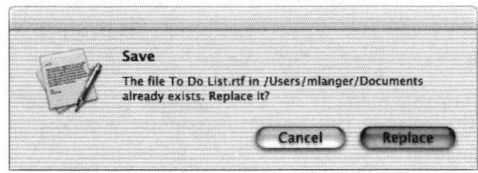

Figure 29 This dialog box appears when you try to save a file with the same name as another file in a folder.

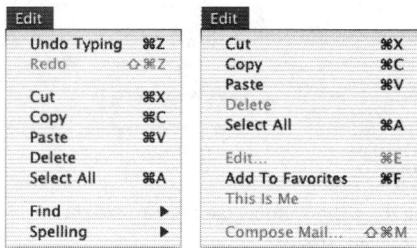

Figures 30 & 31 The Edit menus for TextEdit (left) and Address Book (right).

The Edit Menu

The Edit menu (**Figures 30** and **31**) includes commands for modifying the contents of document. Here's a quick list of the commands you're likely to find, along with their standard keyboard commands:

◆ **Undo** (⌃⌘Z) reverses the last editing action you made.

◆ **Redo** reverses the last undo.

◆ **Cut** (⌃⌘X) removes a selection from the document and puts a copy of it in the Clipboard.

◆ **Copy** (⌃⌘C) puts a copy of a selection in the Clipboard.

◆ **Paste** (⌃⌘V) inserts the contents of the Clipboard into the document.

◆ **Clear** or **Delete** removes a selection from the document. This is the same as pressing Delete when document contents are selected.

◆ **Select All** (⌃⌘A) selects all text or objects in the document.

✔ Tips

■ As you can see in **Figures 30** and **31**, not all Edit menu commands are available in all applications.

■ Edit menu commands work with selected text or graphic objects in a document.

■ Most Edit menu commands are discussed in greater detail in **Chapter 7**, which covers TextEdit.

The Window Menu

The Window menu (**Figures 32** and **33**) includes commands for working with open document windows as well as a list of the open windows.

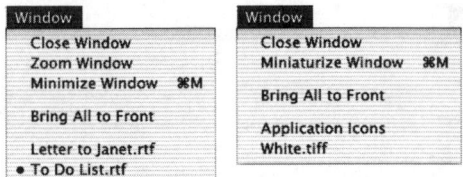

Figures 32 & 33 The Window menus for TextEdit (left) and Preview (right).

✔ Tips

- The windows within applications have the same basic parts and controls as Finder windows, which are discussed in detail in **Chapter 2**.

- A bullet character beside the name of a window in the Window menu indicates that the window contains a document with unsaved changes.

To close a window

1. Choose Window > Close Window (**Figures 32** and **33**).

2. If the window contains a document with changes that have not been saved, a Save Changes dialog sheet like the one in **Figure 14** appears.

   ▲ Click Don't Save to close the window without saving the document.

   ▲ Click Cancel or press (Esc) to keep the window open.

   ▲ Click Save or press (Return) or (Enter) to save the document.

To zoom a window

Choose Window > Zoom Window (**Figure 32**).

The window toggles between its full size and a custom size you create with the window's resize control.

CLOSING & ZOOMING WINDOWS

Figure 34 The icon for a minimized window appears in the Dock.

To minimize a window

Choose Window > Minimize Window (**Figure 32**).

or

Choose Window > Miniaturize Window (**Figure 33**).

or

Press ⌃ ⌘ M.

An animation shows the window shrink down to the size of an icon and slip into the Dock (**Figure 34**).

To display a minimized window

With the application active, choose the window's name from the Window menu (**Figures 32** and **33**).

or

Click the window's icon in the Dock (**Figure 34**).

The window expands out of the Dock and appears onscreen.

To bring all of an application's windows to the front

Choose Window > Bring All to Front (**Figures 32** and **33**).

All of the application's open windows are displayed on top of open windows for other applications.

✔ Tip

- This concept is brand new to Mac OS X, which allows an application's windows to be mingled in layers with other applications' windows.

To activate a window

Choose the window's name from the Window menu (**Figures 32** and **33**).

MINIMIZING & DISPLAYING WINDOWS

The Help Menu

The Help menu (**Figures 35** and **36**) includes commands for viewing onscreen help information specific to the application. Choosing the primary Help command launches the Help Viewer application with help information and links (**Figures 37** and **38**).

✔ Tips

- Onscreen help is covered in detail in **Chapter 12**.

- Although the Help menu may only have one command for a simple application (**Figures 35** and **36**), it can have multiple commands to access different kinds of help for more complex applications.

Figures 35 & 36 The Help menu for Sherlock (left) and TextEdit (right).

Figure 37 Choosing Sherlock Help from Sherlock's Help menu displays this window,...

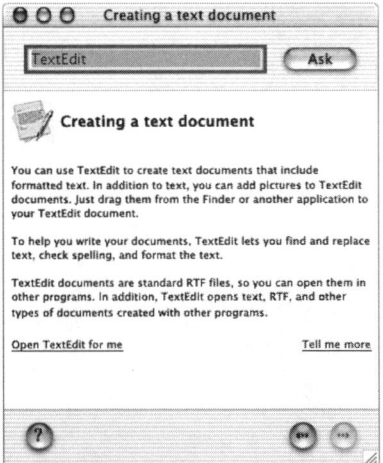

Figure 38 ...while choosing TextEdit Help from TextEdit's Help menu displays this window.

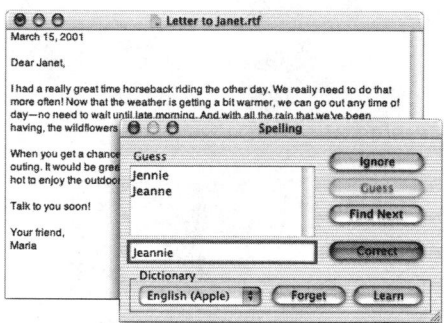

Figure 39 This Spelling dialog in TextEdit is an example of a modeless dialog—you can interact with the document while the dialog is displayed.

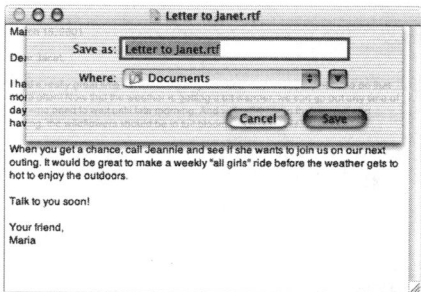

Figure 40 A standard Save Location dialog sheet is an example of a document modal dialog—you must address and dismiss it before you can continue working with the document it is attached to.

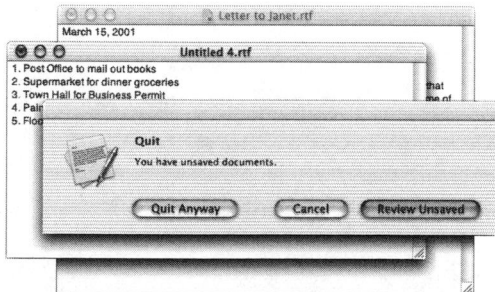

Figure 41 An application modal dialog like this Quit dialog requires your attention before you can continue working with the application.

Dialogs

Mac OS applications use *dialogs* to tell you things and get information from you. Think of them as the way your computer has a conversation—or dialog—with you.

Mac OS X has three main types of dialogs:

- *Modeless* dialogs enable you to work with the dialog while interacting with document windows. These dialogs usually have their own window controls to close and move them (**Figure 39**).

- *Document modal* dialogs usually appear as dialog *sheets* attached to a document window (**Figure 40**). These dialogs must be addressed and dismissed before you can continue working with the window, although you can switch to another window or application while the dialog is displayed.

- *Application modal* dialogs appear as movable dialogs (**Figure 41**). These dialogs must be addressed and dismissed before you can continue working with the application, although you can switch to another application while the dialog is displayed.

This part of the chapter identifies and explains the standard parts of a dialog that you'll see over and over in every application you use.

✔ Tips

- You don't need to remember the modeless vs. modal terminology to work with Mac OS X. Just understand how the dialogs differ and what the differences mean.

- Some dialogs are basically the same from one application to another. This chapter covers some of these standard dialog types, including Open (**Figure 20**), Save Location (**Figures 24, 25,** and **40**), Save Changes (**Figure 14**), and Replace Confirmation (**Figure 29**). Two more standard dialog types—Page Setup and Print—are covered in **Chapter 8**.

To use dialog parts

◆ Click a *tab control* to view a *pane* full of related options (**Figure 42**).

◆ Enter text or numbers into *entry fields* (**Figure 44**), including those that are part of combination boxes (**Figure 43**).

◆ Use *scroll bars* to view the contents of *scrolling lists* (**Figure 43**). Click a list item once to select it or to enter it in a *combination box* (**Figure 43**).

◆ Click a *pop-up menu* (**Figures 43** and **44**) to display its options. Click a menu option to select it.

◆ Click a *check box* (**Figure 45**) to select or deselect it. (A check box is selected when a check mark or X appears inside it.)

◆ Click a *radio button* (**Figure 45**) to select it. (A radio button is selected when a bullet appears inside it.)

◆ Drag a *slider* thumb control (**Figure 45**) to change a setting.

◆ Consult a preview area (**Figure 42**) to see the effects of your changes.

◆ Drag an image file into an *image well* (**Figure 44**).

◆ Click a *push button* (**Figures 42** and **44**) to select it.

Pane   Tab controls   Preview area

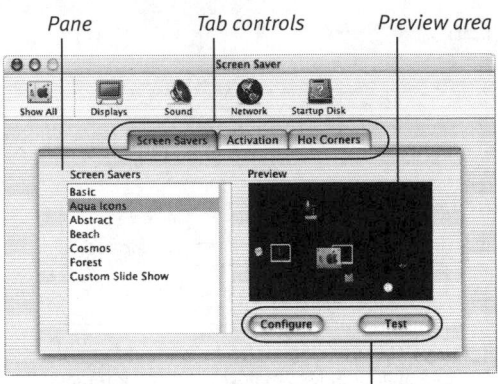

Figure 42 The Screen Saver pane of the System Preferences application.   Push buttons

Scrolling lists   Combination box

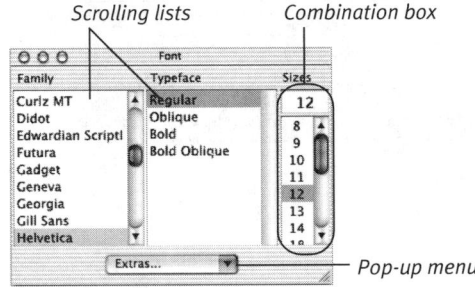

Figure 43 TextEdit's Font pane.   Pop-up menu

Entry field (active)   Pop-up menu   Entry field (inactive)   Image well

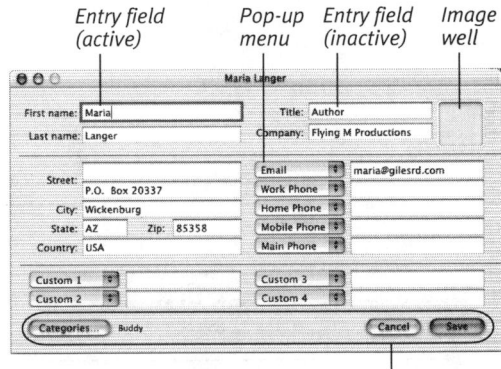

Figure 44 Address Book's Edit Address Card window.   Push buttons

Radio button *Check box* *Slider control*

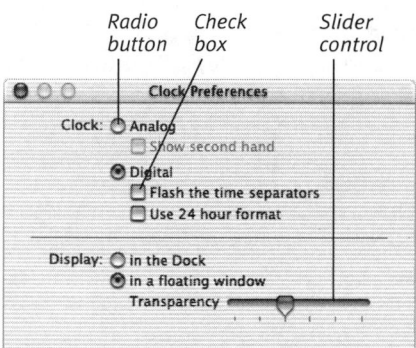

Figure 45 The Clock Preferences dialog for the Clock application.

✔ Tips

- An entry field with a dark border around it is the active field (**Figure 44**). Typing automatically enters text in this field. You can advance from one entry field to the next by pressing Tab.

- If an entry field has a pair of arrows or triangles beside it you can click the triangles to increase or decrease a value already in the field.

- The default push button is the one that pulsates (such as the Save button in **Figure 44**). You can always select a default button by pressing Enter and often by pressing Return.

- You can usually select a Cancel button (**Figure 44**) by pressing Esc.

- You can select as many check boxes (**Figure 45**) in a group as you like.

- One and only one radio button in a group must be selected (**Figure 45**). If you try to select a second radio button, the first button becomes deselected.

- If you click the Cancel button in a dialog (**Figure 44**), any options you set are lost.

- To select multiple items in a scrolling list, hold down ⌃ ⌘ while clicking each one. Be aware that not all dialogs support multiple selections in scrolling lists.

- There are other standard controls in Mac OS X dialogs. These are the ones you'll encounter most often.

USING DIALOGS

Using Classic Applications

When you open an application that isn't Mac OS X compatible, Mac OS X automatically launches the Classic environment, then opens the application within it. The application runs under Mac OS 9.1, which has slightly different interface elements.

This part of the chapter explains how you can manually start and stop the Classic environment, as well as how to use standard Open and Save As dialogs within Mac OS 9.1 applications.

To start the Classic environment

Open any application that is not Mac OS X compatible. The Classic environment launches automatically, and the application opens within it (**Figure 51**).

or

1. Choose Apple menu > System Preferences (**Figure 46**).

2. In the System Preferences window that appears, click the Classic icon (**Figure 47**) to display the Classic pane (**Figure 48**).

3. If necessary, select the hard disk on which Mac OS 9.1 is installed.

4. Click the Start button.

5. Wait while the Classic environment starts. A window with a progress bar (**Figure 49**) tracks its progress. When it's finished, the progress window disappears and the message "Classic is running" appears in the Classic pane (**Figure 50**).

✔ Tip

■ If you often use Mac OS 9.1 applications, you can configure your computer to automatically start the Classic environment when you start or log in to your computer. Just turn on the Start up Classic on login to this computer check box in the Classic pane of System Preferences (**Figure 48**).

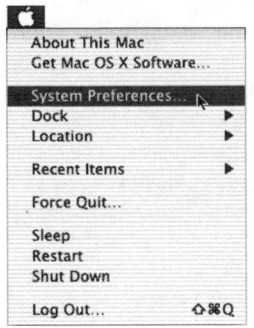

Figure 46
Choose System Preferences from the Apple menu.

Figure 47
The Classic icon in the System Preferences window.

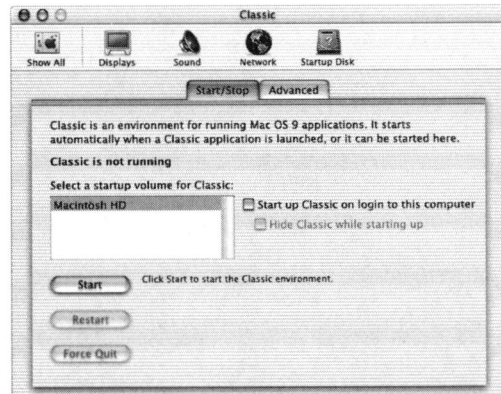

Figure 48 The Classic pane of System Preferences.

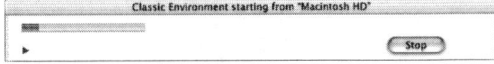

Figure 49 This window appears while the Classic environment starts up.

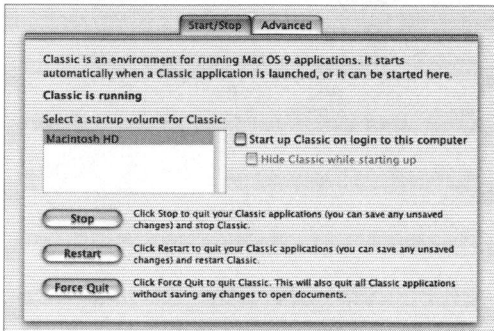

Figure 50 Once the Classic environment is running, you can use the Classic pane to stop it.

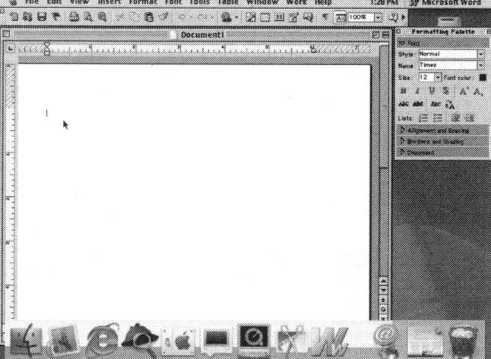

Figure 51 Microsoft Word 2001 running in the Classic environment.

To stop the Classic environment

1. Choose Apple menu > System Preferences (**Figure 46**).

2. In the System Preferences window that appears, click the Classic icon (**Figure 47**) to display the Classic pane (**Figure 50**).

3. Click the Stop button.

4. Your computer switches to the Classic environment and attempts to Quit each open Mac OS 9.1 application. Use any dialog boxes that appear to save changes to unsaved documents.

STOPPING THE CLASSIC ENVIRONMENT

111

To use a Mac OS 9.1 Open dialog

1. Choose File > Open (**Figure 52**), or press
   ⌘⌘O.

   A dialog similar to the one in **Figure 53** or
   54 appears.

2. Use any combination of these techniques
   to navigate to the file you want to open:

   ▲ To open an item in a scrolling list, click
   to select it and then click Open or
   double-click it.

   ▲ To back up out of the current folder to
   a previous folder in the file hierarchy,
   choose a folder from the pop-up menu
   above the scrolling list (**Figure 55**) or
   press ⌘⌘↑ to back up one folder
   level at a time.

   ▲ Click the triangle to the left of the name
   of a disk or folder that you want to open
   (**Figure 54**) to display its contents along
   with the contents of other disks or
   folders (**Figure 56**).

   ▲ Open several files at once by holding
   down [Shift] while clicking the names of
   the files you want to open. (This only
   works in applications that support it.)

   ▲ Choose an option from the Shortcuts
   button menu (**Figure 57**) to quickly
   access the desktop, mounted disks, or
   disks available over the network or
   Internet.

   ▲ Choose an item from the Favorites
   button menu (**Figure 58**) to open a
   Favorite item.

   ▲ Choose an item from the Recent
   button menu (**Figure 59**) to open an
   item you recently opened with that
   application.

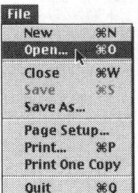

Figure 52
Choose Open from the
application's—in this case
SimpleText's—File menu.

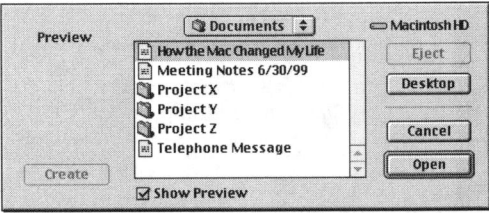

Figure 53 An Open dialog can look like this...

Favorites
Shortcuts | *Recent*

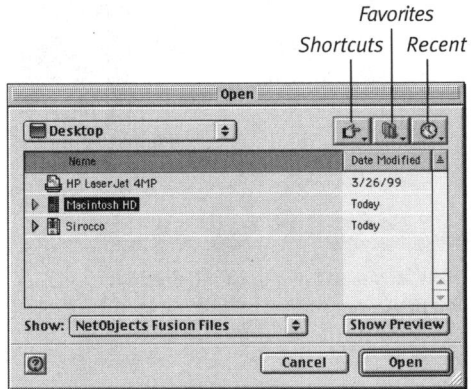

Figure 54 ...or like this.

Figure 55 Use the pop-up menu above the scrolling
list to choose a different folder in the hierarchy.

USING THE OPEN DIALOG

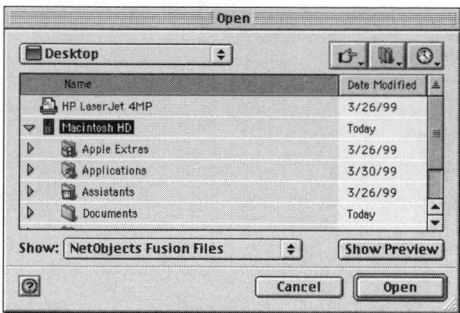

Figure 56 Click a triangle to display the items within its folder or disk.

Figure 57
The Shortcuts button displays the desktop, network connections, and other mounted disks.

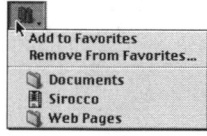

Figure 58
The Favorites button displays your Favorites.

Figure 59 The Recent button displays items recently opened with that application.

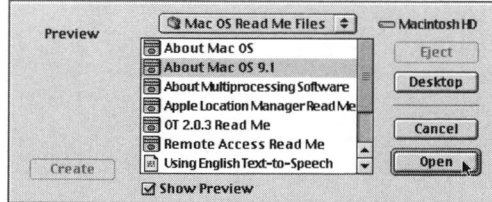

Figure 60 Select the file's name and click Open to open it within the application.

3. Click to select the name of the file that you want to open and then click Open (**Figure 60**) or press [Return] or [Enter].

or

Double-click the name of the file that you want to open.

✔ Tips

- ■ To quickly view the items on the Desktop, click the Desktop button (**Figure 53**) or press [⌃ ⌘ D]. This enables you to open folders, files, and other disks on your Desktop.

- ■ Some Open dialogs offer a Show pop-up menu that lets you narrow down a file list by document or file type (**Figure 54**).

To use the Mac OS 9.1 Save As dialog

1. Choose File > Save As (**Figure 61**). A dialog similar to the one in **Figure 62** or **63** appears.

2. Use any combination of these techniques to navigate to the folder in which you want to save the document:

   ▲ To open an item in a scrolling list, click to select it and then click Open or double-click it.

   ▲ To back up out of the current folder to a previous folder in the file hierarchy, choose a folder from the pop-up menu above the scrolling list (**Figure 55**) or press ⌘↑ to back up one folder level at a time.

   ▲ Choose an option from the Shortcuts button menu (**Figure 57**) to quickly access the desktop, mounted disks, or disks available over the network or Internet.

   ▲ Choose an item from the Favorites button menu (**Figure 58**) to open a Favorite folder.

   ▲ Choose an item from the Recent button menu (**Figure 59**) to open an folder you recently opened with that application.

3. In the edit box beneath the scrolling list, enter the name that you want to give the document.

4. Click Save, or press Return or Enter.

✔ Tips

■ If you have never saved the document, you can also choose Save from the application's file menu or press ⌘S to display the Save As dialog.

■ To quickly view the items on the Desktop, click the Desktop button (**Figure 62**) or press ⌘D. This enables you to open folders and other disks on your Desktop.

Figure 61
Choose Save As from the application's—in this case, SimpleText's— File menu.

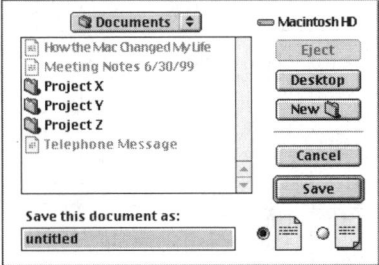

Figure 62 A Save As dialog could look like this...

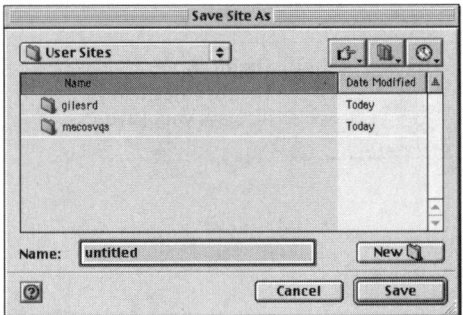

Figure 63 ...or like this.

USING MAC OS SOFTWARE

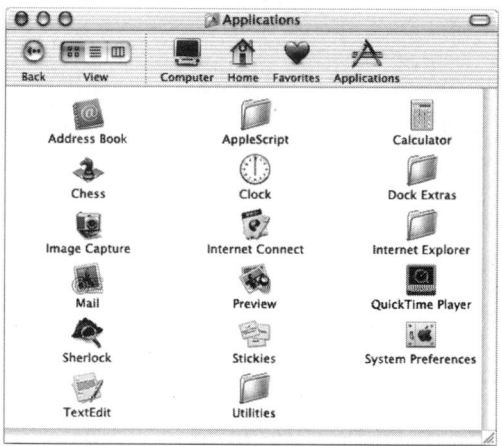

Figure 1 The software that comes with Mac OS can be found in the Applications folder...

Figure 2 ...and the Utilities folder within the Applications folder.

Mac OS Software

Mac OS X includes a variety of software programs that you can use to perform tasks on your computer.

This chapter covers the following programs in the Applications folder (**Figure 1**):

◆ **Address Book**, which enables you to keep track of contact information for friends, family members, and business associates.

◆ **Calculator**, which enable you to perform quick calculations and graph formulas.

◆ **Chess**, which is a computerized version of the game of chess.

◆ **Clock**, which displays a live-action digital or analog clock.

◆ **Preview**, which enables you to view images.

◆ **QuickTime Player**, which enables you to view QuickTime movies and streaming video.

◆ **Stickies**, which enables you to place colorful notes on your computer screen.

It also covers the following program in the Utilities Folder (**Figure 2**):

◆ **Key Caps**, which displays the characters in any installed font.

✔ Tips

■ Installing Mac OS and using Setup Assistant is covered in **Chapter 1**.

■ Mac OS X includes a number of other applications and utilities that are discussed elsewhere in this book and in *Mac OS X: Visual QuickPro Guide*:

▲ TextEdit is covered in **Chapter 7**.

▲ Print Center is covered in **Chapter 8**.

▲ Internet Connect, Internet Explorer, and Mail are covered in **Chapter 9**.

▲ Sherlock is covered in **Chapter 10**.

▲ System Preferences is covered in **Chapter 11**.

▲ AppleScript, Apple System Profiler, Applet Launcher, Battery Monitor, ColorSync Utility, Console, CPU Monitor, DigitalColor Meter, Directory Setup, Disk Copy, Disk Utility, Display Calibrator, Grab, Image Capture, Installer, Keychain Access, NetInfo Manager, Network Utility, Process Viewer, StuffIt Expander, and Terminal are covered in *Mac OS X: Visual QuickPro Guide*.

Address Book

Figure 3
The Address
Book icon.

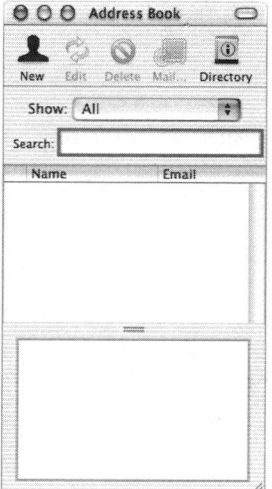

Figure 4
The main Address
Book window.

Address Book

The new Address Book application enables you to keep track of the names, addresses, phone numbers, and e-mail addresses of people you know. Its built-in directory search feature enables you to search LDAP directories on the Internet for contact information. Once an e-mail address is stored within Address Book, you can use it to send e-mail messages with Mac OS's new Mail application.

✔ Tips

- You must have an Internet connection to search LDAP directories and send e-mail.

- **Chapter 9** covers Mac OS X's Mail application.

To launch Address Book

Double-click the Address Book icon (**Figure 3**) in the Applications folder (**Figure 1**).

or

Click the Address Book icon (**Figure 3**) in the Applications folder (**Figure 1**) and choose File > Open, or press ⌃ ⌘ O.

Address Book's main window appears (**Figure 4**).

✔ Tips

- You can also open Address Book from within the Mail application, as discussed in **Chapter 9**.

- *LDAP*, which is short for *Lightweight Directory Access Protocol*, is used for accessing information directories.

To add a new contact record

1. Click the New button in the toolbar (**Figure 4**).

2. Enter information into appropriate fields of the untitled Address Card window that appears (**Figure 5**). You can enter information into any combination of fields. Press [Tab] to move from field to field and use pop-up menus when necessary to identify information.

3. To set a category for the contact, click the Categories button to display the Choose Categories dialog sheet (**Figure 6**). Turn on the check box beside each category you want to assign to the record and click OK.

4. When you are finished entering data for the contact, click Save in the Address Card window. The information is saved and the contact appears in the main Address Book window (**Figure 7**).

✔ Tips

- You can also include a photo or logo for the contact. Simply drag a graphic file icon from a Finder window onto the image well in the Address Card window (**Figure 8**). When you release the mouse button, the image appears. The image also appears in the Address Book main window when the contact is selected (**Figure 9**).

- By assigning categories to contacts, you can use the Show pop-up menu in the Address Book window to narrow down the contact list.

- You can add additional categories to Address Book by clicking the + button in the Choose Categories dialog sheet (**Figure 6**). This adds a blank category line (**Figure 10**), which you can fill in with the name of a category. Likewise, you can delete a custom category by selecting it and clicking the – button.

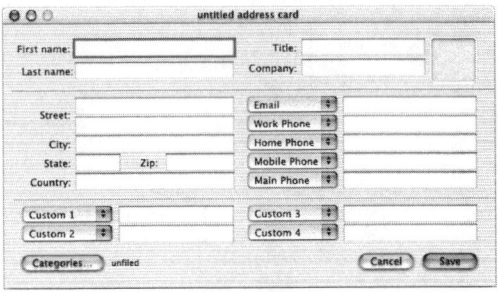

Figure 5 Use this form to enter data for a contact.

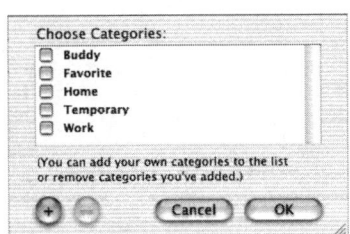

Figure 6 This dialog sheet enables you to specify categories for a contact.

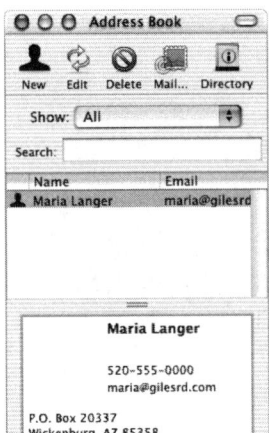

Figure 7 When you save the contact information, it appears in the Address Book window.

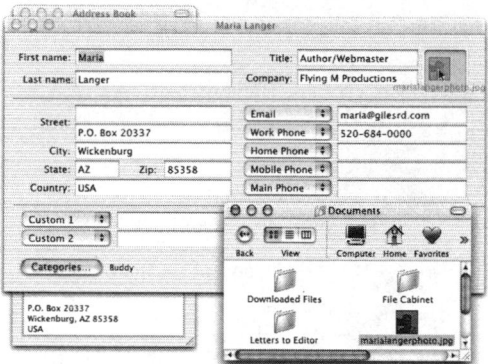

Figure 8 To add a picture for a record, simply drag its icon into the image well.

Figure 9
The picture is added to the record and appears in the Address Book window.

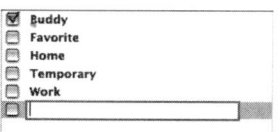

Figure 10
You can add categories to the list.

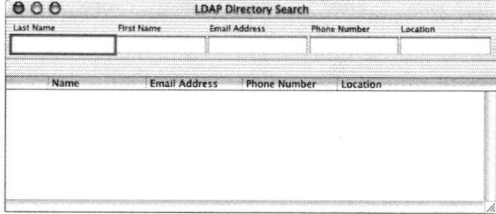

Figure 11 The LDAP Directory Search window.

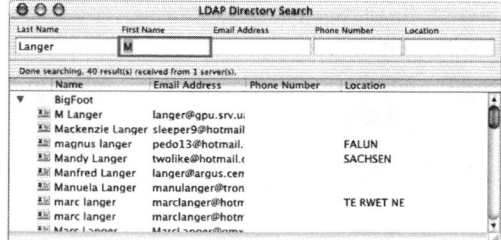

Figure 12 Search results appear in the bottom half of the window.

To edit a contact record

1. In the Address Book window, select the contact you want to edit.

2. Click the Edit button on the toolbar.

3. Use the Address Card window to make changes as desired to the contact's information.

4. When you are finished making changes, click Save. Your changes are saved with the contact record.

To delete a contact record

1. In the Address Book window, select the contact you want to delete.

2. Click the Delete button on the toolbar. The contact disappears.

✔ Tip

- Be sure you have selected the correct contact in step 1. Deleting a contact is permanent and cannot be undone.

To use the LDAP Directory

1. In the Address Book window, click the Directory button on the toolbar.

2. In the LDAP Directory Search window that appears (**Figure 11**) enter search criteria for the person you want to find. You can make entries in any combination of the fields; the more entries, the narrower the search.

3. Press Return. After a moment, the results of the search appear in the bottom half of the window (**Figure 12**).

✔ Tip

- To add one of the contacts in the LDAP Directory Search window to your Address Book, drag the tiny card icon to the left of the name into the Address Book window. A new record for that contact is added.

EDITING CONTACTS, SEARCHING LDAP

Calculator

Calculator displays a simple calculator that can perform addition, subtraction, multiplication, and division.

Figure 13
Calculator The Calculator icon.

✔ Tip

■ The Calculator has been around since the Mac's early days. For Mac OS X, it got a facelift, but it still works the same way.

To launch Calculator

Double-click the Calculator icon (**Figure 13**) in the Applications folder (**Figure 1**).

or

Click the Calculator icon (**Figure 13**) in the Applications folder (**Figure 1**) and choose File > Open or press ⌘ O.

The Calculator window appears (**Figure 14**).

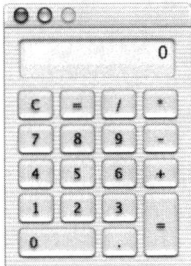

Figure 14
The Calculator looks and works just like a $3 pocket calculator.

To use the Calculator

Use your mouse to click buttons for numbers and operators.

or

Press keyboard keys corresponding to numbers and operators.

The numbers you enter and the results of your calculations appear at the top of the Calculator window.

✔ Tip

■ You can use the Cut, Copy, and Paste commands to copy the results of calculations into documents. **Chapter 7** covers the Cut, Copy, and Paste commands.

USING THE CALCULATOR

Figure 15
Chess The Chess icon.

Figure 16 The Chess window displays a three-dimensional chess board.

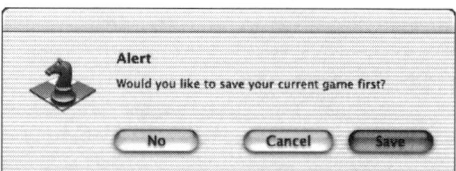

Figure 17 This Alert appears if you try to start a new game while another game is active.

Chess

Chess is a computerized version of the classic strategy game of chess. Your pieces are white and you go first; the computer's pieces are black.

To launch Chess

Double-click the Chess icon (**Figure 15**) in the Applications folder (**Figure 1**).

or

Click the Chess icon (**Figure 15**) in the Applications folder (**Figure 1**), and choose File > Open or press ⌃ ⌘ O.

The Chess window appears (**Figure 16**).

To move a chess piece

Drag the piece onto any valid square on the playing board.

✔ Tips

■ The computer moves automatically after each of your moves.

■ If you attempt to make an invalid move, an alert sounds and the piece returns to where it was.

■ If Speakable Items is enabled, you can use spoken commands to move chess pieces. You can learn about speakable items in *Mac OS X: Visual QuickPro Guide*.

To start a new game

1. Choose File > New.

2. If you are already in the middle of a game, an alert dialog (**Figure 17**) appears:

   ▲ **No** starts a new game without saving the current one.

   ▲ **Cancel** dismisses the dialog and returns you to the current game.

   ▲ **Save** displays a Save Location dialog that you can use to save the game.

CHESS

Clock

Clock displays an analog or digital clock, either in the Dock or in a floating window on screen.

To launch Clock

Double-click the Clock icon (**Figure 18**) in the Applications folder (**Figure 1**).

or

Click the Clock icon (**Figure 18**) in the Applications folder (**Figure 1**) and choose File > Open or press ⌃ ⌘ O.

The Clock either appears in the Dock (**Figure 19**) or as a floating window (**Figure 20**).

To set Clock preferences

1. Choose Clock > Preferences to display the Clock Preferences window (**Figure 21**).

2. Set Clock options by selecting a radio button and toggling check boxes as desired:

   ▲ **Analog** displays an analog clock (**Figures 19** and **20**). Use the check box to determine whether you want the second hand to display.

   ▲ **Digital** displays a digital clock (**Figure 22**). Use check boxes to determine whether it should flash time separators to mark seconds or use 24-hour format.

3. Set Display options as desired by selecting a radio button:

   ▲ **In the Dock** displays the clock in the Dock (**Figure 19**).

   ▲ **In a floating window** displays the clock in a floating window on screen (**Figures 20** and **22**). If you select this option, you can use the slider to set the transparency of the window.

4. Close the Clock Preferences window to save your changes.

Figure 18

Clock The Clock icon.

Figure 19 The Clock in the Dock (not to be confused with the Cat in the Hat).

Figure 20
A floating analog clock window.

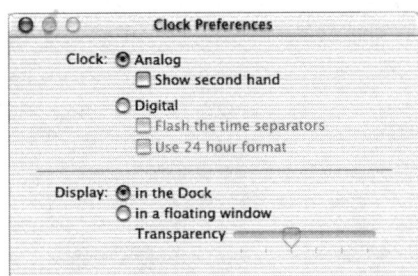

Figure 21 The Clock Preferences window.

Figure 22
A floating digital clock window.

✔ Tip

■ The clock that appears in the menu bar can be customized with the Date & Time pane of the System Preferences application, which is discussed in **Chapter 11**.

USING THE CLOCK

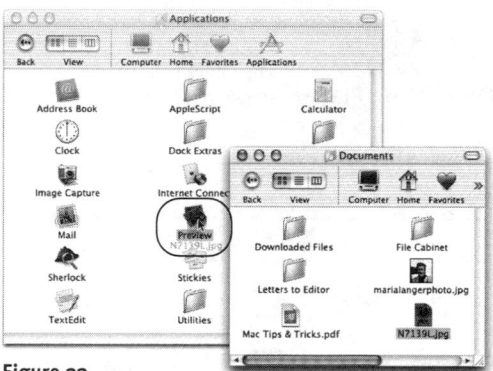

Figure 23
One way to open a file with Preview is to drag the file's icon onto the Preview icon.

Mac Tips & Tricks.pdf

Figure 24
You can also simply double-click a PDF file's icon.

Figure 25
Here's an image file opened with Preview...

Figure 26 ...and here's a PDF file opened with Preview.

Preview

Preview is a program that enables you to open and view two kinds of files:

◆ **Image files**, including files in JPEG, TIFF, PICT, and GIF formats.

◆ **PDF**, or **Portable Document Format**, files created with Adobe Acrobat software.

To open a file with Preview

Drag the file's icon onto the Preview icon in the Applications folder (**Figure 23**).

or

Double-click a PDF file's icon (**Figure 24**).

Preview launches and displays the file in its window (**Figures 25** and **26**).

✔ Tips

■ A PDF format file must end with the characters ".pdf" for Preview to recognize and open it when you double-click it.

■ You can use options on Preview's Display menu (**Figure 27**) to zoom in or out or rotate the window's contents to better view the document.

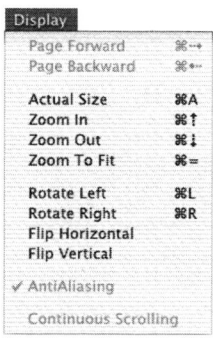

Figure 27
Here's the Display menu with an image file open. Other commands are available when a PDF file is open.

QuickTime Player

QuickTime is a video and audio technology developed by Apple Computer, Inc. It is widely used for digital movies as well as streaming audio and video available via the Internet. QuickTime Player is an application you can use to view QuickTime movies and streaming Internet content.

QuickTime Player

Figure 28
The QuickTime Player icon.

✔ Tips

■ QuickTime version 5, which is included with Mac OS X, has fewer features than the Pro version, which also enables you to edit and save QuickTime files. You can learn more about QuickTime Pro in *QuickTime 5 for Macintosh and Windows: Visual QuickStart Guide*.

■ **Chapter 9** covers Internet access.

■ You may be prompted to enter QuickTime settings when you use QuickTime to access Internet content. QuickTime settings are covered in **Chapter 11**.

Figure 29 When you launch QuickTime Player, a windowful of QuickTime TV channel buttons appears.

To launch QuickTime Player

Double-click the QuickTime Player icon (**Figure 28**) in the Applications folder (**Figure 1**).

or

Click the QuickTime Player icon (**Figure 28**) in the Applications folder (**Figure 1**) and choose File > Open or press ⌃ ⌘ O.

A QuickTime Player window displaying QuickTime TV channels appears (**Figure 29**).

Figure 30
A QuickTime
1984.mov   movie file icon.

Movie

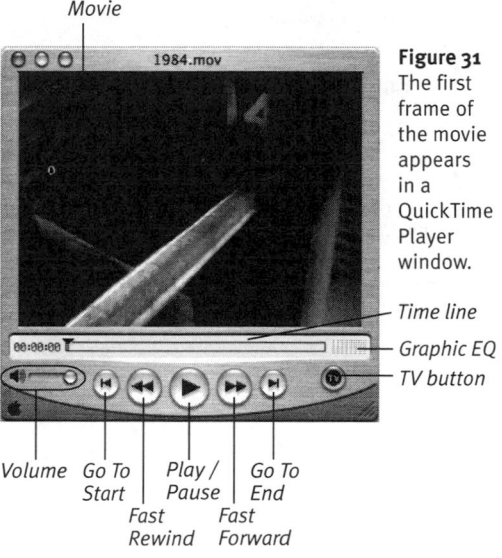

Figure 31
The first
frame of
the movie
appears
in a
QuickTime
Player
window.

Time line
Graphic EQ
TV button

Volume   Go To   Play /   Go To
*   Start   Pause   End*
*   Fast   Fast*
*   Rewind   Forward*

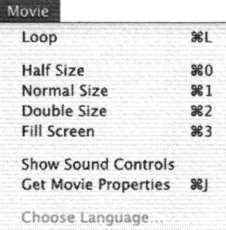

File	
New Player	⌘N
Open Movie...	⌘O
Open URL...	⌘U
Close	⌘W
Page Setup...	
Print...	⌘P

Figure 32
QuickTime Player's File
menu. There are more
menu commands in
QuickTime Pro.

Movie	
Loop	⌘L
Half Size	⌘0
Normal Size	⌘1
Double Size	⌘2
Fill Screen	⌘3
Show Sound Controls	
Get Movie Properties	⌘J
Choose Language...	

Figure 33
Use the Movie menu
to change the size of
the movie's window.

To open a QuickTime movie file

Double-click the QuickTime movie file's icon
(**Figure 30**).

QuickTime Player launches. The movie's first
frame appears in a window (**Figure 31**).

✔ Tip

■ You can also open a QuickTime movie file
by using the Open Movie command on
QuickTime Player's File menu (**Figure 32**).
The Open dialog is covered in **Chapter 5**.

To control movie play

You can click buttons and use controls in the
QuickTime Player window (**Figure 31**) to
control movie play:

◆ **Go To Start** displays the first movie frame.

◆ **Fast Rewind** plays the movie backward
quickly, with sound.

◆ **Play** starts playing the movie. When the
movie is playing, the Play button turns to a
Pause button, which pauses movie play.

◆ **Fast Forward** plays the movie forward
quickly, with sound.

◆ **Go To End** displays the last movie frame.

◆ **Time line** tracks movie progress. By dragging the slider, you can scroll through the
movie without sound.

◆ **Volume** changes movie volume; drag the
slider left or right.

To specify movie size

Select a size option from the Movie menu
(**Figure 33**). The size of the movie's window
changes accordingly.

To open QuickTime content on the Internet

1. With QuickTime Player running, choose File > Open URL (**Figure 32**).

2. Enter the Internet address or URL for the movie you want to watch in the Open URL dialog that appears (**Figure 34**), and click OK.

   Your computer connects to the Internet and downloads the movie you specified. Its first frame appears in a QuickTime Player window (**Figure 31**).

To watch QuickTime TV

1. Choose one of the channels on the Quick-Time TV submenu on the QTV menu (**Figure 35**).

   or

   Click the TV button in a QuickTime window to display QuickTime TV channel buttons (**Figure 29**). Then click one of the channel buttons.

2. The main screen for the Channel appears. In many cases, it will include buttons to access specific content (**Figure 36**). Click a button for the content that interests you.

   Your computer connects to the Internet and downloads the content. It will appear in a QuickTime Player steaming video window (**Figure 37**).

✔ Tips

- Some QuickTime TV channels display *streaming* audio or video. This requires a constant connection to the Internet while content is downloaded to your computer. Streaming content will not stop downloading until you close its QuickTime Player window or quit QuickTime Player.

- You can access other QuickTime TV channels from Apple's QuickTime Web site, http://www.apple.com/quicktime/.

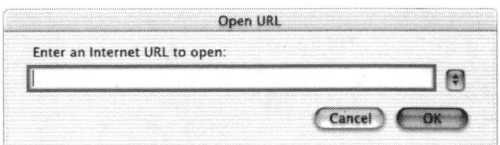

Figure 34 Use this dialog to enter the URL for the movie you want to watch.

Figure 35 The QuickTime TV submenu lists all of the QuickTime TV channels that are programmed into QuickTime Player.

Figure 36 Here's what CNN.com's QuickTime TV channel looked like on the day I wrote this page.

Figure 37 A QuickTime TV news report.

Figure 38
The Stickies
Stickies application icon.

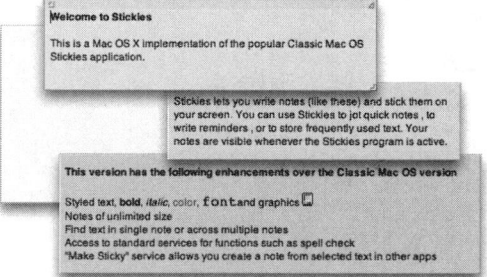

Figure 39 The default windows that appear when you first launch Stickies tell you a little about the program.

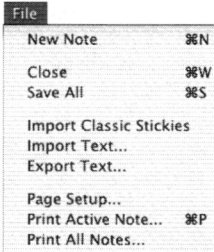

Figure 40
Stickies' File
menu.

Figure 41 Here's a blank new sticky note...

Figure 42 ...and here's the same note with a reminder typed in.

Stickies

Stickies is an application that displays computerized "sticky notes" that you can use to place reminders on your screen.

To launch Stickies

Double-click the Stickies icon (**Figure 38**) in the Applications folder (**Figure 1**).

or

Click the Stickies icon (**Figure 38**) in the Applications folder (**Figure 1**) and choose File > Open or press ⌘O.

The default Stickies windows appear (**Figure 39**).

✔ Tips

- Read the text in the default Stickies windows (**Figure 39**) to learn more about Stickies and how the Mac OS X version differs from previous versions.

- Stickies notes remain on the Desktop until you quit Stickies.

- When you quit Stickies, all notes are automatically saved to disk and will reappear the next time you launch Stickies.

To create a sticky note

1. Choose File > New Note (**Figure 40**) or press ⌘N to display a blank new note (**Figure 41**).

2. Type the text that you want to include in the note (**Figure 42**).

To format a sticky note

◆ To change the color of the note, choose a color from the Color menu (**Figure 43**).

◆ To change the style of note text, select the text you want to format and choose Note > Font Panel (**Figure 44**) or press ⌃ ⌘ T. Then set options in the Font panel window that appears (**Figure 45**). You can leave the Font panel open while you select and format other text in the note as desired. When you're finished formatting text, click the Font panel's close button to dismiss it.

✔ Tips

■ The Font panel works the same in Stickies as it does in TextEdit, which is covered in detail in **Chapter 7**.

■ To apply bold or italic formatting to selected text in a sticky note, simply select Bold or Italic from the Note menu (**Figure 44**).

■ To set the default style for all new sticky notes, format a note as desired and choose Note > Use as Default (**Figure 44**). All new notes will be created with that formatting.

To print sticky notes

1. To print just one sticky note, click it to activate it and then choose File > Print Active Note (**Figure 40**) or press ⌃ ⌘ P.

   or

   To print all sticky notes, choose File > Print All Notes (**Figure 40**).

2. Use the Print dialog that appears (**Figure 46**) to set options for printing and click the Print button.

✔ Tip

■ **Chapter 8** covers the Print dialog and printing.

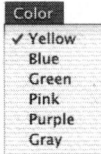

Figure 43
Use the Color menu to set a note's color.

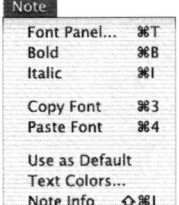

Figure 44
The Note menu offers a number of formatting options.

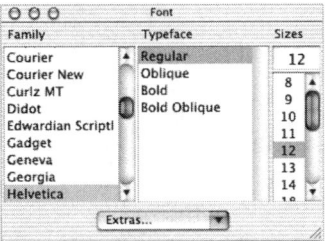

Figure 45
The Font panel enables you to set the font, typeface style, and size for selected text.

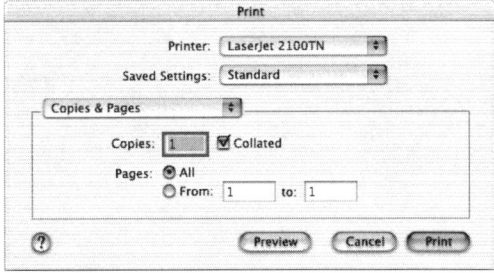

Figure 46 The Print dialog. **Chapter 8** explains its options.

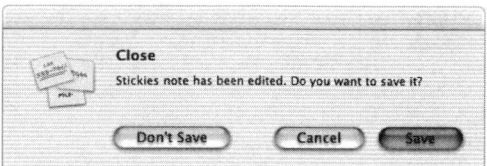

Figure 47 The Close dialog asks if you want to save note contents.

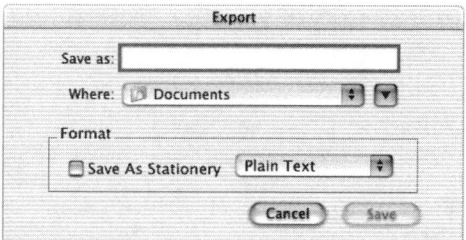

Figure 48 Use the Export dialog to save a note as plain or formatted text in a file on disk.

To close a sticky note

1. Click the close box for the sticky note you want to close.

   or

   Activate the sticky note you want to close and choose File > Close (**Figure 40**) or press ⌃ ⌘ W.

2. A Close dialog like the one in **Figure 47** may appear.

   ▲ Don't Save closes the note without saving its contents.

   ▲ Cancel leaves the note open.

   ▲ Save displays the Export dialog (**Figure 48**), which you can use to save the note as plain or formatted text in a file on disk. Enter a name and select a disk location for the note's contents, then choose a file format and click Save.

✔ Tip

■ Once a sticky note has been saved to disk, it can be opened and edited with TextEdit or any other program capable of opening text files.

Key Caps

Key Caps enables you to see and locate the characters in your fonts.

To launch Key Caps

Double-click the Key Caps icon (**Figure 49**) in the Utilities folder (**Figure 2**).

or

Click the Key Caps icon (**Figure 49**) in the Utilities folder (**Figure 2**) and choose File > Open or press ⌃ ⌘ O.

The Key Caps window appears (**Figure 50**).

To use Key Caps

◆ To see what the characters of a different font look like, choose the font name from the Font menu (**Figure 51**).

◆ To see what characters look like with a modifier key (such as Shift or Option) pressed, press the modifier key (**Figure 52**).

✔ Tips

■ You can type in the Key Caps window to see what a string of text looks like.

■ You can use Key Caps to learn special characters. For example, hold down Option while looking at the Key Caps window (**Figure 52**) to see a bullet (•), registered trademark symbol (®), and copyright symbol (©). To type one of these characters, hold Option while pressing the appropriate keyboard key: Option 8 for •, Option R for ®, Option G for ©.

■ Accented characters (for example, é, ñ, and ü), require two keystrokes to type. First type the keystroke for the accent, then type the character that you want the accent to appear over. For example, to type á, press Option E and then A. The two-stroke characters appear in Key Caps with a white box around them (**Figure 52**).

Figure 49
Key Caps The Key Caps icon.

Figure 50 The Key Caps window, displaying characters from the Lucidia Grand Regular font. (The keyboard in this example is a standard iMac keyboard; your keyboard layout may be different.)

Figure 51
The Font menu displays all the fonts properly installed in your system. (Your font list may vary from this one.)

The font menu contains:
Andale Mono
Apple Chancery
Arial ▶
Arial Black
Arial Narrow ▶
Arial Rounded MT Bold
Big Caslon
Brush Script MT
Capitals
Century Gothic ▶
Charcoal
Chicago
Comic Sans MS ▶
Copperplate Gothic ▶
Copperplate Gothic Bold
Copperplate Gothic Light
Courier ▶
Courier New ▶
Curlz MT
Didot ▶
Edwardian Script ITC
Gadget
Geneva
Georgia ▶
Helvetica ▶
Helvetica Neue ▶
Herculanum
Hiragino Kaku Gothic Pro ▶

Figure 52 In this example, holding down Option displays additional characters in the font.

USING TEXTEDIT

TextEdit

Figure 1
The TextEdit application icon.

Letter.rtf

Figure 2
A TextEdit document's icon.

TextEdit

TextEdit (**Figure 1**) is a basic text editing application that comes with Mac OS. As its name implies, TextEdit lets you create, open, edit, and print text documents (**Figure 2**), including the "Read Me" files that come with many applications.

This chapter explains how to use TextEdit to create, edit, format, open, and save documents.

✔ Tips

- Although TextEdit offers many of the basic features found in a word processing application, it falls far short of the feature list of word processors such as Microsoft Word and the word processing components of integrated software such as AppleWorks.

- If you're new to computers, don't skip this chapter. It not only explains how to use TextEdit but provides instructions for basic text editing skills—like text entry and the Copy, Cut, and Paste commands— that you'll use in all Mac OS-compatible applications.

Launching & Quitting TextEdit

Like any other application, you must launch TextEdit before you can use it. This loads it into your computer's memory so your computer can work with it.

To launch TextEdit

Double-click the TextEdit application icon.

or

1. Select the TextEdit application icon (**Figure 1**).

2. Choose File > Open (**Figure 3**), or press ⌘⌥O.

   TextEdit launches. An untitled document window appears (**Figure 4**).

✔ Tips

- TextEdit is normally found in the Applications folder on your hard drive.

- As illustrated in **Figure 4**, the TextEdit document window has the same standard window parts found in Finder windows. I tell you how to use Finder windows in **Chapter 2**; TextEdit and other application windows work the same way.

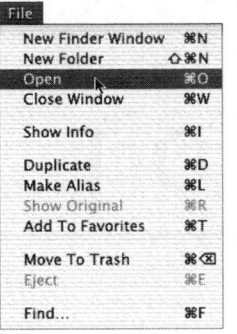

Figure 3
Choose Open from the Finder's File menu.

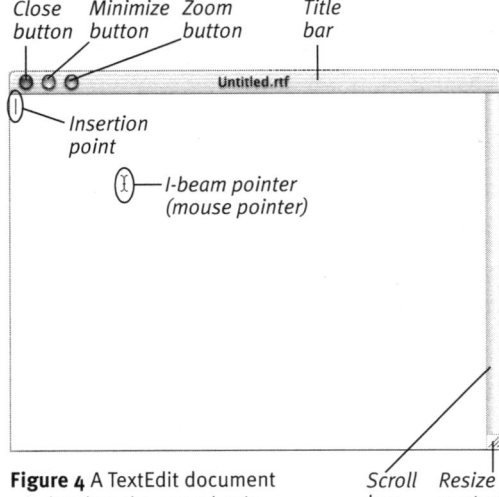

Figure 4 A TextEdit document window has the same basic parts as a Finder window.

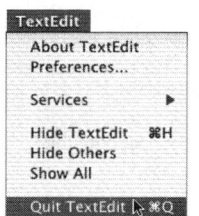

Figure 5
Choose Quit TextEdit from the TextEdit menu.

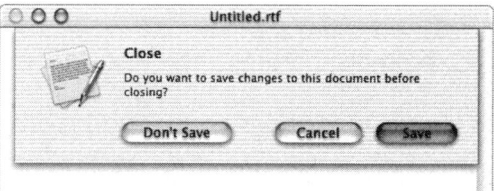

Figure 6 A dialog sheet like this appears when you quit TextEdit with an unsaved document open.

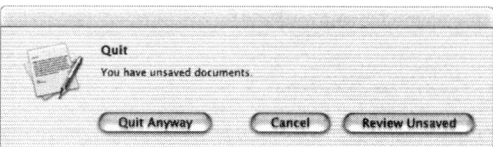

Figure 7 A dialog like this appears when you quit TextEdit with multiple unsaved documents open.

To quit TextEdit

1. Choose TextEdit > Quit TextEdit (**Figure 5**), or press ⌘Q.

2. If a single unsaved document is open, a Close dialog sheet like the one in **Figure 6** appears, attached to the document window.

   ▲ Click Don't Save to quit without saving the document.

   ▲ Click Cancel or press Esc to return to the application without quitting.

   ▲ Click Save or press Return or Enter to save the document.

   or

   If multiple unsaved documents are open, a Quit dialog like the one in **Figure 7** appears:

   ▲ Click Quit Anyway to quit TextEdit without saving any of the documents.

   ▲ Click Cancel or press Esc to return to the application without quitting.

   ▲ Click Review Unsaved or press Return or Enter to view each unsaved document with a dialog like the one in **Figure 6** to decide whether you want to save it.

   TextEdit closes all windows and quits.

✔ Tip

■ You learn more about saving TextEdit documents later in this chapter.

QUITTING TEXTEDIT

Entering & Editing Text

You enter text into a TextEdit document by typing it in. Don't worry about making mistakes; you can fix them as you type or when you're finished. This section tells you how.

✔ Tip

■ The text entry and editing techniques covered in this section work exactly the same in most word processors, as well as many other Mac OS applications.

To enter text

Type the text you want to enter. It appears at the blinking insertion point (**Figure 8**).

✔ Tips

■ It is not necessary to press Return at the end of a line. When the text you type reaches the end of the line, it automatically begins a new line. This is called *word wrap* and is a feature of all word processors. By default, in TextEdit, word wrap is determined by the width of the document window.

■ The insertion point moves as you type.

■ To correct an error as you type, press Delete. This key deletes the character to the left of the insertion point.

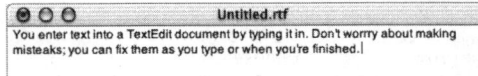

Figure 8 The text you type appears at the blinking insertion point.

ENTERING TEXT

Figure 9 Position the mouse pointer...

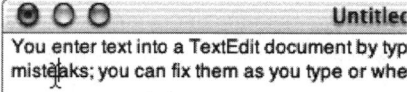

Figure 10 ...and click to move the insertion point.

Figure 11 Position the insertion point...

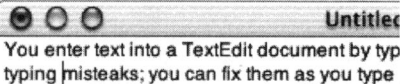

Figure 12 ...and type the text that you want to appear.

To move the insertion point

Press ⬅, ➡, ⬆, or ⬇ to move the insertion point left, right, up, or down one character or line at a time.

or

1. Position the mouse pointer, which looks like an I-beam pointer, where you want the insertion point to appear (**Figure 9**).

2. Click the mouse button once. The insertion point appears at the mouse pointer (**Figure 10**).

✔ Tips

■ Since the text you type appears at the insertion point, it's a good idea to know where the insertion point is *before* you start typing.

■ When moving the insertion point with the mouse, you must click to complete the move. If you simply point with the I-beam pointer, the insertion point will stay right where it is (**Figure 9**).

To insert text

1. Position the insertion point where you want the text to appear (**Figure 11**).

2. Type the text that you want to insert. The text is inserted at the insertion point (**Figure 12**).

✔ Tip

■ Word wrap changes automatically to accommodate inserted text.

MOVING THE INSERTION POINT, INSERTING TEXT

To select text by dragging

Drag the I-beam pointer over the text you want to select (**Figure 13**).

To select text with shift-click

1. Position the insertion point at the beginning of the text you want to select (**Figure 14**).

2. Hold down [Shift] and click at the end of the text you want to select. All text between the insertion point's original position and where you clicked becomes selected (**Figure 15**).

✔ Tip

■ This is a good way to select large blocks of text. After positioning the insertion point as instructed in step 1, use the scroll bars to scroll to the end of the text you want to select. Then shift-click as instructed in step 2 to make the selection.

To select a single word

Double-click the word (**Figure 16**).

✔ Tip

■ In some applications, double-clicking a word also selects the space after the word.

To select an entire document

To select the entire document, choose Edit > Select All (**Figure 17**) or press [⌘ ⌘ A].

✔ Tip

■ There are other selection techniques in TextEdit and other applications. The techniques on this page work in every application.

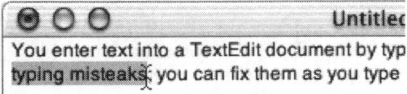

Figure 13 Drag the mouse pointer over the text that you want to select.

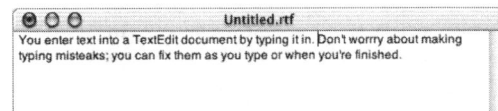

Figure 14 Position the insertion point at the beginning of the text you want to select.

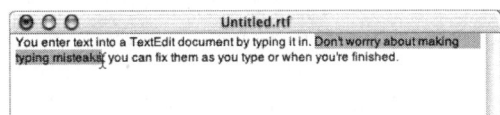

Figure 15 Hold down [Shift] and click at the end of the text you want to select.

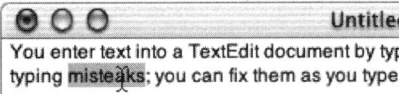

Figure 16 Double-click the word that you want to select.

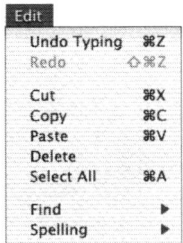

Figure 17 Choose Select All from the Edit menu.

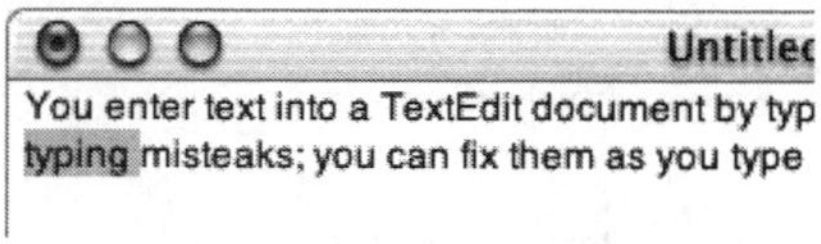

Figure 18 Select the text that you want to delete.

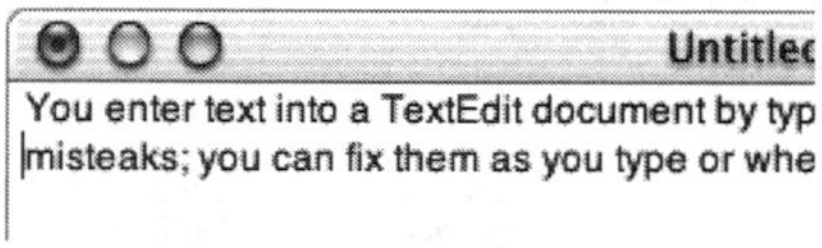

Figure 19 When you press [Delete], the selected text disappears.

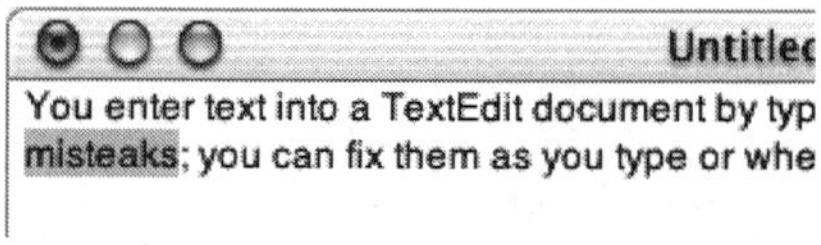

Figure 20 Select the text that you want to replace.

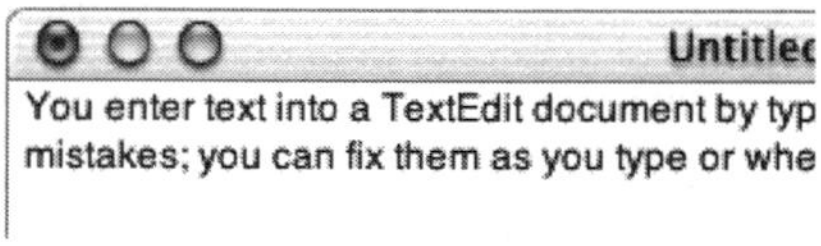

Figure 21 The text you type replaces the selected text.

To delete text

1. Select the text that you want to delete (**Figure 18**).

2. Press [Delete] or [Del]. The selected text disappears (**Figure 19**).

✔ Tip

■ You can delete a character to the left of the insertion point by pressing [Delete]. You can delete a character to the right of the insertion point by pressing [Del].

To replace text

1. Select the text that you want to replace (**Figure 20**).

2. Type the new text. The selected text is replaced by what you type (**Figure 21**).

DELETING & REPLACING TEXT

Basic Text Formatting

TextEdit also offers formatting features that you can use to change the appearance of text.

✔ Tip

■ This chapter covers the most commonly used formatting options in TextEdit. You can explore the other options on your own.

To apply font formatting

1. Select the text to which you want to apply a different font or font size (**Figure 22**).

2. Choose Format > Font > Font Panel (**Figure 23**), or press ⌃⌘T to display the Font Panel (**Figure 24**).

3. To change the font, select a font family from the Family scrolling list. If the family contains more than one typeface, you can also make a selection from the Typeface scrolling list.

4. To change the character size, either enter a new size in the Sizes text entry field or select one of the sizes in the Sizes scrolling list.

5. Preview your changes in the document window behind the Font panel (**Figure 25**). Make additional changes as desired.

6. Repeat steps 1 and 3 through 5 for any other text you want to apply formatting to.

7. When you are finished using the Font panel, close it by clicking its close button.

✔ Tips

■ Generally speaking, a *font* is a style of typeface.

■ The Font panel's Family scrolling list displays all fonts that are properly installed in your System. This list may differ from the one illustrated in **Figure 24**.

■ The larger the text size, the less text appears on screen or on a printed page.

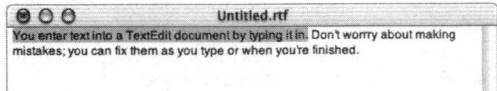

Figure 22 Select the text you want to format.

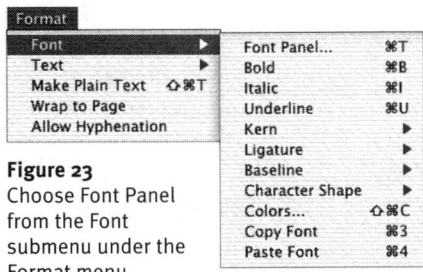

Figure 23 Choose Font Panel from the Font submenu under the Format menu.

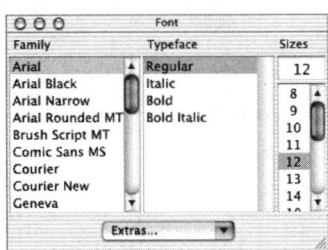

Figure 24 The Font panel.

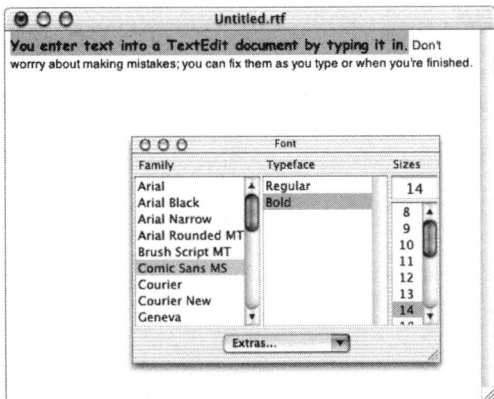

Figure 25 The changes you make in the Font panel are immediately applied to the selected text.

APPLYING FONT FORMATTING

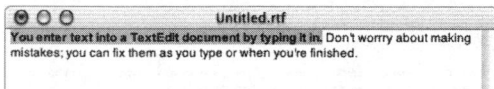

Figure 26 The style you chose is applied.

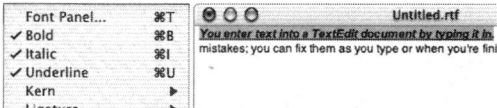

Figure 27 A check mark appears beside the name of each style applied to selected text.

To apply a different font style

1. Select the text you want to apply a different style to (**Figure 22**).

2. Choose a style command from the Font submenu under the Format menu (**Figure 23**) or press its keyboard equivalent. The style options are:

   ▲ **Bold**, or ⌃⌘B, makes text characters appear thicker or darker.

   ▲ **Italic**, or ⌃⌘I, makes text appear slanted.

   ▲ **Underline**, or ⌃⌘U, puts a single underline under text.

   The style you chose is applied to the selected text (**Figure 26**).

✔ Tips

- You can apply more than one style to text (**Figure 27**). Simply select each style you want to apply.

- A check mark appears on the Font submenu beside each style applied to a selection (**Figure 27**).

- To remove an applied style, choose it from the Font submenu again.

- Some styles are automatically applied when you select a specific typeface for a font family in the Font panel (**Figure 25**). Similarly, if you select a typeface in the Font panel, certain style options become unavailable for characters with that typeface applied. For example, if you apply Comic Sans MS Bold font, as shown in **Figure 25**, the Italic option is not available on the Font submenu for that text.

To change paragraph alignment

1. Select the paragraph(s) you want to change the alignment of (**Figure 28**).

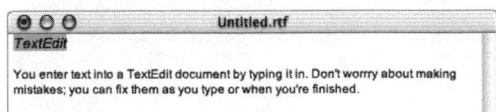

Figure 28 Select the paragraph you want to change the alignment of.

2. Choose an alignment option from the Text submenu under the Format menu (**Figure 29**) or press its keyboard equivalent. The alignment options are:

   ▲ **Align Left**, or ⌃⌘{, aligns text characters against the left side of the window.

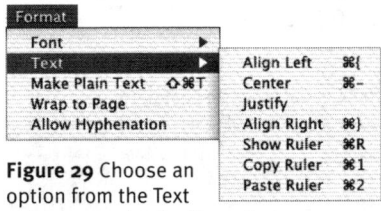

Figure 29 Choose an option from the Text submenu under the Format menu.

   ▲ **Center**, or ⌃⌘-, centers text characters between the left and right side of the window (**Figure 30**).

   ▲ **Justify** adjusts the spacing between words so all lines of the paragraph except the last fill the space between the left and right sides of the window.

   ▲ **Align Right**, or ⌃⌘}, aligns text characters against the right side of the window.

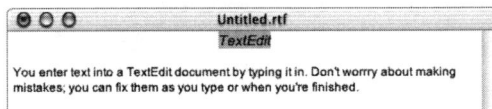

Figure 30 The alignment option you chose is applied.

The alignment option you chose is applied to the selected paragraph(s) (**Figure 30**).

✔ Tip

■ Alignment options affect all lines in a paragraph. To begin a new paragraph, position the insertion point where you want the paragraph to begin and press Return.

CHANGING ALIGNMENT

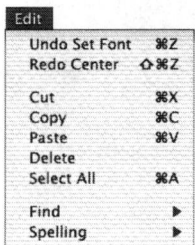

Figure 31
The Edit menu with Undo and Redo commands displayed. If one of these commands were not available, it would be gray.

Undoing & Redoing Actions

The Undo command enables you to reverse your last action, thus offering an easy way to fix errors immediately after you make them. The Redo command, which is available only when your last action was to use the Undo command, reverses the undo action.

✔ Tips

- The Undo and Redo commands are available in most applications and can always be found at the top of the Edit menu.

- Unlike most applications, TextEdit supports multiple levels of undo (and redo). That means you can undo (or redo) several actions, in the reverse order that they were performed (or undone).

- The exact wording of the Undo (and Redo) command depends on what was last done (or undone). For example, if the last thing you did was apply some font formatting, the Undo command will be Undo Set Font (**Figure 31**).

To undo the last action

Choose Edit > Undo (**Figure 31**), or press ⌥ ⌘ Z. The last thing you did is undone.

✔ Tip

- To undo multiple actions, choose Edit > Undo repeatedly.

To redo an action

After using the Undo command, choose Edit > Redo (**Figure 31**), or press Shift ⌥ ⌘ Z. The last thing you undid is redone.

✔ Tip

- To redo multiple actions, choose Edit > Redo repeatedly.

Copy, Cut, & Paste

The Copy, Cut, and Paste commands enable you to duplicate or move document contents. Text that is copied or cut is placed on the Clipboard, where it can be viewed if desired.

✔ Tip

■ Almost all Mac OS applications include the Copy, Cut, and Paste commands on the Edit menu. These commands work very much the same in all applications that support them.

To copy text

1. Select the text that you want to copy (**Figure 32**).

2. Choose Edit > Copy (**Figure 33**), or press ⌘ ⌘ C.

   The text is copied to the Clipboard so it can be pasted elsewhere. The original remains in the document.

To cut text

1. Select the text that you want to cut (**Figure 32**).

2. Choose Edit > Cut (**Figure 33**), or press ⌘ ⌘ X.

   The text is copied to the Clipboard so it can be pasted elsewhere. The original is removed from the document.

To paste Clipboard contents

1. Position the insertion point where you want the Clipboard contents to appear (**Figure 34**).

2. Choose Edit > Paste (**Figure 33**), or press ⌘ ⌘ V.

   The Clipboard's contents are pasted into the document (**Figure 35**).

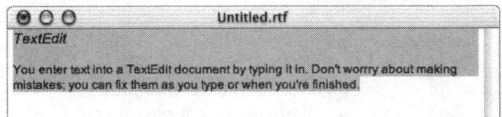

Figure 32 Select the text you want to copy or cut.

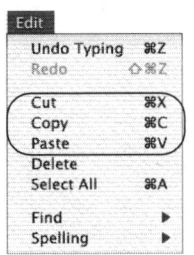

Figure 33 The Copy, Cut, and Paste commands are all on the Edit menu.

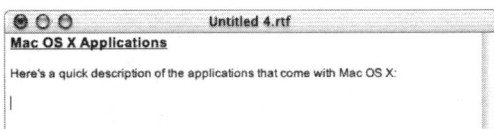

Figure 34 Position the insertion point where you want the contents of the Clipboard to appear.

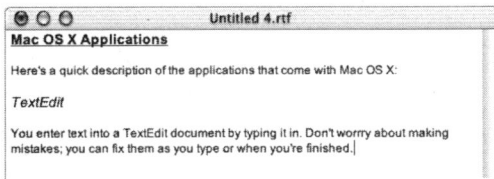

Figure 35 The contents of the Clipboard are pasted into the document.

COPYING, CUTTING, & PASTING TEXT

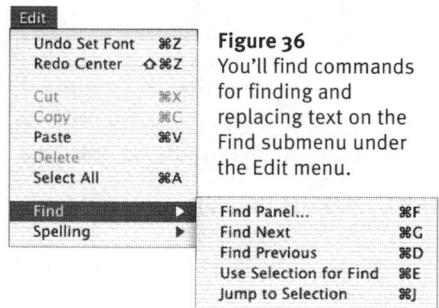

Figure 36
You'll find commands for finding and replacing text on the Find submenu under the Edit menu.

Figure 37 The Find panel.

Find & Replace

TextEdit's find and replace features enable you to quickly locate or replace occurrences of text strings in your document.

✔ Tip

- Most word processing and page layout applications include find and replace features. Although these features are somewhat limited in TextEdit, full-featured applications such as Microsoft Word and Adobe InDesign enable you to search for text, formatting, and other document elements as well as plain text.

To find text

1. Choose Edit > Find > Find Panel (**Figure 36**), or press ⌃⌘F. The Find panel appears (**Figure 37**).

2. Enter the text that you want to find in the Find field.

3. If necessary, select one of the options in the Replace All Scope area:

   ▲ **Entire File** searches the entire file.

   ▲ **Selection** searches only selected text.

4. To perform a case-sensitive search, turn off the Ignore Case check box in the Find Options area. With this check box turned off, *word* will not match *Word*.

5. Click Next, or press (Return) or (Enter). If the text you entered in the Find field is found, it is highlighted in the document.

✔ Tip

- To find subsequent or previous occurrences of the Find field entry, choose Edit > Find > Find Next or Edit > Find Previous (**Figure 36**) or press ⌃⌘G or ⌃⌘D.

FINDING TEXT

To replace text

1. Choose Edit > Find > Find Panel (**Figure 36**), or press ⌃⌘F. The Find panel appears (**Figure 37**).

2. Enter the text that you want to replace in the Find field.

3. Enter the replacement text in the Replace with field (**Figure 38**).

4. If necessary, select one of the options in the Replace All Scope area:

   ▲ **Entire File** searches the entire file.

   ▲ **Selection** searches only selected text.

5. To perform a case-sensitive search, turn off the Ignore Case check box in the Find Options area. With this check box turned off, *word* will not match *Word*.

6. Click the buttons at the bottom of the Find pane to find and replace text:

   ▲ **Replace All** replaces all occurrences of the Find word with the Replace word.

   ▲ **Replace** replaces the currently selected occurrence of the Find word with the Replace word.

   ▲ **Replace & Find** replaces the currently selected occurrence of the Find word with the Replace word and then selects the next occurrence of the Find word.

   ▲ **Previous** selects the previous occurrence of the Find word.

   ▲ **Next** selects the next occurrence of the Find word.

7. When you're finished replacing text, click the Find panel's close button to dismiss it.

✔ Tip

■ Use the Replace All button with care! It will not give you an opportunity to preview and approve any of the replacements it makes.

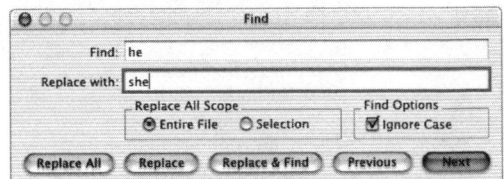

Figure 38 You can set up the Find panel to find and replace text.

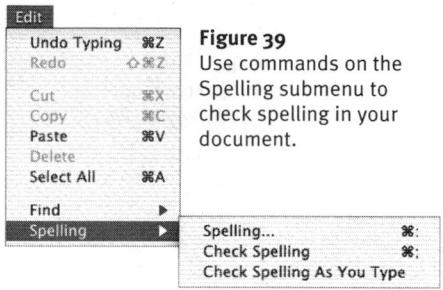

Figure 39
Use commands on the Spelling submenu to check spelling in your document.

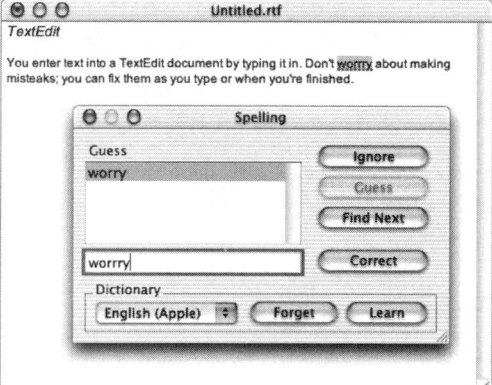

Figure 40 Use the Spelling panel to resolve possible misspelled words.

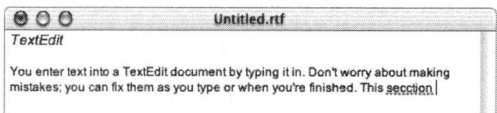

Figure 41 With automatic spelling check enabled, Text-Edit underlines possible misspelled words as you type.

Checking Spelling

TextEdit includes a spelling checker that you can use to check spelling in your document.

To check spelling

1. Choose Edit > Spelling > Spelling (**Figure 39**) or press ⌃⌘: to display the spelling panel and start the spelling check.

   TextEdit selects and underlines the first possible misspelled word it finds. The word appears in a field in the Spelling panel and any suggested corrections appear in the Guess scrolling list (**Figure 40**).

2. You have several options:

   ▲ To replace the word with a guess, select the replacement word and click Correct.

   ▲ To enter a new spelling for the word, enter it in the field where the incorrect spelling appears and click Correct.

   ▲ To ignore the word, click Ignore.

   ▲ To skip the word and continue checking, click Find Next.

   ▲ To add the word to TextEdit's dictionary, click Learn. TextEdit will never stop at that word again in any document.

3. Repeat step 2 for each word that TextEdit identifies as a possible misspelling.

4. When you're finished checking spelling, click the Spelling panel's close button to dismiss it.

✔ Tip

■ You can choose Edit > Spelling > Check Spelling As You Type to have TextEdit check your spelling automatically as you type. With this feature enabled, each time you type a word that isn't in TextEdit's dictionary, a red dotted underline appears beneath it (**Figure 41**).

Saving & Opening Document Files

When you're finished working with a TextEdit document, you may want to save it. You can then open it another time to review, edit, or print it.

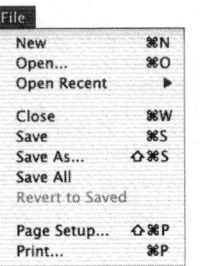

Figure 42
The File menu includes commands for working with files.

To save a document for the first time

1. Choose File > Save (**Figure 42**), or press ⌃ ⌘ S.

   or

   Choose File > Save As (**Figure 42**), or press Shift ⌃ ⌘ S.

2. Use the Save Location dialog sheet that appears (**Figure 43**) to enter a name and select a location for the file.

3. Click Save, or press Return or Enter.

   The document is saved with the name you entered in the location you specified. The name of the document appears on the document's title bar (**Figure 44**).

Figure 43 Use the Save As dialog to enter a name and select a location for saving a file.

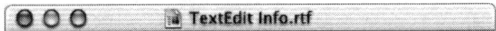

Figure 44 The name of a saved document appears in its title bar.

✔ Tips

- I explain how to use the Save Location dialog in **Chapter 5**.

- There's only one difference between the Save and Save As commands:

  ▲ The Save command opens the Save Location dialog only if the document has never been saved.

  ▲ The Save As command always opens the Save Location dialog.

- By default, TextEdit creates Rich Text Format (RTF) files and appends the *.rtf* extension to all files it saves.

SAVING DOCUMENTS

Figure 45 A bullet in the document window's close button...

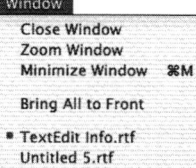

Figure 46
...or beside its name in the Window menu indicates that the document has unsaved changes.

To save changes to an existing document

Choose File > Save (**Figure 42**), or press ⟨⌘ S⟩.

The document is saved. No dialog appears.

✔ Tips

■ TextEdit identifies a document with changes that have not been saved by displaying a bullet in the document window's close button (**Figure 45**) and to the left of the document's name in the Window menu (**Figure 46**).

■ It's a good idea to save changes to a document frequently as you work with it. This helps prevent loss of data in the event of a system crash or power outage.

To save an existing document with a new name or in a new location

1. Choose File > Save As (**Figure 42**).

2. Use the Save Location dialog sheet that appears (**Figure 43**) to enter a different name or select a different location (or both) for the file.

3. Click Save, or press ⟨Return⟩ or ⟨Enter⟩.

   A copy of the document is saved with the name you entered in the location you specified. The new document name appears in the document's title bar. The original document remains untouched.

✔ Tip

■ You can use the Save As command to create a new document based on an existing document—without overwriting the original document with your changes.

SAVING DOCUMENTS

To open a document

1. Choose File > Open (**Figure 42**), or press ⌃ ⌘ O.

2. Use the Open dialog that appears (**Figure 47**) to locate and select the document that you want to open.

3. Click Open, or press Return or Enter.

✔ Tip

■ I explain how to use the Open dialog in **Chapter 5**.

To close a document

1. Choose File > Close (**Figure 42**), or press ⌃ ⌘ W.

2. If the document contains unsaved changes, a Close dialog sheet like the one in **Figure 6** appears.

   ▲ Click Don't Save to close the document without saving it.

   ▲ Click Cancel or press Esc to return to the document without closing it.

   ▲ Click Save or press Return or Enter to save the document.

   The document closes.

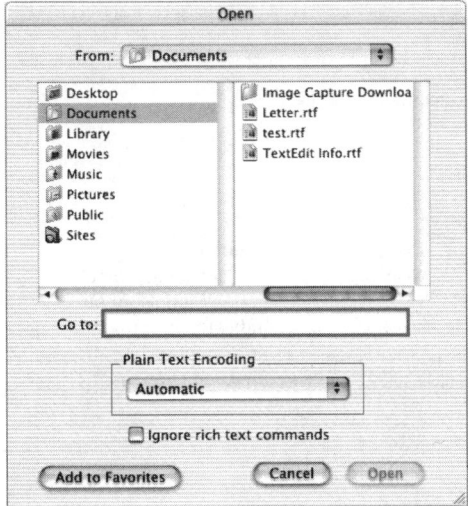

Figure 47 Use the Open dialog to locate and open a file.

PRINTING

Printing

On a Mac OS system, printing is handled by the operating system rather than the individual applications. You choose the Print command in the application that created the document you want to print. Mac OS steps in, displaying the Print dialog and telling the application how to send information to the printer. There are two main benefits to this:

◆ If you can print documents created with one application, you can probably print documents created with any application on your computer.

◆ The Page Setup and Print dialogs, which are generated by Mac OS, look very much the same in every application.

This chapter covers most aspects of printing on a computer running Mac OS X.

To print (an overview)

1. If necessary, add your printer to the Printer List.

2. Open the document that you want to print.

3. If desired, set options in the Page Setup dialog and click OK.

4. Set options in the Print dialog, and click Print.

Printer Drivers

A *printer driver* is software that Mac OS uses to communicate with a specific kind of printer. It contains information about the printer and instructions for using it. You can't open and read a printer driver, but your computer can.

There are basically two kinds of printers:

◆ A **PostScript** printer uses PostScript technology developed by Adobe Systems. Inside the printer is a *PostScript interpreter*, which can process PostScript language commands to print high-quality text and graphics. Examples of PostScript printers include most Apple LaserWriter printers and Hewlett-Packard LaserJet printers.

◆ A **non-PostScript** printer relies on the computer to send it all of the instructions it needs for printing text and graphics. It cannot process PostScript commands. Examples of non-PostScript printers include Apple ImageWriters and Style-Writers, Hewlett-Packard DeskJet printers, and most Epson Stylus printers.

A standard installation of Mac OS X installs many commonly used printer drivers. When you buy a printer, it should come with a CD that includes its printer driver software; if your computer does not recognize your printer, you'll need to install this software to use it.

✔ Tips

■ If you do not have a printer driver for your printer, you may not be able to print.

■ If you need to install printer driver software for your printer, make sure it is Mac OS X compatible. If your printer did not come with Mac OS X compatible printer software, you may be able to get it from the printer manufacturer's Web site.

■ To install a printer driver, follow the instructions that came with its installation disk.

Figure 1 Print Center can be found in the Utilities folder inside the Applications folder.

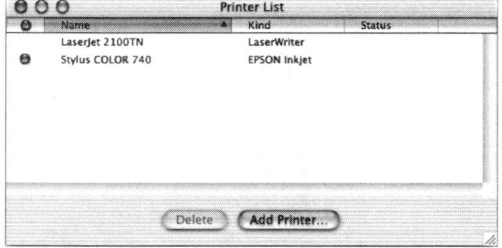

Figure 2 The Printer List window with two printers.

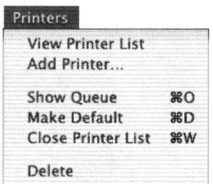

Figure 3
The Printers menu includes commands for working with the Printer List and printers.

Print Center

Print Center (**Figure 1**) is an application that enables you to manage printers and print jobs. It has two main components:

◆ **Printer List** window (**Figure 2**) lists all of the printers your computer "sees." Use this window to select and configure printers.

◆ **Printer Queue** window (**Figure 35** and **36**) lists all the print jobs sent to a specific printer. Use this window to check the status of and cancel print jobs, as discussed later in this chapter.

✔ Tip

■ Print Center replaces the Chooser and Desktop Printer Utility software that were used for the same functions in Mac OS 9.1 and earlier. Desktop printers are not available in Mac OS X.

To open Print Center

1. Click the Applications icon in the toolbar of any Finder window to open the Applications folder.

2. Open the Utilities folder.

3. Open the Print Center icon (**Figure 1**).

The Printer List window (**Figure 2**) should appear automatically. If it does not, follow the instructions below to display it.

To display the Printer List window

Choose Printers > View Printer List (**Figure 3**).

The Printer List window appears (**Figure 2**).

✔ Tip

■ If a question mark appears beside a printer in the Printer List window, you may need to install printer driver software for that printer. Printer drivers are covered on the previous page.

To add a printer

1. Choose Printers > Add Printer (**Figure 3**).

   or

   Click the Add Printer button in the Printer List window (**Figure 2**).

2. A dialog sheet appears. Choose an option from the pop-up menu (**Figure 4**) to indicate the type of printer connection.

3. If you chose AppleTalk, wait while Print Center looks for printers and displays a list of what it finds (**Figure 5**). Select the printer you want to add, and click Add.

   or

   If you chose LPR Printers using IP, enter an IP (or Internet Protocol) address or domain name and set other options in the dialog sheet (**Figure 6**). Then click Add.

   or

   If you chose USB, Print Center displays a list of USB printers connected to the computer (**Figure 7**). Select the printer you want to add, and click Add.

   The printer appears in the Printer List window (**Figure 2**).

✔ Tips

- You only have to add a printer if it does not already appear in the Printer List window (**Figure 2**). This needs to be done only once; Mac OS will remember all printers that you add.

- In step 3, if you chose AppleTalk and your network includes AppleTalk zones, you must select a zone from the pop-up menu that appears in the dialog (**Figure 5**) to see a list of printers.

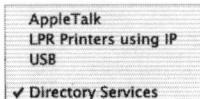

Figure 4
Use this pop-up menu to choose the type of printer connection.

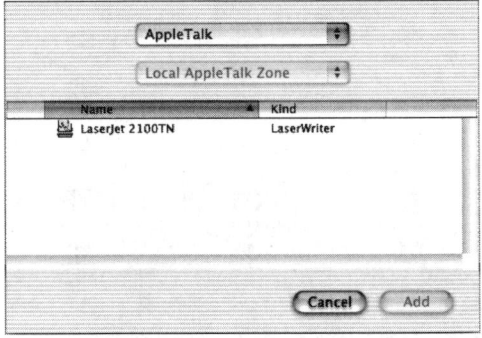

Figure 5 Options for adding an AppleTalk printer,...

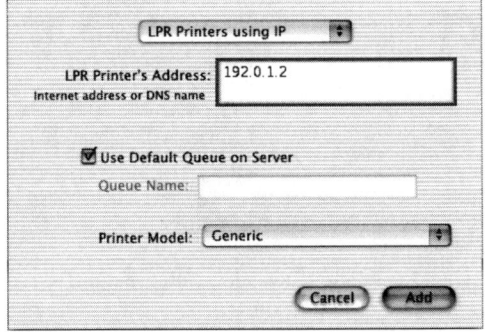

Figure 6 ...an LPR Printer using IP, ...

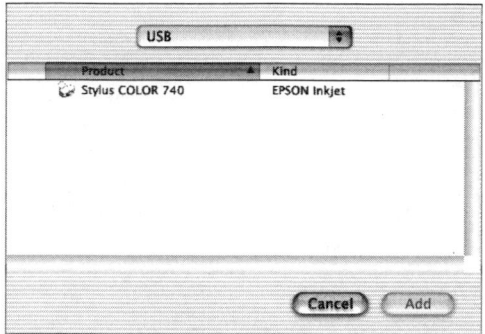

Figure 7 ...and a USB printer.

■ If your AppleTalk or USB printer is properly connected but it does not appear in step 3 (**Figures 5** and **7**), you may have to install printer driver software for it. Printer drivers are discussed earlier in this chapter.

■ If you're not sure how to set options for an LPR Printer using IP (**Figure 6**), ask your network administrator.

To delete a printer

1. In the Printer List window (**Figure 2**), select the printer you want to delete.

2. Choose Printers > Delete (**Figure 3**).

    or

    Click the Delete button in the Printer List window (**Figure 2**).

    The printer is removed from the list.

To set the default printer

1. In the Printer list window (**Figure 2**), select the printer you want to set as the default.

2. Choose Printers > Make Default (**Figure 3**), or press ⌃ ⌘ D.

    A colored bullet appears beside the printer you selected, indicating that it is the default printer.

✔ Tip

■ The default printer is the one that is selected by default when you open the Print dialog.

DELETING & SETTING DEFAULT PRINTERS

The Page Setup Dialog

The Page Setup dialog lets you set page attributes prior to printing, including the printer the document should be formatted for, paper size, orientation, and scale.

To set Page Attributes

1. Choose File > Page Setup (**Figures 8a**, **8b**, and **8c**) to display the Page Setup dialog sheet (**Figure 9**).

2. If necessary, choose Page Attributes from the settings pop-up menu (**Figure 10**).

3. If necessary, select the correct printer from the Format for pop-up menu (**Figure 11**).

4. Select a paper size from the Paper Size pop-up menu (**Figure 12**).

5. Select an Orientation option by clicking it.

6. Enter a scaling percentage in the Scale field.

7. Click OK to save your settings and dismiss the Page Setup dialog.

✔ Tips

- The Format for pop-up menu should list all of the printers that appear in the Print Center's Printer List window (**Figure 2**).

- Options in each of the above steps vary depending on the printer selected from the Format for pop-up menu. Additional options may be available for your printer; check the documentation that came with the printer for details.

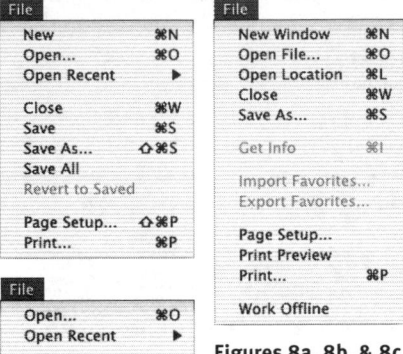

Figures 8a, 8b, & 8c
The Page Setup and Print commands appear on most File menus, including TextEdit (top left), Preview (bottom left), and Internet Explorer (right).

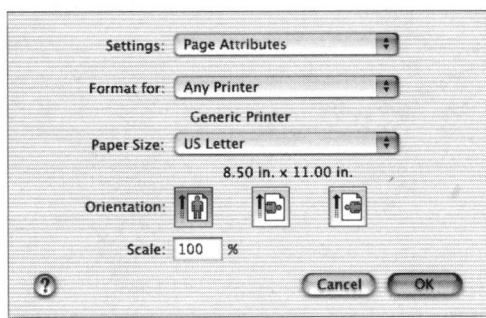

Figure 9 The Page Setup dialog sheet.

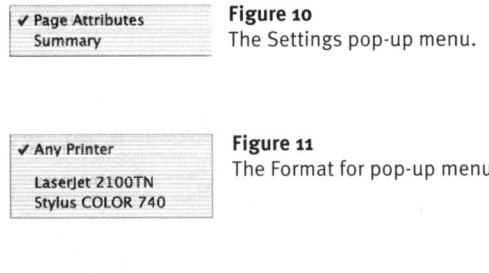

Figure 10
The Settings pop-up menu.

Figure 11
The Format for pop-up menu.

Figure 12
The Paper Size pop-up menu when Any Printer is chosen from the Format for pop-up menu.

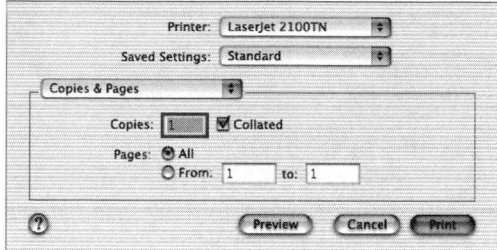

Figure 13 The Copies & Pages pane of the Print dialog.

| ✓ LaserJet 2100TN |
| Stylus COLOR 740 |
| Edit Printer List... |

Figure 14
The Printer pop-up menu.

The Print Dialog

The Print dialog enables you to set printing options and send the print job to the printer. Like the Page Setup dialog, the Print dialog is a standard dialog, but two things can cause its appearance and options to vary:

◆ Print options vary depending on the selected printer.

◆ Additional options may be offered by specific applications.

This section explains how to set the options available for most printers and applications.

✔ Tips

■ If your Print dialog includes options that are not covered here, check the documentation that came with your printer for help.

■ For information about using Print options specific to an application, consult the documentation that came with the application.

To open the Print dialog

Choose File > Print (**Figures 8a**, **8b**, and **8c**), or press ⌃ ⌘ P.

The Copies & Pages pane of the Print dialog appears (**Figure 13**).

To select a printer

In the Print dialog (**Figure 13**) choose a printer from the Printer pop-up menu (**Figure 14**).

✔ Tips

■ The Printer pop-up menu (**Figure 14**) includes all printers that appear in Print Center's Printer List window (**Figure 2**).

■ Choosing Edit Printer List from the Printer pop-up menu (**Figure 14**) opens Print Center and displays its Printer List window so you can add a printer. Adding printers is covered earlier in this chapter.

THE PRINT DIALOG

To set Copies & Pages options

1. In the Print dialog, choose Copies & Pages from the third pop-up menu (**Figure 15a** or **15b**) to display Copies & Pages options (**Figure 13**).

2. In the Copies field, enter the number of copies of the document to print.

3. To collate multiple copies, turn on the Collated check box.

4. In the Pages area, select either the All radio button to print all pages or enter values in the From and To fields to print specific pages.

To set Layout options

1. In the Print dialog, choose Layout from the third pop-up menu (**Figure 15a** or **15b**) to display Layout options (**Figure 16**).

2. To set the number of pages that should appear on each sheet of paper, choose an option from the Pages per Sheet pop-up menu (**Figure 17**). The preview area of the dialog changes accordingly (**Figure 18**).

3. To indicate the order in which multiple pages should print on each sheet of paper, select a Layout Direction option. The preview area of the dialog changes accordingly (**Figure 18**).

4. To place a border around each page, choose an option from the Border pop-up menu (**Figure 19**).

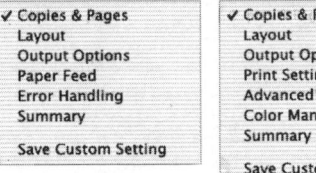

Figures 15a & 15b
The pop-up menu beneath the Saved Settings pop-up menu offers different options depending on the printer that is selected. The menu on the left is for a Hewlett-Packard LaserJet printer connected via network and the menu on the right is for an Epson Sylus Color printer connected directly to the computer via USB.

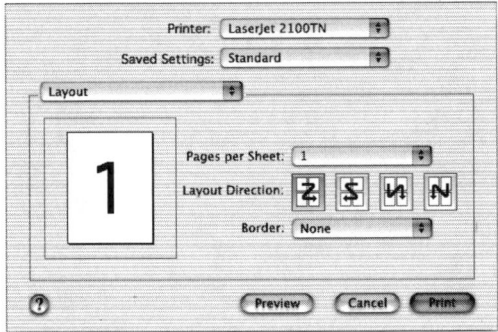

Figure 16 The Layout pane of the Print dialog.

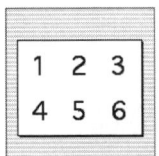

Figure 17
The Pages per Sheet pop-up menu.

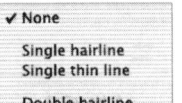

Figure 18
The Preview area indicates the number of pages to be printed per sheet, as well as the page order.

Figure 19
The Border pop-up menu.

SETTING COPIES, PAGES, & LAYOUT OPTIONS

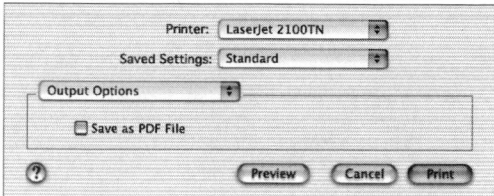

Figure 20 The Output Options pane of the Print dialog.

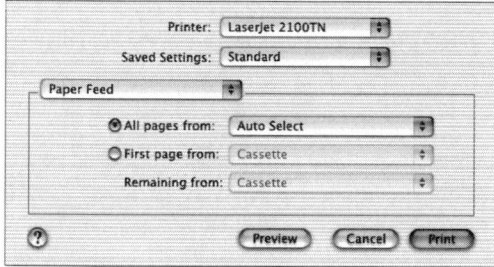

Figure 21 The Paper Feed pane of the Print dialog.

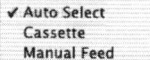

Figure 22
Use this pop-up menu to choose the paper source.

To set Output options

1. In the Print dialog, choose Output Options from the third pop-up menu (**Figure 15a** or **15b**) to display the Output Options pane (**Figure 20**).

2. To save the document as a PDF file (instead of printing it), turn on the Save as PDF File check box.

✔ Tip

■ When you turn on the Save as PDF File check box, the Print button in the Print dialog turns into a Save button.

To set Paper Feed options

1. In the Print dialog, choose Paper Feed from the third pop-up menu (**Figure 15a**) to display Paper Feed options (**Figure 21**).

2. To specify how paper trays should be used for paper feed, select one of the radio buttons.

3. To specify which paper tray(s) should be used for paper feed, choose options from the pop-up menu(s) (**Figure 22**).

✔ Tip

■ The options offered in the Paper Feed pane of the Print dialog (**Figure 21**) vary greatly depending on your printer. The options shown here are for a Hewlett-Packard LaserJet 2100TN printer.

SETTING OUTPUT & PAPER FEED OPTIONS

To set Error Handling options

1. In the Print dialog, choose Error Handling from the third pop-up menu (**Figure 15a**) to display Error Handling options (**Figure 23**).

2. To specify how the printer should report PostScript errors, select one of the Post-Script™ Errors radio buttons.

3. To specify how the printer should handle an out-of-paper situation for a multiple-tray printer, select one of the Tray Switching radio buttons.

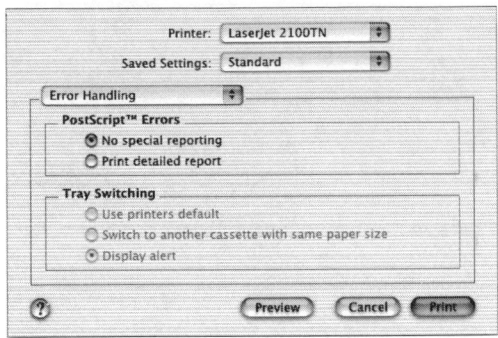

Figure 23 The Error Handling pane of the Print dialog.

✔ Tips

- These options are only available for Post-Script printers.

- Tray switching options are only available for printers with multiple paper trays.

To set Print Settings options

1. In the Print dialog, choose Print Settings from the third pop-up menu (**Figure 15b**) to display the Print Settings pane (**Figure 24**).

2. Select the type of paper you will print on from the Media Type pop-up menu (**Figure 25**).

3. For a color printer, select an Ink option.

4. Set Mode options as desired. These options vary from printer to printer; check the documentation that came with your printer for details.

Figure 24 The Print Settings pane of the Print dialog for an Epson Stylus Color printer.

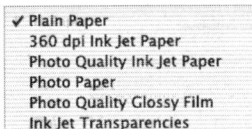

Figure 25
The Media Type pop-up menu for an Epson Stylus Color printer.

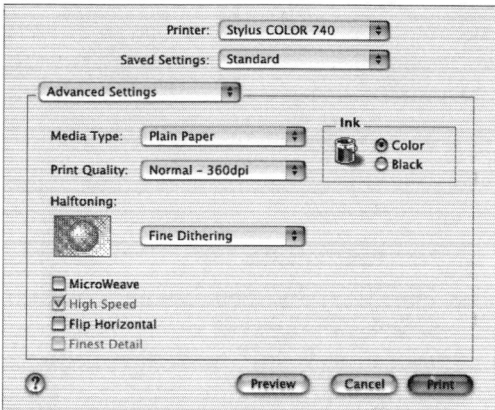

Figure 26 The Advanced Settings pane of the Print dialog for an Epson Stylus Color printer.

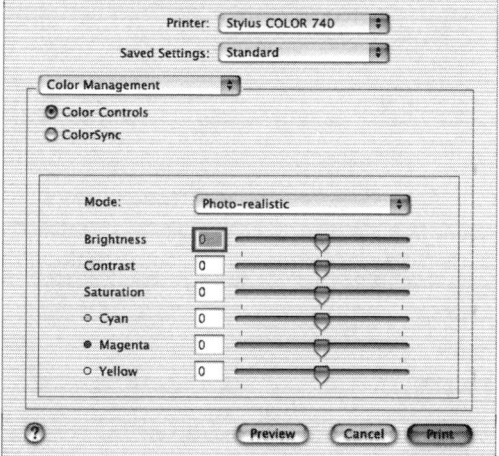

Figure 27 The Color Management pane of the Print dialog with Color Controls selected...

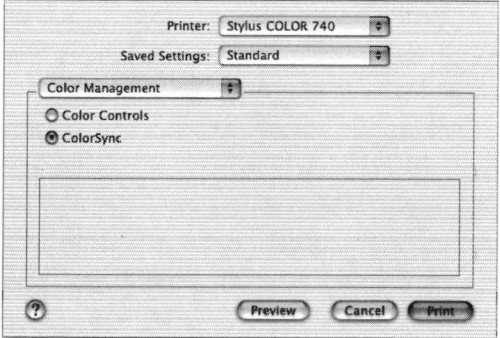

Figure 28 ...and with ColorSync selected.

To set Advanced Settings options

1. In the Print dialog, choose Advanced Settings from the third pop-up menu (**Figure 15b**) to display the Advanced Settings pane options (**Figure 26**).

2. Set options as desired. These options vary from printer to printer; check the documentation that came with your printer for details.

To set Color Management options

1. In the Print dialog, choose Color Management from the third pop-up menu (**Figure 15b**) to display Color Management options (**Figure 27**).

2. To indicate the color management method, select one of the radio buttons near the top of the pane. The options in the dialog change depending on the method you select (**Figures 27** and **28**).

3. If you selected Color Controls, set options in the dialog as desired.

✔ Tips

- Color management methods and options are far beyond the scope of this book.

- ColorSync is discussed in the sequel to this book, *Mac OS X: Visual QuickPro Guide*.

SETTING ADVANCED & COLOR OPTIONS

To save settings

In the Print dialog (**Figures 13**, **16**, **20**, **21**, **23**, **24**, **26**, **27**, and **28**), choose Save Custom Setting from the third pop-up menu (**Figure 15a** or **15b**).

Custom is automatically selected from the Saved Settings pop-up menu (**Figure 29**).

✔ Tip

■ It's a good idea to save settings if you often have to change the Print dialog's settings. This can save time when you need to print.

To use saved settings

In the Print dialog, choose Custom from the Saved Settings pop-up menu (**Figure 29**). All Print dialog settings are restored to what they were the last time you saved settings.

To preview a document

1. In the Print dialog (**Figure 13**), click the Preview button. The Print dialog disappears and Mac OS opens Preview. A moment later, the document appears in a Preview window (**Figure 30**).

2. If necessary, use controls at the bottom of the preview window to scroll from one page to the next.

3. When you're finished previewing the document, you have two options:

   ▲ Choose File > Print (**Figure 8b**) or press ⌃ ⌘ P to display the Print dialog and print the document from Preview.

   ▲ Choose Preview > Quit Preview (**Figure 31**) or press ⌃ ⌘ Q to quit Preview.

✔ Tips

■ Preview is covered in **Chapter 6**.

■ Some applications, such as Internet Explorer, include a Print Preview command on their File menu (**Figure 8c**).

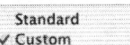

Figure 29
The Saved Settings pop-up menu.

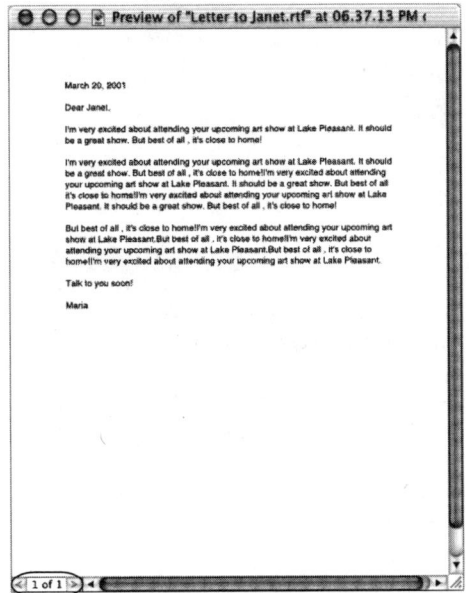

Figure 30 The Preview button displays the document in a Preview window. You can use controls at the bottom of the window to scroll from page to page.

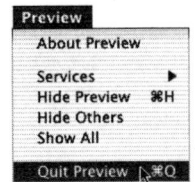

Figure 31
Quit Preview by choosing Quit Preview from the Preview menu.

SAVING SETTINGS, PREVIEWING DOCUMENTS

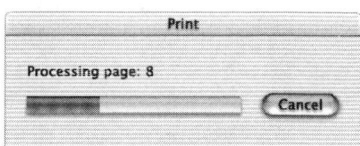

Figure 32 A progress window like this appears as a print job is spooled to the print queue.

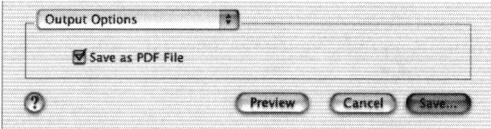

Figure 33 When you turn on the Save as PDF File check box, the Print button turns into a Save button.

Figure 34 Use this Save Location dialog to enter a name, select a location, and Save a document as a PDF file.

To print

In the Print dialog (**Figures 13**, **16**, **20**, **21**, **23**, **24**, **26**, **27**, and **28**), click Print.

The print job is sent to the print queue, where it waits for its turn to be printed. A progress window like the one in **Figure 32** appears as it is sent or *spooled*.

✔ Tips

■ You can normally cancel a print job as it is being spooled to the print queue or printer by pressing ⌃ ⌘ . . Any pages spooled *before* you press ⌃ ⌘ . , however, may be printed anyway.

■ Canceling a print job that has already been spooled to a print queue is discussed later in this chapter.

To save a document as a PDF file

1. In the Output Options pane of the Print dialog (**Figure 20**), turn on the Save as PDF File check box.

2. Set other options in other panes of the Print dialog as desired.

3. Click Save (**Figure 33**).

4. A Save Location dialog like the one in **Figure 34** appears. Use it to enter a name and choose a disk location for the PDF file.

✔ Tip

■ Using the Save Location dialog is covered in **Chapter 5**.

PRINTING, SAVING AS PDF FILES

Print Queues

As mentioned earlier in this chapter, Print Center can also be used to manage print queues. A *print queue* is a list of documents waiting to be printed. When you click the Print button to send a document to a printer, you're really sending it to the printer's queue, where it waits its turn to be printed.

Print Center's queue windows enable you to check the progress of documents that are printing; to stop printing; and to hold, resume, or cancel a specific print job.

To open a printer's queue window

1. Open Print Center.

2. In the Printer List window (**Figure 2**), double-click the name of the printer for which you want to open the queue.

   or

   In the Printer List window (**Figure 2**) select the name of the printer for which you want to open the queue, and choose Printers > Show Queue (**Figure 3**) or press ⌃⌘O.

   The printer's queue window appears (**Figure 35** or **36**).

✔ Tips

- Instructions for opening Print Center are provided earlier in this chapter.

- When a document is in the print queue, the Print Center icon appears in the Dock (**Figure 37**). Click the icon to open the Print Center.

To stop the print queue

Choose Queue > Stop Queue (**Figure 38**).

Any printing stops and the words "Queue stopped" appear near the top of the queue window (**Figure 39**).

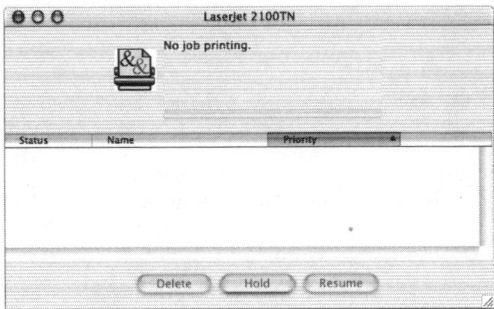

Figure 35 A printer's queue window, with no documents in the queue...

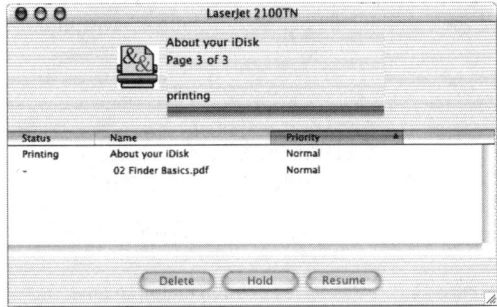

Figure 36 ...and the same printer's queue window with two documents in the queue, one of which is printing.

Figure 37 When print jobs are in a printers queue, the Print Center icon appears in the Dock.

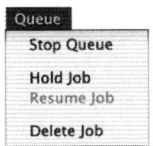

Figure 38 The Queue menu.

Figure 39 The queue status appears near the top of the queue window.

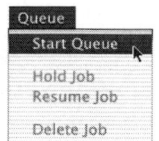

Figure 40
Choose Start Queue from the Queue menu to restart the print queue.

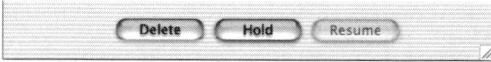

Figure 41 When you select a print job that is not on hold, the Delete and Hold buttons become active.

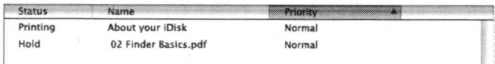

Figure 42 The word "Hold" appears in the status column for any job on hold.

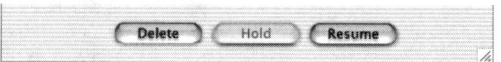

Figure 43 When you select a print job that is on hold, the Resume button becomes active.

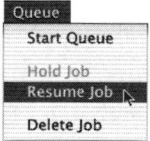

Figure 44
To resume a print job on hold, choose Resume Job from the Queue menu.

To restart the print queue

Choose Queue > Start Queue (**Figure 40**).

The next waiting print job starts printing.

To hold a specific print job

1. In the printer's queue window (**Figure 36**), select the print job you want to hold.

2. Click the Hold button (**Figure 41**).

or

Choose Queue > Hold Job (**Figure 38**).

The word "Hold" appears in the Status column beside the job name in the queue window (**Figure 42**). If the job was printing, printing stops and another job in the queue begins to print.

To resume a specific print job

1. In the printer's queue window (**Figure 36**), select the print job you want to resume.

2. Click the Resume button (**Figure 43**).

or

Choose Queue > Resume Job (**Figure 44**).

The word "Hold" disappears from the Status column beside the job name in the queue window. If no other jobs are printing, the job begins to print.

To cancel a specific print job

1. In the printer's queue window (**Figure 36**), select the print job you want to cancel.

2. Click the Delete button (**Figure 41**).

or

Choose Queue > Delete Job (**Figure 38**).

The job is removed from the print queue. If it was printing, printing stops.

MANAGING THE PRINT QUEUE & PRINT JOBS

Troubleshooting Printing Problems

When a printing problem occurs, Mac OS can often give you hints to help you figure out why. Here are some examples:

◆ A dialog like the one in **Figure 45** appears when your printer has a paper jam. Clear the jam.

◆ A dialog like the one in **Figure 46** appears when your computer can't find the selected printer. Check to make sure the printer is properly connected and turned on.

◆ A dialog like the one in **Figure 47** appears when your printer is out of paper. Add paper!

When you get one of these error messages, click the Stop Job button and fix the problem (if you can). Then select the document in the queue window (**Figure 48**) and click the Retry button. If the problem is fixed, the document should print.

✔ Tip

■ If you have printing problems that Mac OS can't help you identify, check the trouble-shooting section of the documentation that came with your printer.

Figure 45 This dialog appeared when the printer got a paper jam.

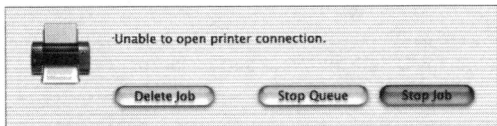

Figure 46 This dialog appeared when the printer wasn't turned on.

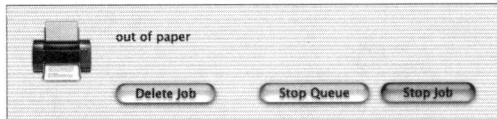

Figure 47 This dialog appeared when the printer ran out of paper.

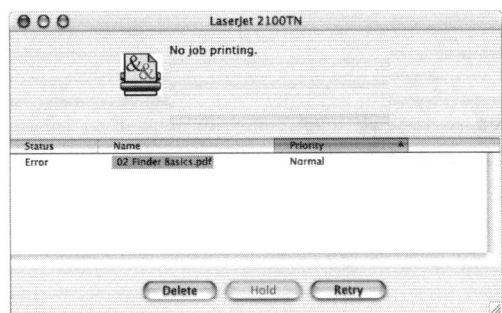

Figure 48 The word "Error" appears in the Status column beside a document that couldn't print. Fix the problem, select the document's name, and click Retry.

CONNECTING TO THE INTERNET

9

Connecting to the Internet

The *Internet* is a vast, worldwide network of computers that offers information, communication, online shopping, and entertainment for the whole family.

There are two ways to connect to the Internet:

◆ In a *direct* or *network connection*, your computer has a live network connection to the Internet all the time. This is relatively common for workplace computers on companywide networks. For home use, *DSL*, a type of direct connection, is gaining popularity, although it can be costly.

◆ In a *modem* or *dial-up connection*, your computer uses its modem to dial in to a server at an *Internet Service Provider* (*ISP*), which gives it access to the Internet. This is a cheaper way to connect, but your access speed is limited by the speed of your modem.

This chapter explains how to configure your system for an Internet connection, connect to the Internet, and use the Internet applications and utilities included with Mac OS X.

✔ Tips

■ An ISP is an organization that provides access to the Internet for a fee.

■ The *World Wide Web* is part of the Internet. The Web and the *Web browser* software you use to access it are covered later in this chapter.

TCP/IP, PPP, & Internet Connect

Your computer accesses the Internet via a TCP/IP connection. *TCP/IP* is a standard Internet *protocol*, or set of rules, for exchanging information.

A TCP/IP connection works like a pipeline. Once established, Internet applications—such as your Web browser and e-mail program—reach through the TCP/IP pipeline to get the information they need. When the information has been sent or received, it stops flowing through the pipeline. But the pipeline is not disconnected.

If you have a direct or network connection to the Internet, the Internet is accessible all the time. But if you connect via modem, you need to use Internet Connect software. This software, which comes with Mac OS, uses PPP to connect to TCP/IP networks via modem. *PPP* is a standard protocol for connecting to networks.

When you connect via modem using Internet Connect, you set up a temporary TCP/IP pipeline. Internet applications are smart enough to automatically use Internet Connect to connect to the Internet when necessary. When you're finished accessing Internet services you should tell Internet Connect to disconnect.

✔ Tip

■ Internet Connect is brand new to Mac OS X. It replaces the Remote Access software found in previous versions of Mac OS.

Manually Setting Internet Configuration Options

If you set up your Internet connection as part of the setup process discussed in **Chapter 1**, your computer should be all ready to connect to the Internet and you can skip ahead to the sections that discuss Internet connection software. But if you didn't set up your connection or your Internet connection information has changed since setup, you'll have to do some manual configuration.

Mac OS X includes two System Preferences panels that you can use to manually set up an Internet configuration:

◆ **Network** enables you to set server IP address and domain name information, as well as proxy and PPP dialup information.

◆ **Internet** enables you to set a wide variety of configuration options, including personal, e-mail, Web, and news information.

The following two sections explain the configuration options in these System Preference panels in case you ever need or want to modify settings.

✔ Tip

■ If your Internet configuration is working fine, don't change it! Internet connections follow one of the golden rules of computing: *If it ain't broke, don't fix it.*

Network Preferences

The Network panel of System Preferences enables you to configure your modem or network connection:

◆ For **modem or network connections**, you can set options to configure your TCP/IP address and proxy information.

◆ For **modem connections only**, you can set options for your PPP connection to the Internet and your modem.

◆ For **network connections only**, you can set options for your PPPoE connection to a DSL server and AppleTalk connection to an internal network.

✔ Tips

■ A discussion of AppleTalk network connections is beyond the scope of this book. You can learn more about networking in the sequel to this book, *Mac OS X: Visual QuickPro Guide*.

■ Before you set Network preferences, make sure you have all the information you need to properly configure the options. You can get all of the information you need from your ISP or network administrator.

To open Network preferences

1. Choose Apple > System Preferences (**Figure 1**).

   or

   Click the System Preferences icon in the Dock (**Figure 2**).

2. In the System Preferences window that appears, click the Network icon to display its options (**Figure 3**).

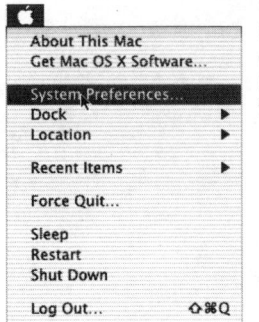

Figure 1
Choose System Preferences from the Apple menu...

Figure 2 ...or click the System Preferences icon in the Dock.

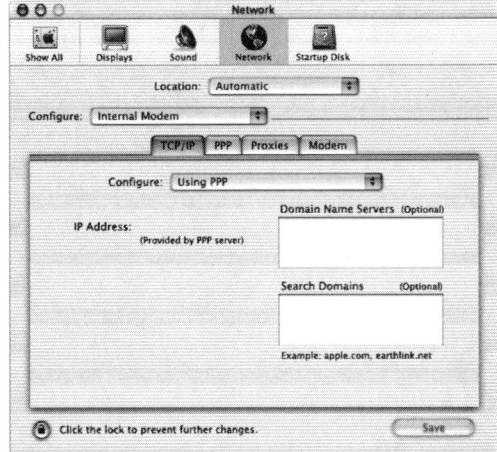

Figure 3 The Network panel of System Preferences with the TCP/IP tab selected for a modem connection.

NETWORK PREFERENCES

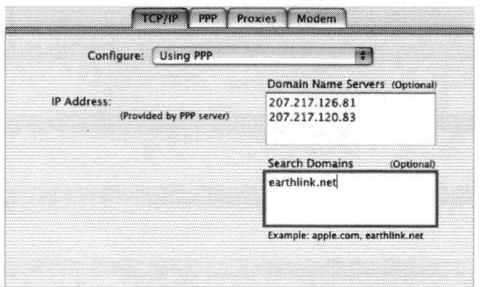

Figure 4 If your ISP has not provided you with a static IP address, the TCP/IP pane might look like this.

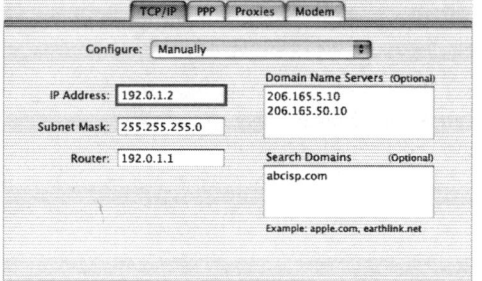

Figure 5 If your ISP has provided you with a static IP address, the TCP/IP pane should include all address information.

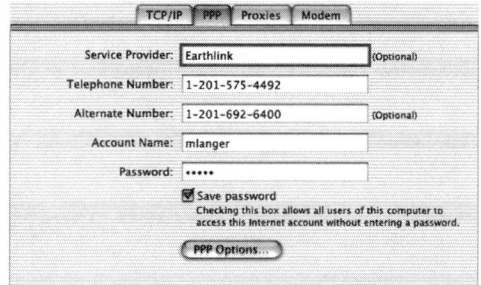

Figure 6 The PPP pane should include all of the information your computer needs to dial in and log on to the ISP's server.

To set up a modem connection

1. In the Network panel of System Preferences, choose Modem or Internal Modem from the Configure pop-up menu above the tabs.

2. If necessary, click the TCP/IP tab to display its options (**Figure 3**).

3. If your ISP's instructions say that IP address and domain name information will be assigned automatically (i.e., you have a *dynamic* IP address), choose Using PPP from the Configure pop-up menu in the TCP/IP pane. Then enter the domain information in the fields. **Figure 4** shows an example. (This is the most commonly used option for dial-up connections to ISPs.)

   or

   If your ISP provided a *static* IP address and domain name server information for your connection, choose Manually from the Configure pop-up menu in the TCP/IP pane and enter the information provided in each of the fields that appear. **Figure 5** shows an example.

4. Click the PPP tab to display its options.

5. Enter the dialup information provided by your ISP. **Figure 6** shows an example.

6. Click the Modem tab to display its options (**Figure 7**).

7. Choose your modem type from the Modem pop-up menu.

8. Select a Sound radio button:

   ▲ **On** plays dialing and connection sounds through the modem or computer speaker.

   ▲ **Off** dials and connects silently.

Continued on next page...

SETTING UP A MODEM CONNECTION

Continued from previous page.

9. Select a dialing radio button:

   ▲ **Tone** enables you to dial with touch-tone dialing.

   ▲ **Pulse** enables you to dial with pulse dialing. Select this option only if touch-tone dialing is not available on your telephone line.

10. To instruct your computer to wait until it "hears" a dial tone before it dials, turn on the Wait for dial tone before dialing check box. This, however, can prevent the computer from dialing if you have an unusual dial tone.

11. Click Save to save your changes to Network preferences.

✔ Tips

■ Do not use the settings illustrated here. Use the settings provided by your ISP.

■ In step 5, if you turn on the Save password check box, you won't have to enter your password when you connect to the Internet. Be aware, however, that anyone who accesses your computer with your login will also be able to connect to the Internet with your account.

■ The Modem menu in step 7 includes dozens of modem makes and models, so your modem should be listed. If it isn't, choose another model from the same manufacturer or, if the manufacturer isn't listed, choose one of the Hayes models.

■ In step 8, you may want to keep modem sounds on until you're sure you can connect. This enables you to hear telephone company error recordings that can help you troubleshoot connection problems. You can always turn sound off later.

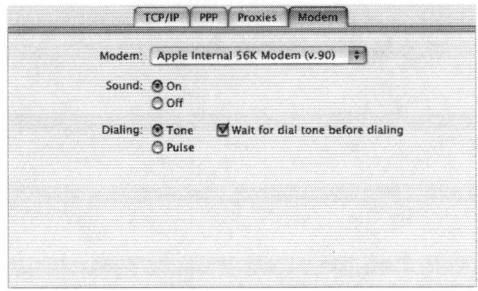

Figure 7 The Modem pane enables you to set options for your modem.

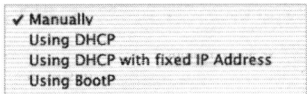

Figure 8 The Configure menu in the TCP/IP pane for a network connection offers four options.

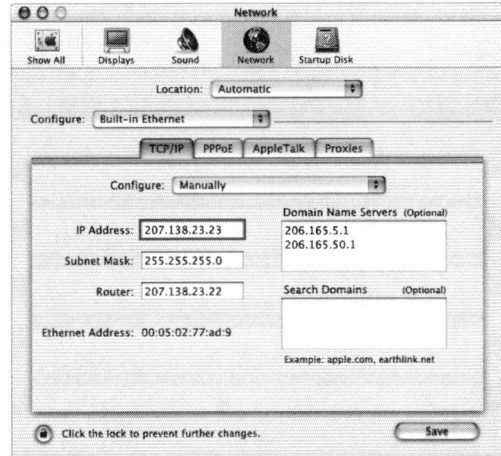

Figure 9 Examples of various configurations for a network TCP/IP connection: manual,...

SETTING UP A MODEM CONNECTION

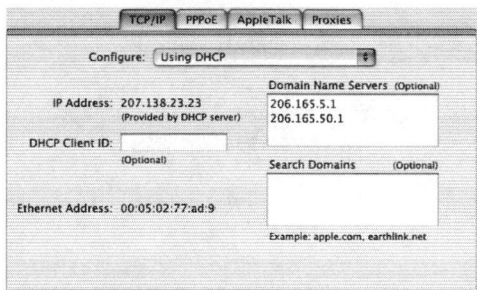

Figure 10 ...DHCP, ...

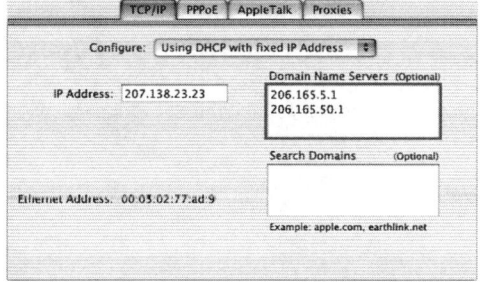

Figure 11 ...DHCP with a fixed IP address,...

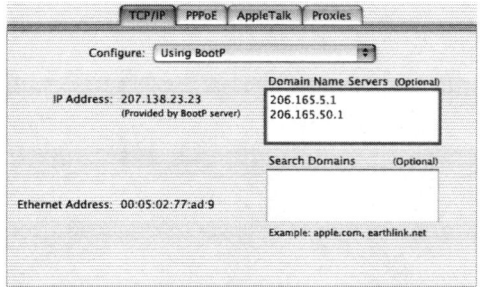

Figure 12 ...and using BootP.

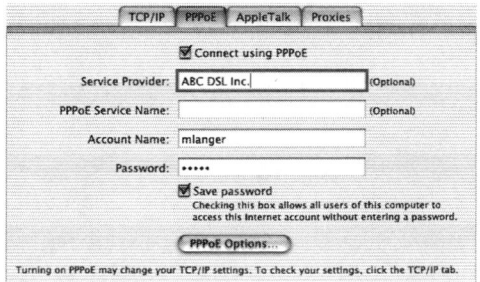

Figure 13 You can use the PPPoE pane to set up a PPPoE connection to a DSL server.

To set up a network connection

1. In the Network panel of System Preferences, choose the network option from the Configure pop-up menu above the tabs. This option will probably be labeled "Built-in Ethernet," but it could have another name.

2. If necessary, click the TCP/IP tab to display its options.

3. Choose one of the options from the Configure pop-up menu in the TCP/IP pane (**Figure 8**). The option you select determines the appearance of the rest of the pane—**Figures 9** through **12** show examples.

4. Enter the appropriate IP addresses and domain names in the fields.

5. If you have a DSL connection via PPPoE, click the PPPoE tab to display its options. Turn on the Connect using PPPoE check box and enter the connection information provided by your ISP. **Figure 13** shows an example.

6. Click Save to save your changes to Network preferences.

✔ Tips

- Do not use the settings illustrated here. Use the settings provided by your ISP or network administrator.

- If you're not sure which option to choose in Step 3, ask your network administrator.

- In step 5, if you turn on the Save password check box, you won't have to enter your password when you connect to the Internet. Be aware, however, that anyone who accesses your computer with your login will also be able to connect to the Internet with your account.

To set proxy options

1. In the Network panel of System Preferences, click the Proxies tab to display its options (**Figure 14**).

2. Turn on the check box beside each proxy option you need to set up. Then enter appropriate information for each one.

3. Click Save to save your changes to Network preferences.

✔ Tips

- Proxies are most often required for network connections; they are seldom required for dialup connections.

- Do not change settings in the Proxies pane of Network preferences unless instructed by your ISP or network administrator. Setting invalid values may prevent you from connecting to the Internet.

- Proxies pane options are the same for modems as for network connections.

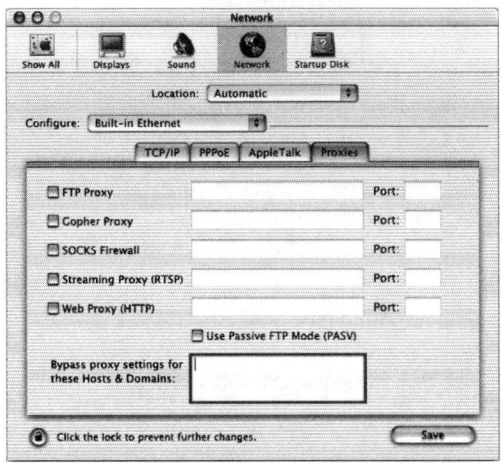

Figure 14 The Proxies pane of the Network panel of System Preferences.

Internet Preferences

The Internet panel of System Preferences includes panes you can use to set options for accessing Internet features:

◆ **Email** enables you to set your default e-mail reader application, e-mail address, and e-mail server information.

◆ **Web** enables you to set your default Web browser, home page, search page, and file download location.

◆ **News** enables you to set your default news reader application, news server information, and connection information.

✔ Tip

■ Internet preferences also enables you to set options for iTools, which is discussed in **Appendix B**.

To open Network preferences

1. Choose Apple > System Preferences (**Figure 1**).

   or

   Click the System Preferences icon in the Dock (**Figure 2**).

2. In the System Preferences window that appears, click the Internet icon to display its options (**Figures 15, 16,** and **17**).

To set Email options

1. In the Internet panel of System Preferences, click the Email tab to display its options (**Figure 15**).

2. To specify your e-mail application, choose an option from the Default Email Reader pop-up menu. The default selection is Mail, which is discussed in this chapter, but you can choose any e-mail program that is listed or choose Select to use an Open dialog to locate and select the program you want to use.

3. Fill in the fields with address and connection information for your e-mail address. This information should have been provided by your ISP or network administrator.

✔ Tip

■ If you turn on the Use iTools Email account check box, all other options are filled in and you can skip step 3. iTools is discussed in **Appendix B**.

To set Web options

1. In the Internet panel of System Preferences, click the Web tab to display its options (**Figure 16**).

2. To specify your Web browser application, choose an option from the Default Web Browser pop-up menu. The default option is Internet Explorer, which is discussed in this chapter, but you can choose any Web browser that is listed or choose Select to use an Open dialog to locate and select the program you want to use.

3. Fill in the fields with URLs for your pre-ferred home page, search page, and file download location.

✔ Tip

■ URL is defined and discussed later in this chapter.

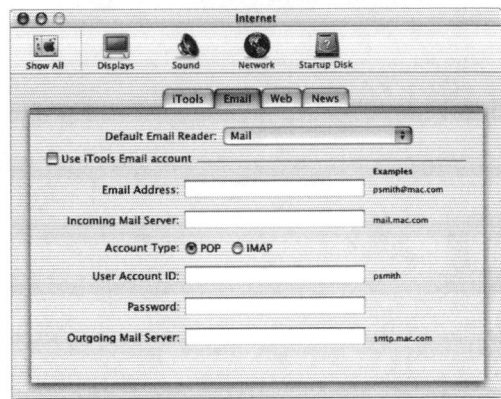

Figure 15 The Internet panel of System Preferences for Email, ...

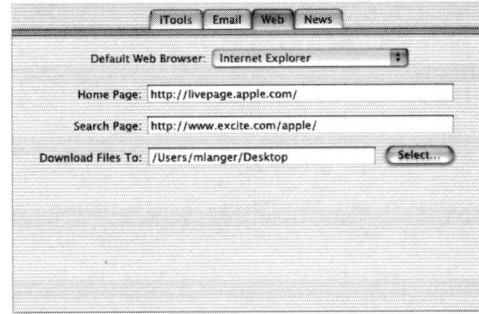

Figure 16 ...Web, ...

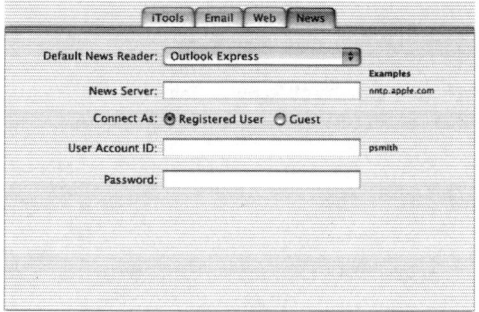

Figure 17 ...and News.

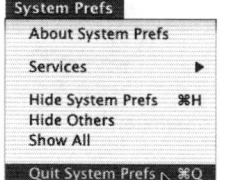

Figure 18
When you quit System Preferences, all of your Internet Preference settings are saved.

To set Web options

1. In the Internet panel of System Preferences, click the News tab to display its options (**Figure 17**).

2. To specify your news reader application, choose an option from the Default News Reader pop-up menu. The default option is Outlook Express, a Classic application that comes with Mac OS 9.1 and is not covered in this book, but you can choose any news reader application that is listed or choose Select to use an Open dialog to locate and select the program you want to use.

3. Fill in the fields with server and connection information to access news groups.

✔ Tip

■ URL is defined and discussed later in this chapter.

To save Internet preferences

Choose System Prefs > Quit System Prefs (**Figure 18**), or press ⌃⌘Q.

The System Preferences application quits, and all of your settings are saved.

SETTING NEWS OPTIONS, SAVING PREFERENCES

Connecting to an ISP

You can establish a PPP connection to your ISP by using Internet Connect to dial in.

✔ Tip

■ If you have a network connection to the Internet, you are always connected.

To connect to an ISP

1. Open the Internet Connect icon in the Applications folder (**Figure 19**).

2. Check the settings in the main Internet Connect window that appears (**Figure 20**).

3. Click the Connect button. Internet Connect dials your modem. It displays the connection status in its Status area (**Figure 21**).

   When Internet Connect has successfully connected, the Connect button turns into a Disconnect button and the Status area fills with connection information(**Figure 22**).

✔ Tips

■ The settings that appear in the Internet Connect window (**Figure 20**) should reflect settings you made in the Network panel of System Preferences. If you need to make changes, click the Edit button and follow the instructions provided earlier in this chapter.

■ You can click the triangle beside the Configuration pop-up menu to collapse the window and display only the status area (**Figure 23**).

■ Internet Connect does not have to be open while you are connected to the Internet.

To disconnect from an ISP

1. Open or switch to Internet Connect (**Figures 20** through **23**).

2. Click the Disconnect button (**Figures 22** and **23**). The connection is terminated.

Figure 19
The Internet Connect application icon.

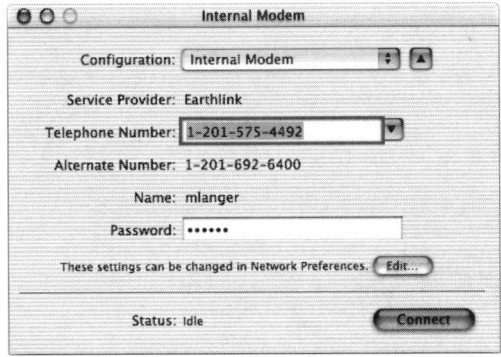

Figure 20 Internet Connect's main window.

Figure 21 The Status area displays connection status information while you are connecting...

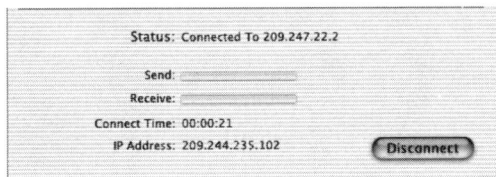

Figure 22 ...and after you have connected.

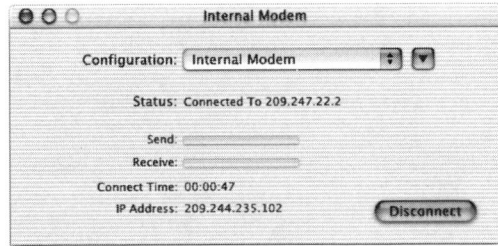

Figure 23 You can collapse Internet Connection's window to show only connection status.

Mail   Internet Explorer

Figures 24 & 25 Mail (left) and Internet Explorer (right) are the two Internet applications that come with Mac OS X.

Figure 26 You can open both Mail and Internet Explorer by clicking their icons in the Dock.

Internet Applications

Mac OS X includes two applications for accessing the Internet:

◆ **Mail** is an Apple program that enables you to send and receive e-mail messages.

◆ **Internet Explorer** is a Microsoft program that enables you to browse Web sites and download files from FTP sites.

This section provides brief instructions for using these two programs. You can explore the other features of these programs on your own.

✔ Tips

■ Mail and Internet Explorer are set as the default e-mail and Web browser programs. If you prefer to use other applications, be sure to change the appropriate settings in the Internet panel of System Preferences, as discussed earlier in this chapter.

■ Mac OS 9.1, which is bundled with Mac OS X to handle Classic applications, includes Outlook Express, an e-mail application and Netscape Communicator, a Web browser.

To open Mail

Use one of the following techniques:

◆ Open the Mail icon in the Applications folder (**Figure 24**).

◆ Click the Mail icon in the Dock (**Figure 26**).

To open Internet Explorer

Use one of the following techniques:

◆ Open the Internet Explorer icon in the Internet Explorer folder in the Applications folder (**Figure 25**).

◆ Click the Explorer icon in the Dock (**Figure 26**).

Mail

Mail (**Figure 27**) is an e-mail application from Apple Computer, Inc. It enables you to send and receive e-mail messages using your Internet e-mail account.

This section provides enough information about Mail to get you started sending and receiving e-mail messages.

To set up an e-mail account

1. Choose Mail > Preferences.

2. In the Mail Preferences window that appears, click the Accounts button to display its options (**Figure 28**).

3. Click the Create Account button.

4. In the Account Information pane of the dialog that appears (**Figure 29**), enter the account and server information for the e-mail account.

5. Click OK to save your settings and dismiss the dialog. The account appears in the Mail Preferences window (**Figure 30**).

6. Click the Mail Preferences window's close button to dismiss it.

✔ Tips

- Your e-mail account may have already been set up for you based on information you provided in the Mac OS X configuration process, which was discussed in **Chapter 1**.

- You only have to set up an e-mail account once.

- Your ISP or network administrator can provide most of the information you need to set up an e-mail account.

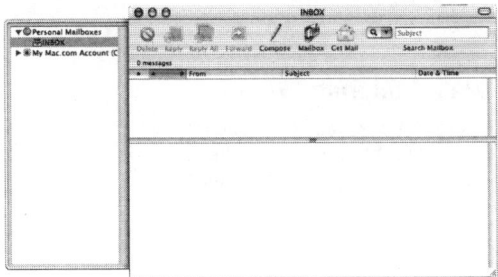

Figure 27 The Mail main window with the Mailbox drawer displayed.

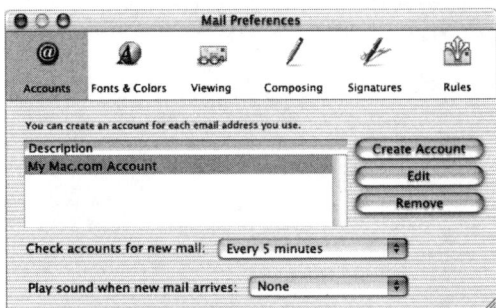

Figure 28 The Account pane of the Mail Preferences window.

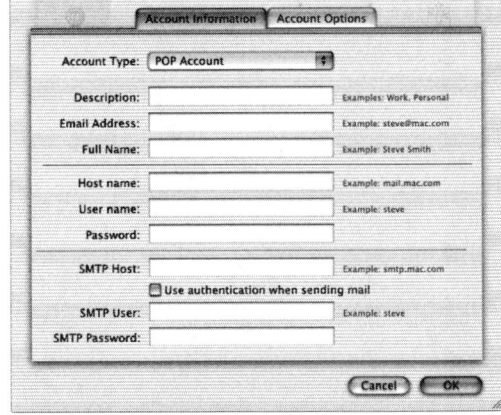

Figure 29 The Account Information pane enables you to enter basic information for your e-mail account.

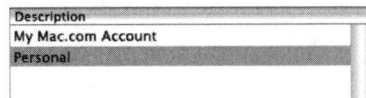

Figure 30 The account you added appears in the list.

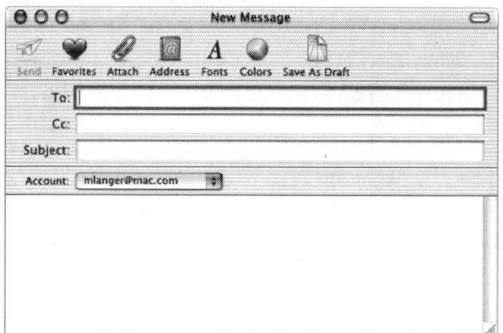

Figure 31 Clicking the Compose button opens a New Message window like this one.

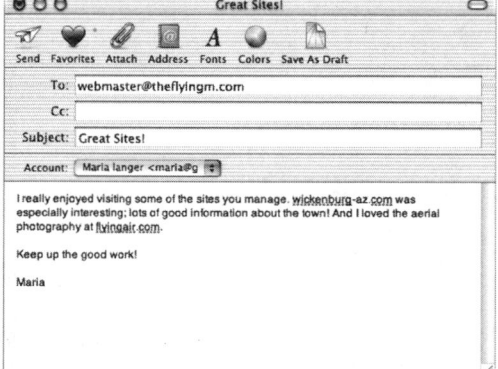

Figure 32 Here's a short message ready to be sent. The dashed underlines indicate potential spelling errors caught by Mail's built-in spelling checker; these lines aren't sent with the messages.

To create & send a message

1. Click the Compose button at the top of the Mail main window (**Figure 27**). The New Message window appears (**Figure 31**).

2. Enter the e-mail address of the message recipient in the To field, and press Tab twice.

3. Enter a subject for the message in the Subject field, and press Tab.

4. Type your message into the large box at the bottom of the window. When you are finished, the window might look like the one in **Figure 32**.

5. Click the Send button near the top of the window. The message window closes and Mail sends the message.

✔ Tips

- You can use the Address Book application to maintain a directory of the people you write to. Select the name of the person in the Address Book list (**Figure 33**) and click the Mail button to launch Mail and display a preaddressed New Message form. Address Book is covered in **Chapter 6**.

- If you have a modem connection to the Internet, you must connect before you can send a message.

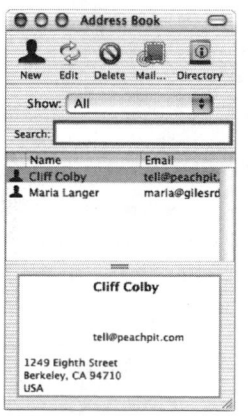

Figure 33
You can use Mail to send an e-mail message to someone in your Address Book by selecting the person's name and clicking the Mail button.

To retrieve e-mail messages

1. Click the Get Mail button at the top of the main window (**Figure 27**).

2. Mail connects to your e-mail server and downloads messages waiting for you. Any incoming messages appear in bold when you select the Inbox icon for the account in the Mailbox drawer (**Figure 34**).

✔ Tips

- You can toggle the display of the Mailbox drawer by clicking the Mailbox button in the main Mail window (**Figure 34**).

- You can view the contents of the Inbox or other mail folders by clicking icons in the Mailbox drawer (**Figure 34**).

To read a message

1. Click the message that you want to read. It appears in the bottom half of the main Mail window (**Figure 34**).

2. Read the message.

✔ Tips

- You can also double-click a message to display it in its own message window (**Figure 35**).

- To reply to the message, click Reply. A preaddressed message window with the entire message quoted appears (**Figure 36**). Type your reply, and click Send.

- To forward the message to another e-mail address, click Forward. A message window containing a copy of the message appears. Enter the e-mail address for the recipient in the To field, and click Send.

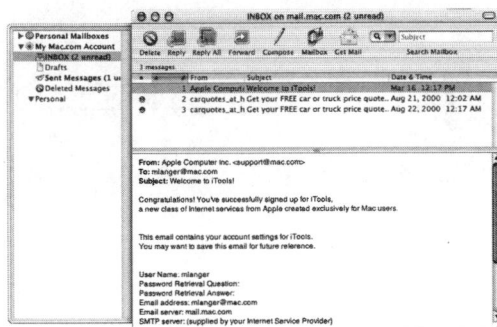

Figure 34 Incoming messages appear in the Inbox. Select a message to display it in the window.

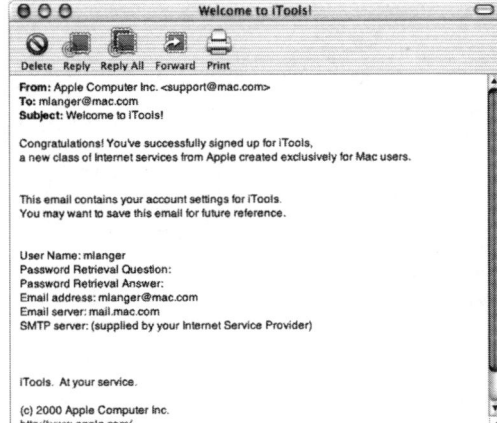

Figure 35 Double-click a message to open it in its own window.

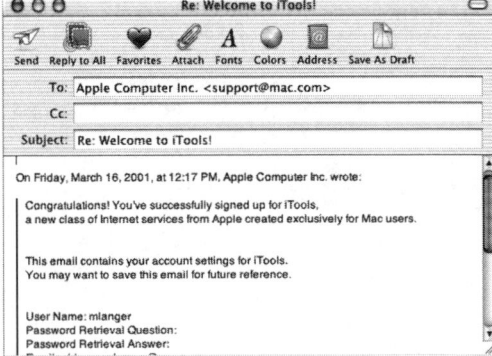

Figure 36 When you click the Reply button, a preaddressed message window appears.

RETRIEVING & READING E-MAIL MESSAGES

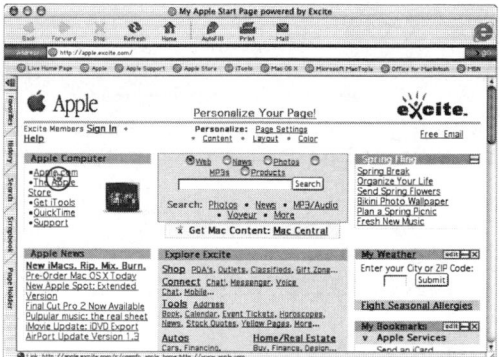

Figure 37 When you launch Internet Explorer, it displays the default home page—in this case, Apple's "Live Page."

Figure 38 Clicking the link in **Figure 37** displays this page.

Internet Explorer

Internet Explorer is a popular Web browser application from Microsoft. It enables you to view, or *browse*, pages on the World Wide Web.

A Web *page* is a window full of formatted text and graphics (**Figures 37** and **38**). You move from page to page by clicking text or graphic links or by opening *URLs* (*uniform resource locators*) for specific Web pages. These two methods of navigating the World Wide Web can open a whole world of useful or interesting information.

✔ Tips

- The version of Internet Explorer included with Mac OS X is Mac OS X compatible. (Older versions run under the Classic environment only.) It has been customized to start with a specific home page and offer buttons with links to Apple and Microsoft pages.

- You can easily identify a link by pointing to it; the mouse pointer turns into a pointing finger and the link destination appears in the status bar at the bottom of the window (**Figure 37**).

To follow a link

1. Position the mouse pointer on a text or graphic link. The mouse pointer turns into a pointing finger (**Figure 37**).

2. Click. After a moment, the page or other location for the link you clicked will appear (**Figure 38**).

To view a specific URL

Enter the URL in the Address field near the top of the Internet Explorer window (**Figure 39**), and press [Return] or [Enter].

To return to the home page

Click the Home button at the top of the Internet Explorer window (**Figure 39**).

✔ Tip

■ You can change the default home page by specifying a different page's URL in the Web tab of the Internet panel of System Preferences. The page you specify will load each time you launch Internet Explorer. The Internet panel is discussed earlier in this chapter.

To save a page as a favorite

1. Display the Web page that you want to save as a favorite.

2. Choose Favorites > Add Page to Favorites (**Figure 40**), or press [⌃][⌘][D].

   The name of the page is added to the Favorites menu (**Figure 41**).

✔ Tips

■ Once a page has been added to the Favorites menu, you can display it by selecting its name from the menu.

■ Favorites are also referred to as *bookmarks*.

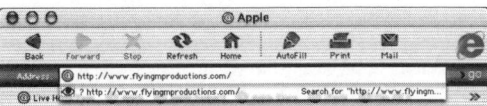

Figure 39 Enter the URL in the Address field at the top of the Internet Explorer window, and press [Enter].

Figure 40 The Add Page to Favorites command adds the currently displayed page to the Favorites menu,...

Figure 41 ...as shown here.

VIEWING URLS, SAVING FAVORITES

USING SHERLOCK

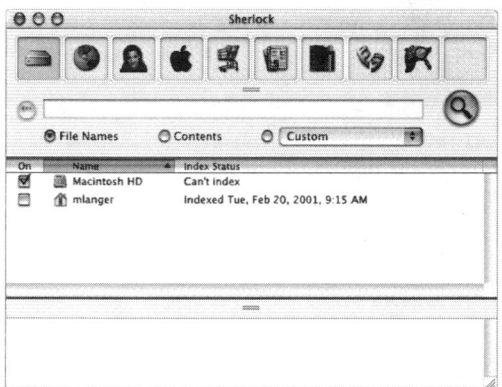

Figure 1 Sherlock enables you to search for files on mounted disks and information on the Internet.

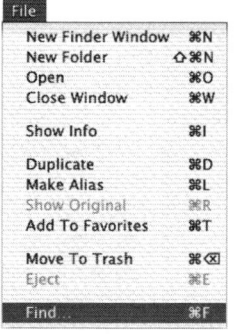

Figure 2
You can launch Sherlock by choosing Find from the Finder's File menu, ...

Figure 3 ...by clicking the Sherlock icon in the Dock, ...

Sherlock

Figure 4
...or by double-clicking the Sherlock icon in the Applications folder.

Sherlock

Sherlock (**Figure 1**) is Apple's powerful search utility. It enables you to perform the following searches:

◆ Search your internal hard disk and other mounted volumes for files based on file name, content, or other criteria.

◆ Search the Internet for information found on Web sites all over the world, including contact information for people you know and merchandise available from online vendors.

This chapter explain show to use Sherlock's search features as well as how to customize Sherlock so it works the way you want it to.

✔ Tips

■ **Chapter 3** tells you more about mounted disks and volumes.

■ Internet access is required to use Sherlock to search the Internet. **Chapter 9** covers accessing the Internet.

To launch Sherlock

Use one of these techniques:

◆ Choose File > Find (**Figure 2**), or press ⌃ ⌘ F.

◆ Click the Sherlock icon in the Dock (**Figure 3**).

◆ Double-click the Sherlock icon in the Applications folder (**Figure 4**).

Channels

Sherlock's interface includes a feature called *channels*, which enables you to organize search sites based on the types of information they can find for you. Sherlock comes preconfigured with nine channels:

- ◆ **Files** is for searching mounted volumes and folders for files. It is the only channel that does not require Internet access to use.

- ◆ **Internet** is for searching the Internet for general information.

- ◆ **People** is for searching the Internet for the e-mail addresses and other contact information of people you know.

- ◆ **Apple** is for searching Apple computer for product and technical information.

- ◆ **Shopping** is for searching online stores for items you may want to purchase.

- ◆ **News** is for searching news and information sites for news articles.

- ◆ **Reference** is for searching reference libraries for information.

- ◆ **Entertainment** is for searching for information from the world of entertainment.

- ◆ **My Channel** is an empty channel you can use to organize your own search sites.

To switch to a specific channel

Click the icon for the channel at the top of the Sherlock window (**Figure 5**).

or

Choose the name of the channel from the Channels menu (**Figure 6**).

Figure 5
Sherlock's default channels.

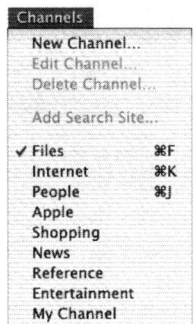

Figure 6
You can switch to a channel by choosing its name from the Channels menu.

Figure 7 Here's an example of search criteria for searching by name...

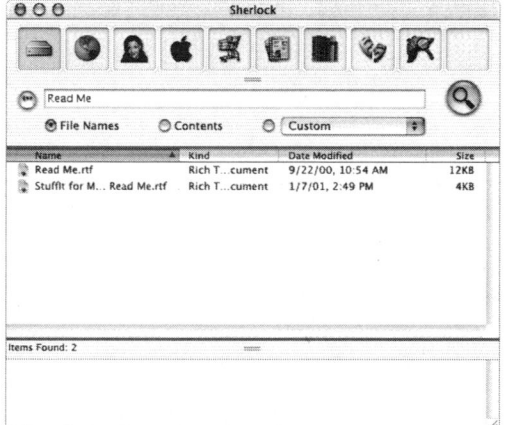

Figure 8 ...and here's what the search results might look like.

Finding Files

Sherlock enables you to search your internal hard disk, user folders, or other mounted volumes, including CD-ROM, floppy, Zip, and networked disks, for files based on a variety of search criteria:

◆ **File Names** enables you to search for files based on all or part of the file name.

◆ **Contents** enables you to search for files based on any part of the document's contents.

◆ **Custom** criteria enables you to search for files based on any combination of criteria, including file name, contents, and other file attributes.

✔ Tip

■ File attributes are covered in greater detail later in this section.

To find files by name

1. Click the Files channel button at the top of the Sherlock window (**Figure 5**) or press ⌃⌘F to display Sherlock's Files channel (**Figure 1**).

2. Select the File Names radio button.

3. Enter all or part of the name of the file you want to find in the text field near the top of the window (**Figure 7**).

4. Turn on the check box beside each disk or folder you want to search.

5. Click the magnifying glass button to begin the search. Sherlock searches the specified disks, displaying its status while it works. The search results appear in the bottom half of the window (**Figure 8**).

To find files by content

1. Click the Files channel button at the top of the Sherlock window (**Figure 5**) or press ⌃⌘F to display Sherlock's Files channel (**Figure 1**).

2. Select the Contents radio button.

3. Enter the text you are searching for within the file's contents in the text field near the top of the window (**Figure 9**).

4. Turn on the check box beside each disk or folder you want to search. If all of the checked items have been recently indexed (as noted beside the item name), skip ahead to step 8.

5. If a disk or folder you want to search has not been recently indexed, select it and choose Find > Index Now (**Figure 10**).

6. Wait while the item is indexed. Information about indexing progress appears beside the item name while Sherlock works (**Figure 11**). When it is finished, the item's Index Status changes to reflect the recent indexing.

7. Repeat steps 5 and 6 for every disk or folder you want to index.

8. Click the magnifying glass button to begin the search. Sherlock searches the specified disks, displaying its status while it works. The search results appear in the bottom half of the window (**Figure 12**).

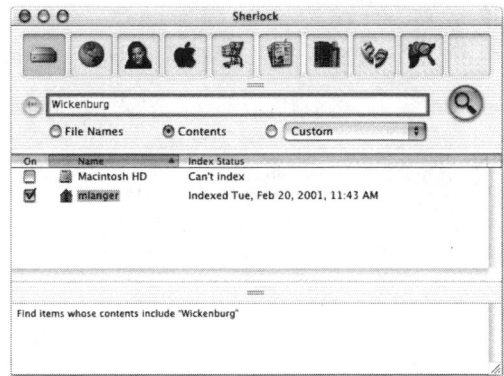

Figure 9 Here's the criteria set up for searching by content.

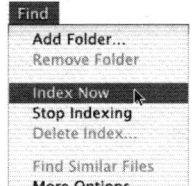

Figure 10 Choose the Index Now command to index a selected volume.

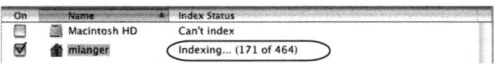

Figure 11 Indexing progress is displayed beside the volume name in Sherlock's window.

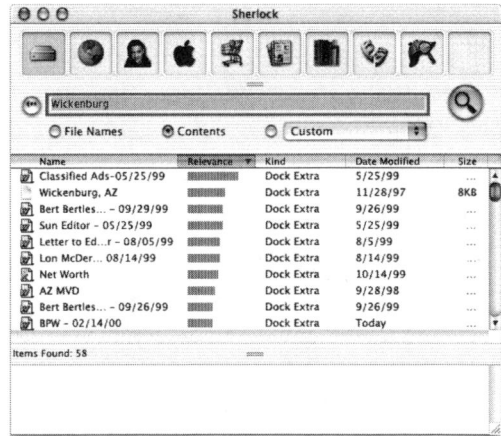

Figure 12 The search results appear in the bottom half of the Sherlock window.

FINDING FILES BY CONTENT

✔ Tips

- The Find by Content feature searches the index, not the actual files. Therefore, it cannot find files that match criteria if the files were created or modified after the index was last updated.

- To index a server disk, you must be the server's administrator. To index a user folder, you must be the folder's owner.

- The amount of time it takes to index a disk or folder depends on how many items it contains. For large hard disks and CD-ROM discs, indexing can take twenty minutes or longer.

- Options for automatically indexing disks and folders are discussed later in this chapter.

- When displaying the results of a search by content, Sherlock includes a Relevance column (**Figure 12**) that indicates how many times the search criteria appeared in the content of the file. Found files are sorted by relevance, so the most likely matches appear at the top of the list.

To find files by custom criteria

1. Click the Files channel button at the top of the Sherlock window (**Figure 5**) or press ⌃ ⌘ F to display Sherlock's Files channel (**Figure 1**).

2. Select the radio button beside the Custom pop-up menu.

3. Choose Edit from the Custom pop-up menu (**Figure 13**).

4. In the More Search Options dialog that appears (**Figure 14**), turn on check boxes and enter search criteria for the attributes you want to use to search for files. Here are your options:

   ▲ **File name** is the name of the file. Choose an option from the pop-up menu (**Figure 15**), and enter all or part of the file name beside it.

   ▲ **Content includes** enables you to specify text to find within a file's contents. Enter the text in the text field. (The volume must be indexed to find by content; see the section titled "To find files by content" for details.)

   ▲ **Date created** is the date the file was created. Choose an option from the pop-up menu (**Figure 16**), and enter a date beside it.

   ▲ **Date modified** is the date the file was last changed. Choose an option from the pop-up menu (**Figure 16**), and enter a date beside it.

   ▲ **Size** is the size of the file in kilobytes (KB). Choose an option from the pop-up menu (**Figure 17**), and enter a size value beside it.

   ▲ **Kind** is the type of file. Choose an option from the first pop-up menu (**Figure 18**), and then choose a type from the pop-up menu beside it (**Figure 19**). (**Chapter 2** covers file types.)

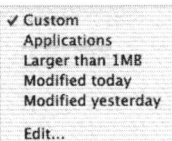

Figure 13
The Custom pop-up menu enables you to choose from predefined searches or create your own custom search.

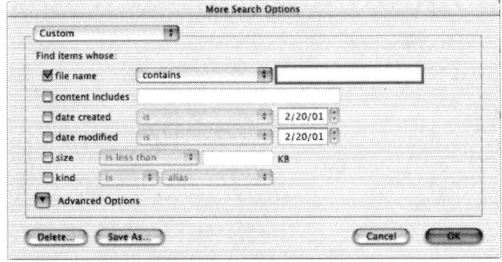

Figure 14 Use the More Search Options dialog to set up custom search criteria.

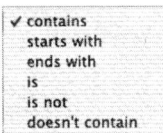

Figure 15
Use this pop-up menu to specify how a file's name should match your entry.

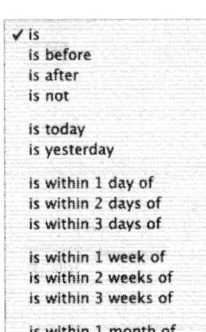

Figure 16
Use a pop-up menu like this one to specify how a date you enter should match the creation or modification date of a file.

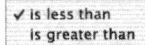

Figure 17 Use this pop-up menu to specify how size should match your criteria.

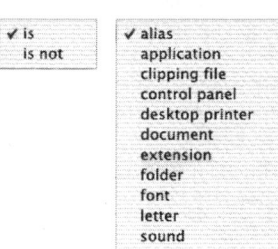

Figures 18 & 19
To specify a kind of document, choose an option from these two pop-up menus.

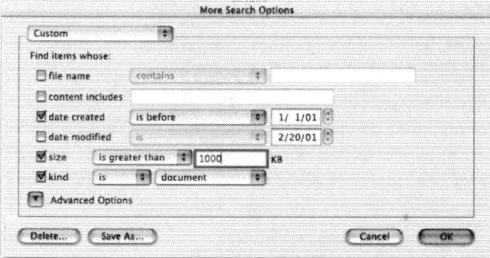

Figure 20 Here's what the More Search Options dialog looks like with some criteria set,...

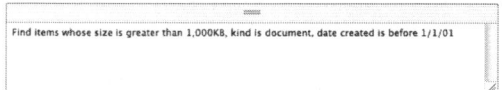

Figure 21 ...here's what the same criteria looks like in the bottom of the Sherlock window,...

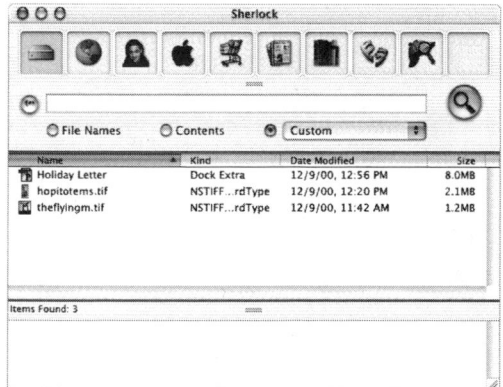

Figure 22 ...and here's what the items found list might look like for that criteria.

5. When you are finished setting up search criteria (**Figure 20**), click OK to return to the Sherlock window. The criteria appears in the bottom of the window (**Figure 21**).

6. Turn on the check box beside each disk or folder you want to search.

7. Click the magnifying glass button to begin the search. Sherlock searches the specified disks, displaying its status while it works. The search results appear in the bottom half of the window (**Figure 22**).

✔ Tips

- The Custom pop-up menu in the Sherlock window includes other predefined custom search options (**Figure 13**). Choose an option and click Sherlock's magnifying glass button to perform the search.

- Sherlock finds files that match *all* search criteria in the More Search Options dialog (**Figure 20**). The more criteria you include, the fewer files you will find.

- Clicking the Advanced Options button in the More Search Options dialog expands the dialog to offer additional options for setting search criteria (**Figure 23**). These options are technical in nature and far beyond the scope of this book.

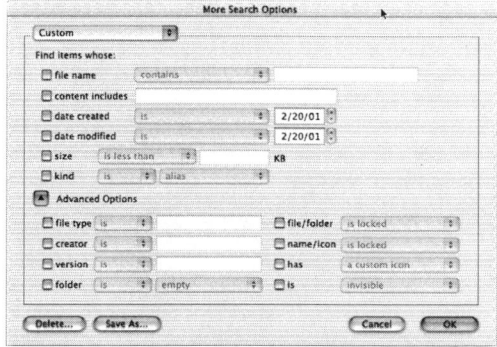

Figure 23 Clicking the triangle beside Advanced Options expands the dialog to offer more options.

To save custom criteria

1. Follow steps 1 through 4 in the section titled "To find files by custom criteria" to set up criteria in Sherlock's More Search Options dialog (**Figure 20**).

2. Click Save.

3. Enter a name for the set of search criteria in the Save Custom Settings dialog that appears (**Figure 24**).

4. Click Save to save the settings and return to the Sherlock window.

✔ Tips

■ Once you've saved custom search criteria, you can use it any time by choosing its name from the Custom pop-up menu in the Sherlock window (**Figure 25**).

■ You can remove a set of custom search criteria by clicking Delete in the More Search Options dialog (**Figure 20**). Select the criteria set you want to delete in the Delete Custom Search Settings dialog that appears (**Figure 26**), and click Delete.

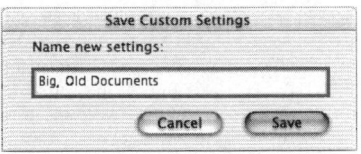

Figure 24 Use this dialog to name and save a set of custom search criteria so you can use it again and again.

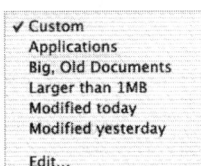

Figure 25
When you save custom search criteria, its name appears in the Custom pop-up menu in the Sherlock window.

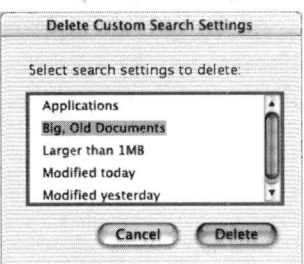

Figure 26 Use this dialog to delete sets of custom search criteria you no longer use.

Figure 27 When you select an item, the complete path to its location appears in Sherlock's window.

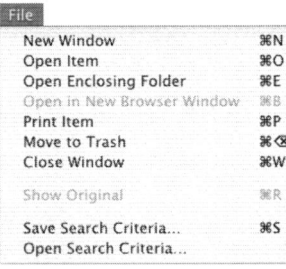

Figure 28 Sherlock's File menu offers all kinds of commands for working with selected items.

Figure 29 You can move an item by dragging it from the Sherlock window to a new place on disk.

Figure 30 When you release the item, its path changes.

To work with the list of items found

1. Scroll through the list of items found (**Figures 8**, **12**, and **22**) to locate an item that interests you.

2. Click the item to select it (**Figure 27**). Then:

   ▲ To see where the item is located, consult the bottom part of the window for the complete path to its location (**Figure 27**).

   ▲ To open the item, double-click it, choose File > Open Item (**Figure 28**), or press ⌘O.

   ▲ To open the folder in which the item is stored, choose File > Open Enclosing Folder (**Figure 28**) or press ⌘E.

   ▲ To print the item (if it is a printable file), choose File > Print Item (**Figure 28**) or press ⌘P. (**Chapter 8** covers printing.)

   ▲ To move the item, drag it from the Sherlock window to a disk, folder, or Finder window (**Figure 29**). When you release the mouse button, the item still appears in the Sherlock window, but its path at the bottom of the window changes (**Figure 30**).

   ▲ To delete the item, drag it from the Sherlock window to the Trash, choose File > Move to Trash (**Figure 28**), or press ⌘Delete. The item still appears in the Sherlock window, but its path at the bottom of the window shows that it is in the Trash.

   ▲ To view the original for the item (if it is an alias), choose File > Show Original or press ⌘R. (**Chapter 4** covers aliases.)

Continued on next page...

WORKING WITH ITEMS FOUND

Continued from previous page.

▲ To find files that are similar to the item, choose Find > Find Similar Files (**Figure 31**). Sherlock performs another find based on the selected file's contents and attributes and displays the results in its window.

Figure 31
The Find menu includes the Find Similar Files command, which searches for files based on the content of the selected file.

✔ Tips

■ To select more than one found item at a time, hold down Shift while clicking each one. The paths for the items do not appear at the bottom of the Sherlock window when more than one item is selected.

■ You can sort the items found list in the Sherlock window (**Figure 27**) by clicking one of its column headings. To reverse the sort order, just click the same column heading again.

■ To remove the items found list so you can perform a new search, click the Files channel button at the top of the Sherlock window (**Figure 5**).

■ To open a separate Sherlock window to perform a new search (without disturbing the items found list), choose File > New Window (**Figure 28**) or press ⌃ ⌘ N.

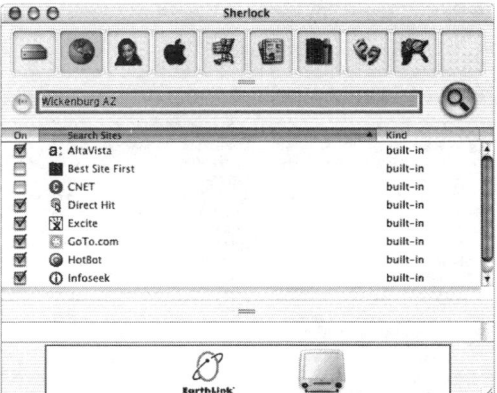

Figure 32 Use Sherlock's Internet channel to search the Internet for information.

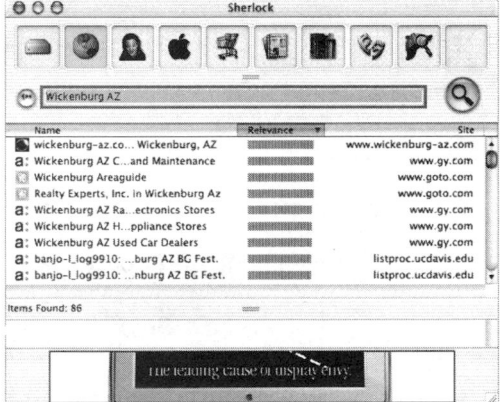

Figure 33 Sherlock displays matches, in order of relevance, in its window.

✔ Tips

- When entering words in step 2, enter at least two or three words you expect to find in documents about the topic you area searching for. This helps narrow down the search, resulting in more useful matches.

- The more search sites you select the longer the search will take.

- Ads appear at the bottom of the Sherlock window. Click an ad to open a corresponding Web page in your Web browser.

Searching the Internet

If you have Internet access, you can use Sherlock to search for Web pages with information about topics that interest you. Unlike most other Internet search engines, Sherlock can search multiple directories (or *search sites*) at once. Best of all, you don't need to know special search syntax. Just enter a search word or phrase in plain English, select the search sites you want to use, and put Sherlock to work. It displays matches in order of relevance, so the most likely matches appear first.

To search the Internet

1. Click the button for one of the Internet search channels:

   ▲ **Internet** (⌃ ⌘ J) is a general purpose search channel, good for finding Web pages that cover specific topics.

   ▲ **Apple** is best for searching for Apple-related information, including products and how-to instructions.

   ▲ **News** is best for finding news stories from news Web sites.

   ▲ **Reference** is good for finding articles about specific topics on reference sites.

   ▲ **Entertainment** is good for finding information about movies, music, and your favorite entertainment artists.

2. Enter a search word or phrase in the text field near the top of the window (**Figure 32**).

3. Turn on the check box beside each search site you want to use to search.

4. Click the magnifying glass button to begin the search. Sherlock searches the Internet, displaying its status while it works.

5. After a moment, the matches begin to appear. You can begin working with matches immediately or wait until Sherlock has finished searching (**Figure 33**).

To work with the items found list of Web pages

1. Scroll through the list of items found (**Figure 33**) to locate an item that interests you.

2. Click the item to select it (**Figure 34**). Then:

   ▲ To learn more about the item, consult the information that appears beneath the items found list (**Figure 34**).

   ▲ To open the item's Web page, double-click it, choose File > Open, or press ⌃⌘○. Your Web browser launches and displays the item in its window (**Figure 35**).

✔ Tips

■ To open a Web page in new Web browser window (rather than in the currently open Web browser window), choose File > Open in New Browser Window or press ⌃⌘B.

■ You can sort the items found list in the Sherlock window (**Figure 33**) by clicking one of its column headings. To reverse the sort order, just click the same column heading again.

■ To remove the items found list so you can perform a new search, click a button for one of the Internet search channels at the top of the Sherlock window (**Figure 5**).

■ To open a separate Sherlock window to perform a new search (without disturbing the items found list), choose File > New Window (**Figure 28**) or press ⌃⌘N.

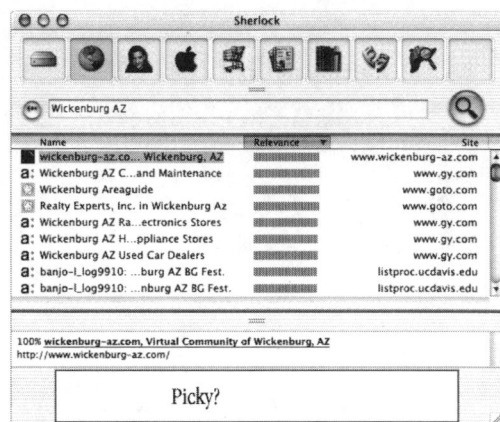

Figure 34 Select a Web page to display information about it.

Figure 35 Double-clicking the name of a Web page displays the page in your Web browser window. Here's my favorite Web site for my favorite western town.

WORKING WITH ITEMS FOUND

Figure 36 Use Sherlock to search for people you know.

Figure 37 Sherlock displays a list of all matches for the name you entered. (Please do not dial these phone numbers; they're not mine!)

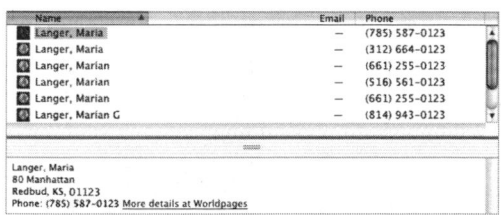

Figure 38 Click an item to see its details in the bottom of the window. (Please do not bother this person. She is not me!)

Searching for People

If you have Internet access, you can use Sherlock to find the contact information for people you know. This feature searches the entries in several popular e-mail directories to find matches.

To search for a person

1. Click the People channel button at the top of the Sherlock window (**Figure 5**) or press ⌃⌘J to display Sherlock's People channel.

2. Enter the complete name for the person in the text field near the top of the window (**Figure 36**).

3. Turn on the check box beside each search site you want to use to search.

4. Click the magnifying glass button to begin the search. Sherlock searches the directories you selected, displaying its status while it works.

5. After a moment, the matches begin to appear. You can begin working with matches immediately or wait until Sherlock has finished searching (**Figure 37**).

6. To get all the information about a matched item, click it once. The information appears in the area beneath the list (**Figure 38**).

✔ Tip

■ Although Sherlock can find people, the search sites it uses may not have complete or up-to-date data. For example, although Sherlock found 8 matches for "Maria Langer," none of them is for me.

Shopping Online

If you have Internet access, you can also use Sherlock to find products that you can buy online. This feature can search various departments at Amazon.com as well as other online retailers and auctions.

To search for a product

1. Click the Shopping channel button at the top of the Sherlock window (**Figure 5**) to display Sherlock's Shopping channel.

2. Enter the name or some key words for the product you want to find in the text field near the top of the window (**Figure 39**).

3. Turn on the check boxes beside each search site where you want to shop.

4. Click the magnifying glass button to begin the search. Sherlock searches the online stores you selected, displaying its status while it works.

5. After a moment, the matches begin to appear. You can begin working with matches immediately or wait until Sherlock has finished searching (**Figure 40**).

6. To get all the information about a matched item, click it once. The information appears in the area beneath the list (**Figure 40**).

7. To learn more about the item or buy it, double-click it. This launches your Web browser and displays the page on the Web site where the item is offered for sale.

Figure 39 Use Sherlock to shop online.

Figure 40 Select one of the matches to get more information about it, along with a clickable link to the Web site where it's available for sale.

Figure 41 Use a standard Save Location dialog to save search criteria as a file on disk.

terms conta...kenburg AZ"

Figure 42 A Sherlock search file's icon looks like this.

Figure 43 You can open a search file from within Sherlock, using a standard Open dialog.

Saving Searches

Sherlock enables you to save search files with the details of frequently used searches. This makes it possible to repeat a search by simply opening a Sherlock search file icon.

To save a search

1. Use Sherlock as described throughout this chapter to set up search criteria and perform a search.

2. Choose File > Save Search Criteria (**Figure 28**), or press $\boxed{\circlearrowleft}\boxed{\mathcal{H}}\boxed{S}$.

3. Use the Save Location dialog sheet that appears (**Figure 41**) to select a disk location and enter a name for the search file.

4. Click Save. The search criteria is saved as a file on disk.

To use a saved search

Double-click the icon for a saved search file (**Figure 42**). Sherlock opens and performs the search, displaying the results in its window.

or

1. Choose File > Open Search Criteria (**Figure 28**).

2. Use the Open dialog sheet that appears (**Figure 43**) to locate, select, and open the saved search criteria file.

   Sherlock performs the search, displaying the results in its window.

SAVING SEARCH CRITERIA

Customizing Sherlock

There are a number of things you can do to customize the way Sherlock works for you. This section explores some of the most useful ones.

To add a folder to the Files channel

1. Click the Files channel button at the top of the Sherlock window (**Figure 5**) or press ⌘ ⌘ F to display Sherlock's Files channel (**Figure 1**).

2. Choose Find > Add Folder (**Figure 44**).

3. Use the Open dialog sheet that appears to select the folder you want to add (**Figure 45**).

4. Click Add. The folder is added to Sherlock's list of disks and folders (**Figure 46**), and if automatic indexing is enabled, Sherlock indexes the folder.

✔ Tips

■ Adding folders to the Files channel makes it easy to search specific folders without searching an entire disk.

■ Automatic indexing options are covered later in this chapter.

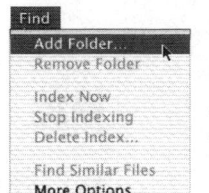

Figure 44
Use the Add Folder command to add a folder to the Files channel.

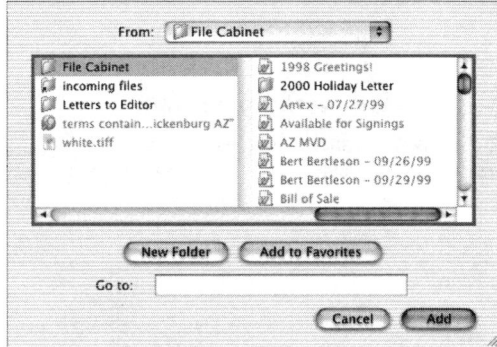

Figure 45 Choose the folder you want to add.

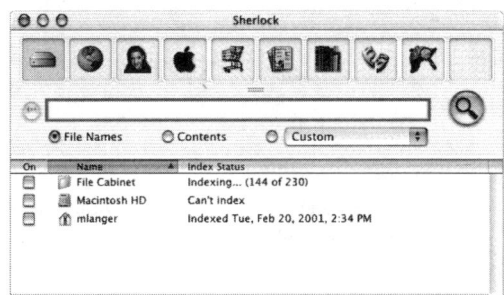

Figure 46 The added folder appears with the rest of the disks and folders in Sherlock's Files channel.

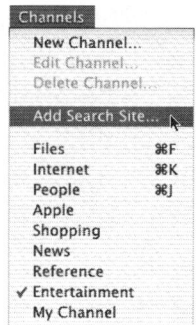

Figure 47
Choose Add Search Site from the Channels menu.

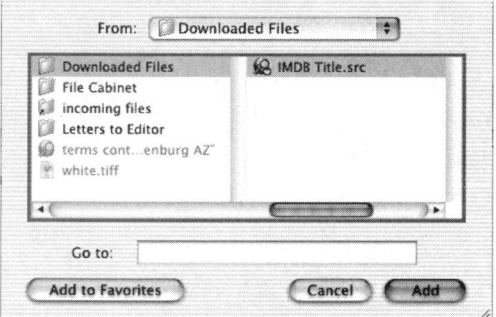

Figure 48 Locate and select the plug-in file you want to add.

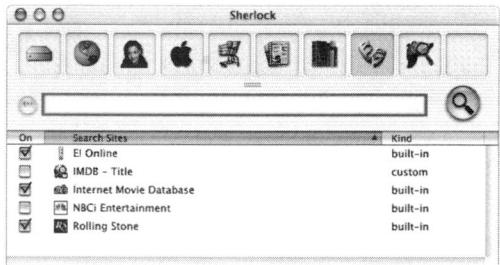

Figure 49 The plug-in appears in the Channel's list of search sites.

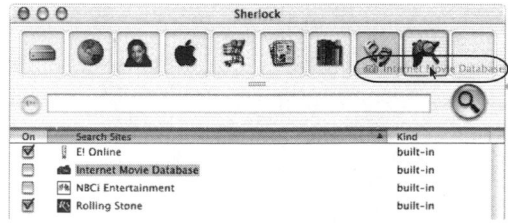

Figure 50 Drag a search site from the channel's window to a channel button.

To add a search site to one of Sherlock's Internet channels

1. Visit Apple's Sherlock Plug-ins Web page (http://www.apple.com/sherlock/plugins.html) to learn more about and download additional search site files.

2. In Sherlock, click the button for the channel you want to add the search site to.

3. Choose Channels > Add Search Site (**Figure 47**).

4. Use the Open dialog sheet that appears to locate and select the search site file you want to add (**Figure 48**).

5. Click Add. The search site file appears in the list of search sites for the channel (**Figure 49**).

✔ Tips

- Search site files are also referred to as *Sherlock plug-ins.*

- Cnet's Downloads.com (http://www.downloads.com/) is another good source for Sherlock plug-ins. Enter a search phrase of *Sherlock plug-in* to see what's available for download.

To move search sites from one channel to another

Drag the search site name from the list of search sites to the button for the channel you want to move it to (**Figure 50**). When you release the mouse button, the search site moves.

✔ Tips

- You can copy a search site from one channel to another by holding down Option while you drag its name as instructed above.

- This is a great way to create a custom channel.

To set automatic indexing options

1. Choose Sherlock > Preferences (**Figure 51**).

2. Set the indexing options in the Preferences dialog that appears (**Figure 52**) by toggling the check boxes:

   ▲ **Automatically index items when Sherlock is opened** tells Sherlock to automatically index disks and folders when you launch it.

   ▲ **Automatically index folders when they're added to the Files channel** tells Sherlock to automatically index a folder when you add a folder to the Files channel list of disks and folders.

3. Click OK.

✔ Tip

■ You may want to turn automatic indexing off if the Files channel includes seldom-searched disks or folders with many files. Just remember to manually index items before you use the search by content feature to search them.

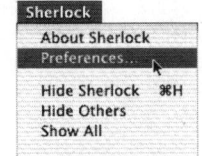

Figure 51
Choose Preferences from the Sherlock menu.

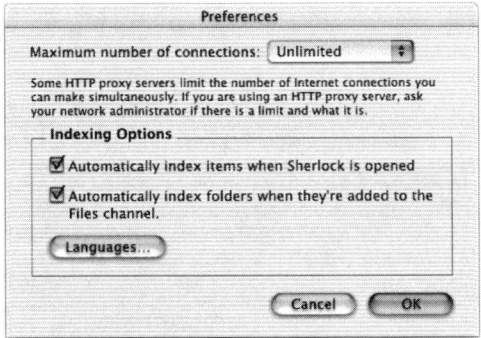

Figure 52 Use the Preferences dialog to set indexing options. These are the default settings.

SETTING SYSTEM PREFERENCES 11

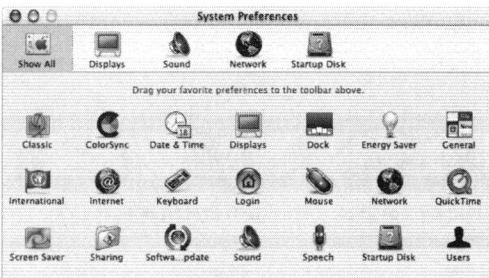

Figure 1 The System Preferences window, with icons for all panes displayed.

✔ Tips

- Other, more advanced System Preferences panes are covered in *Mac OS X: Visual QuickPro Guide*, the sequel to this book, including Classic, ColorSync, Displays, International, Internet, Login, Network, QuickTime, Sharing, Software Update, Speech, Startup Disk, and Users.

- **Chapter 4** explains how you can set Finder preferences and customize the toolbar that appears within Finder windows. Be sure to check out that chapter to see what other customization options are available to you.

System Preferences

One of the great things about Mac OS is the way it can be customized to look and work the way you want it to. For example, you can set the date and time, customize the appearance and functionality of the Dock, fine-tune the way the mouse works, and set up a screen saver.

Mac OS X offers a new way to customize Mac OS: with the System Preferences application (**Figure 1**). It offers access to a variety of panes, each containing settings for a part of Mac OS.

This chapter looks at the following System Preferences panes:

- ◆ **Date & Time** enables you to set the system date and time as well as customize the appearance of the menu bar clock.

- ◆ **Dock** enables you to change the size, magnification, and other settings for the Dock.

- ◆ **Energy Saver** enables you to set options for putting your system, display, or hard disk to sleep after a certain period of inactivity.

- ◆ **General** enables you to set the color scheme and scroll bar functionality.

- ◆ **Keyboard** enables you to fine-tune keyboard operations for the way you type.

- ◆ **Mouse** enables you to set the tracking and double-click speed for the mouse.

- ◆ **Screen Saver** enables you to set up a screen saver for your monitor.

- ◆ **Sound** enables you to set the system volume, speaker balance, and alert sound.

To open System Preferences

Choose Apple > System Preferences (**Figure 2**).

or

Click the System Preferences icon in the Dock (**Figure 3**).

The System Preferences window appears (**Figure 1**).

To open a preferences pane

Click the icon for the pane you want to display.

or

Choose the name of the pane you want to display from the Pane menu (**Figure 4**).

✔ Tips

- To display icons for all System Preferences panes, click the Show All button in the toolbar of the System Preferences window.

- You can customize the System Preferences window's toolbar. Simply drag an icon for a preferences pane into the toolbar. You can then access that pane no matter what pane is displayed in the window.

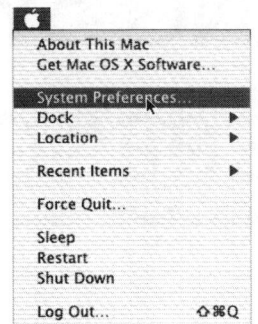

Figure 2
To open System Preferences, choose System Preferences from the Apple menu...

Figure 3 ...or click the System Preferences icon in the Dock.

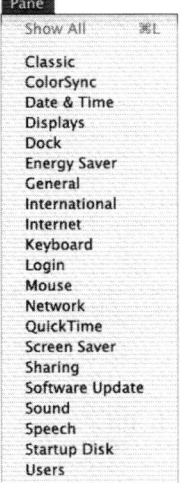

Figure 4
The Pane menu lists all of the System Preferences panes.

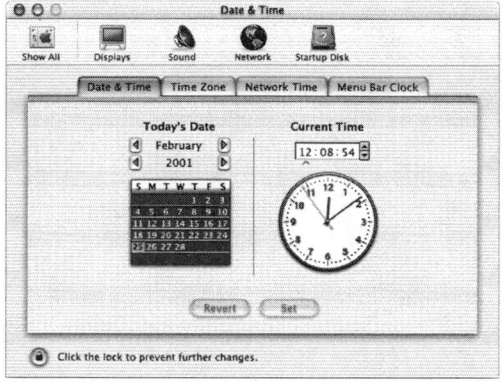

Figure 5 The Date & Time panel of the System Preferences Date & Time pane.

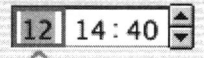

Figure 6 Click a time value and enter a new value to change it.

Date & Time

The Date & Time pane (**Figures 5, 7, 8,** and **9**) includes four panels for setting the system time and clock options:

◆ **Date & Time** (**Figure 5**) enables you to manually set the date and time.

◆ **Time Zone** (**Figure 7**) enables you to set your time zone.

◆ **Network Time** (**Figure 8**) enables you to synchronize your system clock with a network time server.

◆ **Menu Bar Clock** (**Figure 9**) enables you to set options for the appearance of the digital clock in the menu bar.

To manually set the date & time

1. In the Date & Time Pane of System Preferences, click the Date & Time tab to display its panel (**Figure 5**).

2. Make changes as follows:

   ▲ To change the date, click the arrow buttons beside the month and year to set the month and year. Then click the current date on the calendar to set the date.

   ▲ To change the current time, click on the part of the time that you want to change (**Figure 6**) and type in a new value or use the arrow keys beside the time to change the value.

3. Click Set.

✔ Tip

■ Another way to change the time in step 2 is to drag the hands of the analog clock so they display the correct time. (This is kind of cool, but it's tough to be accurate.)

To set the time zone

1. In the Date & Time Pane of System Preferences, click the Time Zone tab to display its panel (**Figure 7**).

2. Click on your approximate location on the map. A white bar indicates the time zone area.

3. Choose the name of your time zone from the pop-up menu beneath the map.

✔ Tips

- In step 3, only those time zones that apply to the white bar on the map are listed in the pop-up menu. If your time zone does not appear in the menu, make sure you clicked the correct area in the map in step 2.

- It's a good idea to choose the correct time zone, since Mac OS uses this information with the network time server (if utilized) and to properly change the clock for daylight saving time.

To use a network time server

1. In the Date & Time Pane of System Preferences, click the Network Time tab to display its panel (**Figure 8**).

2. Click the Start button. Your computer will use its network or Internet connection to periodically get the date and time from a time server and update the system clock automatically.

✔ Tip

- If this feature does not work when the Configure option is set to From NetInfo as shown in **Figure 8**, consult your Network Administrator. You may have to set the Configure option to Manually and enter the IP address of a server.

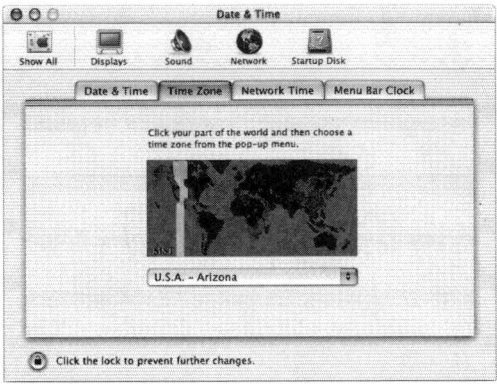

Figure 7 The Time Zone panel of the System Preferences Date & Time pane.

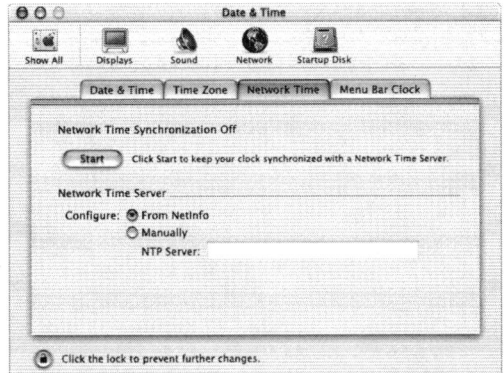

Figure 8 The Network Time panel of the System Preferences Date & Time pane.

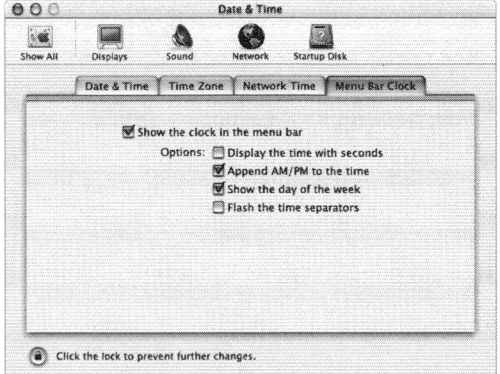

Figure 9 The Menu Bar Clock panel of the System Preferences Date & Time pane. These are the default settings.

To set menu bar clock options

1. In the Date & Time Pane of System Preferences, click the Menu Bar Clock tab to display its panel (**Figure 9**).

2. To enable the menu bar clock, turn on the Show the clock in the menu bar check box.

3. Toggle check boxes to specify how the menu bar clock looks:

   ▲ **Display the time with seconds** displays the seconds as part of the time.

   ▲ **Append AM/PM to the time** displays AM or PM after the time.

   ▲ **Show the day of the week** displays the three-letter abbreviation for the day of the week before the time.

   ▲ **Flash the time separators** blinks the colon(s) in the time every second. (Talk about a potentially annoying distraction!)

   The clock changes immediately to reflect your settings.

✔ Tip

■ The menu bar clock settings have nothing to do with the Clock application, which can place a clock in the Dock. The Clock application is covered in **Chapter 6**.

Dock

The Dock pane (**Figure 10**) offers several options for customizing the Dock's appearance and functionality.

To customize the Dock

1. Display the Dock pane of System Preferences (**Figure 10**).

2. Set options as desired:

   ▲ To set the size of the Dock and its icons, drag the Dock Size slider to the left or right.

   ▲ To enable Dock icon magnification (**Figure 11**), turn on the Magnification check box and drag the slider to the left or right to specify how large the magnified icons should become when you point to them.

   ▲ To hide the Dock until you need it, turn on the Automatically hide and show the Dock check box. With this feature enabled, the Dock disappears until you position the mouse pointer at the bottom of the screen.

   ▲ To display the "jumping icon" animation while a program is launching, turn on the Animate opening applications check box.

✔ Tip

■ If you think the Dock takes up too much valuable real estate on your screen, try one of these options:

   ▲ Set the Dock size smaller, then enable magnification so the icons enlarge when you point to them.

   ▲ Turn on the Automatically hide and show the Dock check box. (This is what I do and it works like a charm.)

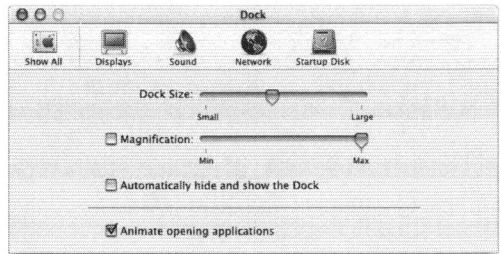

Figure 10 The Dock pane of System Preferences.

Figure 11 With magnification enabled, when you point to an icon in the Dock, it grows so you can see it better.

CUSTOMIZING THE DOCK

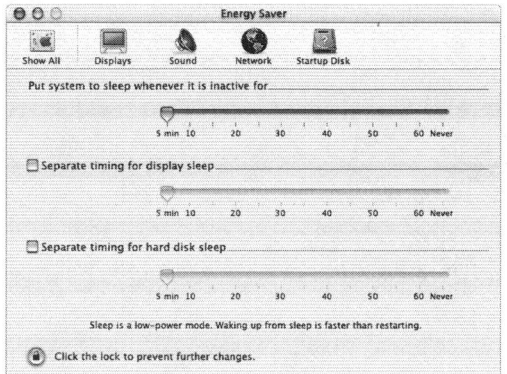

Figure 12 The Energy Saver pane of System Preferences.

Energy Saver

The Energy Saver pane (**Figure 12**) enables you to specify settings for automatic system, display, and hard disk sleep. These settings can reduce the amount of power your computer uses when idle.

✔ Tips

- Energy Saver settings are especially important for PowerBook and iBook users running on battery power.

- System sleep is discussed in **Chapter 2**.

- To wake a sleeping display, move the mouse or press any key.

- A sleeping hard disk wakes automatically when it needs to.

To set Energy Saver options

1. Display the Energy Saver pane of System Preferences (**Figure 12**).

2. Set options as desired:

   ▲ To set the system sleep timing, drag the top slider to the left or right.

   ▲ To set display sleep timing, turn on the check box beside Separate timing for display sleep and drag its slider to the left or right.

   ▲ To set hard disk sleep timing, turn on the check box beside Separate timing for hard disk sleep and drag its slider to the left or right.

General

The General pane (**Figure 13**) enables you to set basic color options as well as scroll bar functionality.

To set General options

1. Display the General pane of System Preferences (**Figure 13**).

2. Set options as desired:

   ▲ Use the Appearance pop-up menu to choose a color for buttons, menus, and windows throughout Mac OS X and Mac OS X applications.

   ▲ Use the Highlight color pop-up menu to choose a highlight color for text in documents, fields, and lists.

   ▲ Select a radio button to specify what happens when you click in the scroll track of a scroll bar. **Jump to next page** scrolls to the next window or page of the document. **Scroll to here** scrolls to the relative location in the document. For example, if you click in the scroll track two-thirds of the way between the top and bottom, you'll scroll two-thirds of the way through the document. (This is the same as dragging the scroller to that position.)

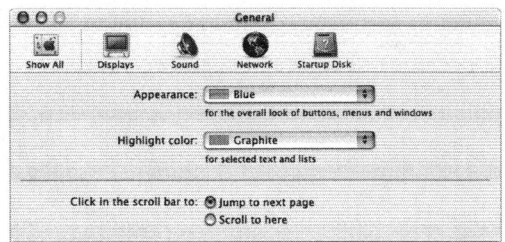

Figure 13 The General pane of System Preferences.

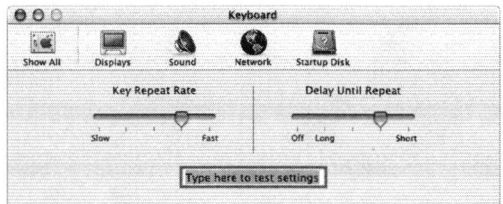

Figure 14 The Keyboard pane of System Preferences.

Keyboard

The Keyboard pane of System Preferences (**Figure 14**) enables you to set key repeat options for keyboard operation.

To set key repeat options

1. Display the Keyboard pane of System Preferences (**Figure 14**).

2. Set options as desired:

   ▲ Use the Key Repeat Rate slider to set how fast a key repeats when held down.

   ▲ Use the Delay Until Repeat slider to set how long a key must be pressed before it starts to repeat.

3. Test your settings by typing in the test field at the bottom of the pane. If necessary, repeat step 2 to fine-tune your settings for the way you type.

✔ Tip

■ Key Repeat settings are especially useful for heavy-handed typists.

Mouse

The Mouse pane (**Figure 15**) enables you to set options that control the way the mouse works, including the tracking and double-click speed.

To set mouse speeds

1. Display the Mouse pane of System Preferences (**Figure 15**).

2. Set options as desired:

   ▲ To set the speed of the mouse movement on your screen, drag the Tracking Speed slider.

   ▲ To set the amount of time between each click of a double-click, drag the Double-Click Speed slider. You can test the double-click speed by double-clicking in the test field; make changes as necessary to fine-tune the double-click speed.

✔ Tip

■ If you're just learning to use a mouse, try setting the tracking and double-click speeds to slower than the default settings.

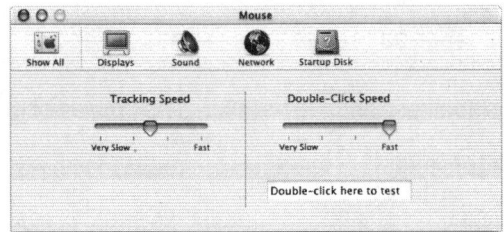

Figure 15 The Mouse pane of System Preferences.

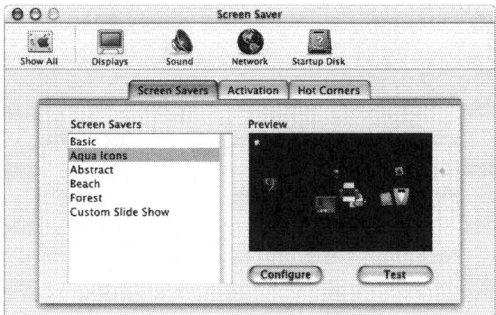

Figure 16 The Screen Savers panel of the System Preferences Screen Saver pane.

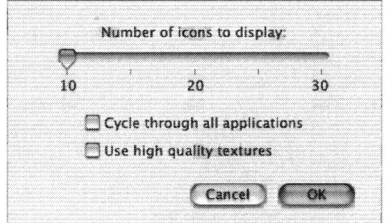

Figure 17 The configuration dialog sheet for the Aqua Icons screen saver.

Screen Saver

The Screen Saver pane (**Figures 16**, **18**, and **19**) includes three panels for setting up the Mac OS screen saver:

◆ **Screen Savers** (**Figure 16**) enables you to select, configure, and test the screen saver you want to use.

◆ **Activation** (**Figure 17**) enables you to specify when the screen saver goes to work and whether you must enter a password to view the screen.

◆ **Hot Corners** (**Figure 19**) enables you to select a corner of the screen to activate the screen saver.

✔ Tip

■ Screen Saver is a new feature in Mac OS X.

To select & configure a screen saver

1. In the Screen Saver pane of System Preferences, click the Screen Savers tab to display its panel (**Figure 16**).

2. Select one of the options in the Screen Savers list. A preview of the screen saver you selected appears in the Preview area.

3. To set options for the screen saver, click Configure. Then use the dialog sheet that appears to set options and click OK. (**Figure 17** shows the configuration options for the Aqua Icons screen saver; other screen savers offer different options.)

4. To see what the screen saver looks like on your screen, click Test. The screen goes black and the screen saver kicks in. To go back to work, move your mouse.

To set screen saver automatic activation options

1. In the Screen Saver pane of System Preferences, click the Activation tab to display its panel (**Figure 18**).

2. Drag the slider to the right or left to set the amount of idle time before the screen saver automatically activates.

3. Select one of the password protection radio buttons:

   ▲ **Do not ask for a password** enables you to clear the screen saver and view the screen without entering a password.

   ▲ **Use my user account password** requires you to enter your user password to clear the screen saver and view the screen. (This can prevent busybodies from viewing your screen or accessing your computer while you're away from your desk.)

To set hot corner activation options

1. In the Screen Saver pane of System Preferences, click the Hot Corners tab to display its panel (**Figure 19**).

2. Click in a corner to select that corner as a hot corner:

   ▲ One click places a check mark in the corner. A check tells Screen Saver to activate when you position your mouse pointer in that corner of the screen.

   ▲ Two clicks places a minus sign in the corner. A minus sign tells Screen Saver never to activate when the mouse pointer is positioned in that corner of the screen.

✔ Tip

■ You can place check marks and minus signs in any combination in the screen corners.

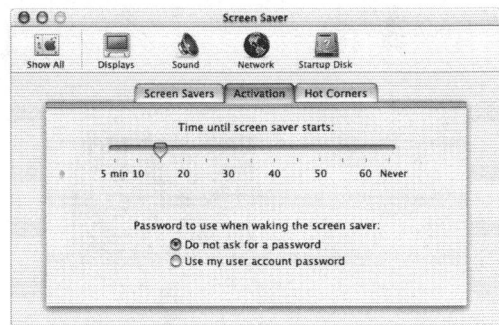

Figure 18 The Activation panel of the System Preferences Screen Saver pane.

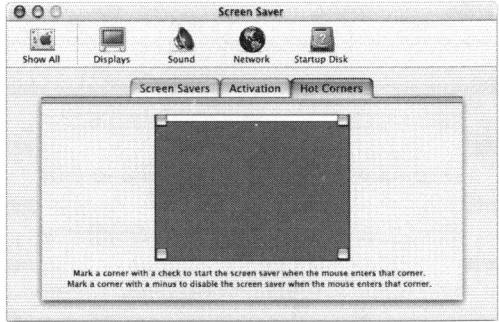

Figure 19 The Hot Corners panel of the System Preferences Screen Saver pane.

SETTING SCREEN SAVER ACTIVATION OPTIONS

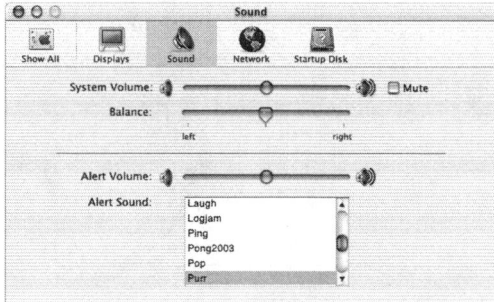

Figure 20 The Sound pane of System Preferences.

Sound

The Sound pane (**Figure 20**) enables you to set system volume and balance as well as the alert sound and volume.

To set system & alert sound options

1. Display the Sound pane of System Preferences (**Figure 20**).

2. Set options as desired:

   ▲ To set the system volume, drag the System Volume slider to the left or right.

   ▲ To set the speaker balance (for built-in speakers or headphones), drag the Balance slider to the left or right.

   ▲ To set the alert volume, drag the Alert Volume slider to the left or right.

   ▲ To set the alert sound, select one of the options in the Alert Sound list.

✔ Tips

- Each time you move and release a slider or select a different alert sound, an alert sounds so you can hear a sample of your change.

- To keep your computer quiet, turn on the Mute check box.

SETTING SYSTEM & ALERT SOUND OPTIONS

Fonts

Fonts are typefaces that appear on screen and in printed documents. When they're properly installed, they appear on all Font menus and in font lists.

Mac OS X supports several font formats, including those created for Mac OS 9.1 and earlier and Windows:

- *TrueType* fonts, in Mac OS or Windows format. These fonts have *.dfont*, *.ttf*, or *.ttc* extensions.

- *OpenType* fonts, in Windows format. These fonts have *.otf* extensions.

- *PostScript* fonts in Mac OS or Windows format. These fonts must be accompanied by corresponding bitmapped font files.

Fonts are stored in two places:

- The Fonts folder inside the Library folder on the startup disk (**Figure 21**) contains fonts that are available to all computer users.

- The Fonts folder inside the Library folder in each user's Home folder (**Figure 22**) contains fonts that are available to only that user.

✔ Tip

- Unless you're sharing your Macintosh with others in a workplace, you'll probably want to store your fonts in the systemwide Fonts folder—in the Library folder for the startup disk (**Figure 21**).

To install a font

Drag all files that are part of the font into the appropriate Fonts folder (**Figure 23**).

To uninstall a font

Drag all files that are part of the font out of the Fonts folder they were installed into (**Figure 24**).

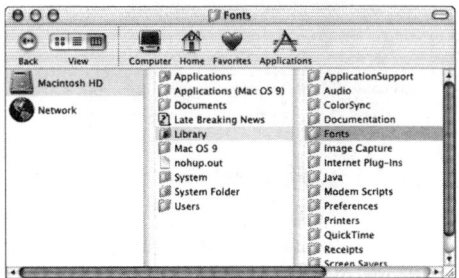

Figure 21 Fonts can be stored in the Fonts folder in the Library folder for the startup disk...

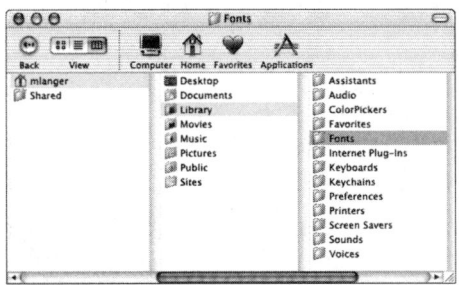

Figure 22 ...or in the Fonts folder in the Library folder for a specific user.

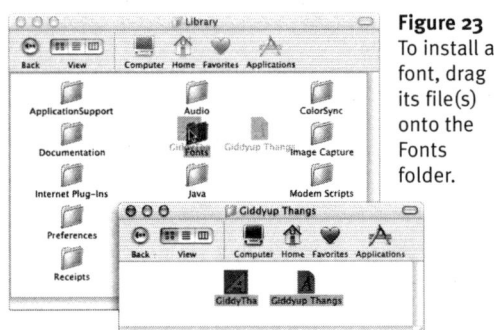

Figure 23 To install a font, drag its file(s) onto the Fonts folder.

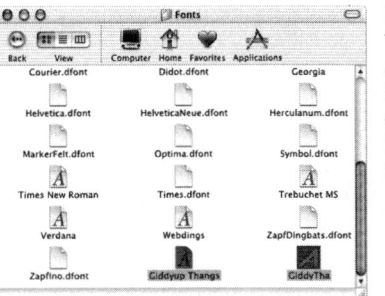

Figure 24 To uninstall a font, drag its file(s) out of the Fonts folder.

GETTING HELP

Getting Help

Mac OS offers two basic ways to get additional information and answers to questions as you work with your computer:

◆ **Help Tags** identify screen items as you point to them. This help feature is supported by many (but not all) applications.

◆ **Apple Help** uses the Help Viewer application to provide information about using Mac OS and Mac OS X applications. This Help feature, which is accessible though commands on the Help menu, is searchable and includes clickable links to information.

This chapter explains how to get help when you need it.

✔ Tip

■ Balloon Help and Guide Help, which were available in previous versions of Mac OS, are no longer available in Mac OS X. You can still find them in applications running in the Classic environment.

Help Tags

Help Tags identify screen elements that you point to by providing information in small yellow boxes (**Figures 1**, **2**, and **3**).

✔ Tips

- Help Tags replace the Balloon Help feature available in Mac OS 9.1 and earlier.

- Help tags are especially useful when first starting out with a new software application.

To use Help Tags

Point to an item for which you want more information. If a Help Tag is available for the item, it appears after a moment (**Figures 1**, **2**, and **3**).

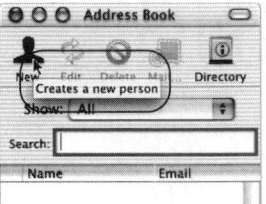

Figure 1 A Help Tag in the Address book main window, ...

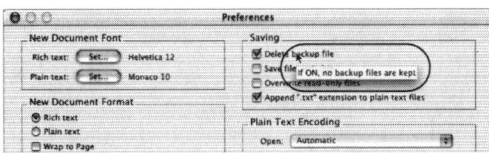

Figure 2 ...in the TextEdit Preferences window, ...

Figure 3 ...and in the Mac Help window.

Apple Help

Apple Help uses the Help Viewer application to display information about Mac OS or a specific application. It includes several features that enable you to find information—and use it—quickly:

- ◆ **Quick Clicks** (**Figures 6a** and **6b**) offers links to answers for frequently asked questions.

- ◆ **Search feature** enables you to search for topics containing specific words or phrases.

- ◆ **Links to related information** enable you to move from one topic to a related topic.

- ◆ **Links to applications** enable you to open an application referenced by a help topic.

- ◆ **Links to online information** enable you to get the latest information from Apple's Web site.

✔ Tips

- ■ Although this feature's generic name is Apple Help, help windows may display the name of the application that help is displayed for.

- ■ Support information available on Apple's Web site is discussed in **Appendix B**.

To open Apple Help

Choose Help > *Application Name* Help (**Figures 4a**, **4b**, and **4c**), or press ⌃ ⌘ ?.

or

Choose Help from a contextual menu (**Figure 5**).

or

Click the Help button in a window or dialog in which it appears (**Figure 6a**).

The main Help window (**Figures 6a** and **6b**) or help topic (**Figure 6c**) appears.

✔ Tip

- Using contextual menus is covered in **Chapter 2**.

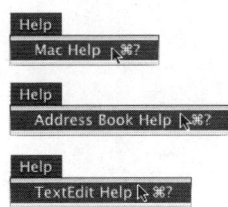

Figures 4a, 4b, & 4c
The Help command on Help menus for the Finder (top), Address Book (middle), and TextEdit (bottom).

Figure 5
The Help command can also be found on some contextual menus.

OPENING APPLE HELP

Help button

Figures 6a, 6b, & 6c These are the main Help windows for the Finder (left) and Address Book (middle). TextEdit's main Help window (right) is also a help topic, providing information in addition to links.

Figure 7 Enter a search word or phrase in the field at the top of the Help window.

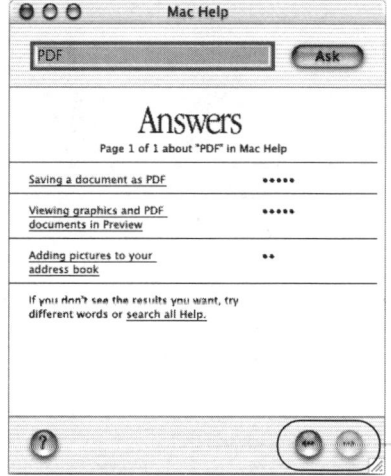

Figure 8 When you click Ask, a list of topics matching the search criteria appears.

Back and Forward buttons

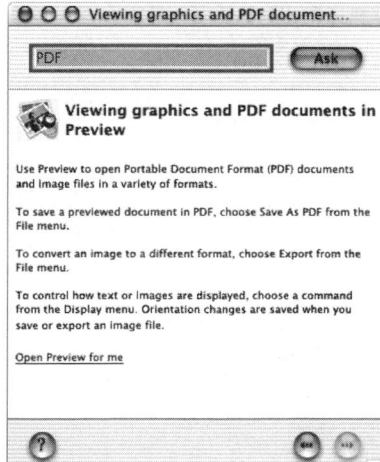

Figure 9 Clicking a link displays information as a Help topic.

To search Help

1. Enter a search word or phrase in the entry field at the top of the Help window (**Figure 7**).

2. Click Ask.

3. After a moment, the Help window fills with a list of search results (**Figure 8**). Click an underlined link to display information about the topic in a window (**Figure 9**).

✔ Tips

- The asterisks to the right of a topic name in the Search Results list indicate how well the topic matches your search criteria. The more asterisks, the more relevant the item.

- You can click the Back and Forward buttons to move backward and forward through Help windows (**Figure 8**).

- The search results window may include a link to automatically search all Help files for your search criteria (**Figure 8**). Clicking this link may display more search results.

- The Help topic window may include links for opening one or more applications (**Figure 9**).

SEARCHING HELP

Application Help

Many applications include extensive online help. The help features of various applications may look and work differently, so it's impossible to cover them in detail here. Most online help features, however, are easy to use.

✔ Tips

- Some applications, such as the Microsoft Office suite of products, include an entire online manual that is searchable and printable.

- Not all applications include online help. If you can't locate an online help feature for an application, check the documentation that came with the application to see if it has one and how you can access it.

To access an application's online help

Choose a command from the Help menu within that application.

or

Click a Help button within a dialog.

Help & Troubleshooting Advice

Here's some advice for getting help with and troubleshooting problems.

- **Join a Macintosh user group.** Joining a user group and attending meetings is probably the most cost-effective way to learn about your computer and get help. You can find a users' group near you by consulting the User Group page at Apple's Web site (http://www.apple.com/usergroups/) or calling 1-800-SOS-APPL.

- **Visit Apple's Web site.** If you have access to the Web, you can find a wealth of information about your computer right online. Start at http://www.apple.com/ and follow links or search for the information you need.

- **Visit the Web sites for the companies that develop the applications you use most.** A regular visit to these sites can keep you up to date on updates and upgrades to keep your software running smoothly. These sites can also provide technical support for problems you encounter while using the software. Learn the URLs for these sites by consulting the documentation that came with the software.

- **Visit Web sites that offer troubleshooting information.** Ted Landau's MaxFixIt (http://www.macfixit.com/) and Ric Ford's MacInTouch (http://www.macintouch.com/) are two excellent resources.

- **Read Macintosh magazines.** A number of magazines, each geared toward a different level of user, can help you learn about your computer: *Macworld*, *Mac Addict*, and *Mac Home Journal* are the most popular. Stay away from PC-centric magazines; the majority of the information they provide will not apply to your Macintosh and may confuse you.

MENUS & KEYBOARD EQUIVALENTS

Menus & Keyboard Equivalents

This appendix illustrates all of Mac OS X's Finder menus and provides a list of corresponding keyboard equivalents.

To use a keyboard equivalent, hold down the modifier key (usually ⌘) while pressing the keyboard key for the command.

Menus and keyboard commands are discussed in detail in **Chapter 2**.

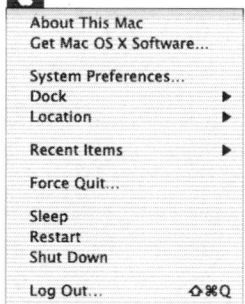

Apple Menu

Shift ⌘ Q	Log Out
Option ⌘ D	Dock > Turn Hiding On/Off

Finder Menu

Shift ⌘ Delete	Empty Trash
⌘ H	Hide Finder

File Menu

⌃ ⌘ N	New Finder Window
Shift ⌃ ⌘ N	New Folder
⌃ ⌘ O	Open
⌃ ⌘ W	Close Window
Option ⌃ ⌘ W	Close All
⌃ ⌘ I	Show Info
⌃ ⌘ D	Duplicate
⌃ ⌘ L	Make Alias
⌃ ⌘ R	Show Original
⌃ ⌘ T	Add To Favorites
⌃ ⌘ Delete	Move To Trash
⌃ ⌘ E	Eject
⌃ ⌘ F	Find

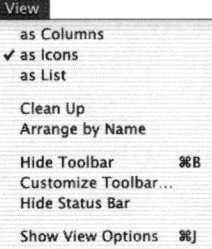

Edit Menu

⌃ ⌘ Z	Undo
⌃ ⌘ X	Cut
⌃ ⌘ C	Copy
⌃ ⌘ V	Paste
⌃ ⌘ A	Select All

View Menu

⌃ ⌘ B	Show/Hide Toolbar
⌃ ⌘ J	Show/Hide View Options

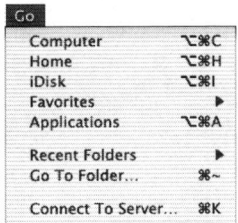

Go Menu

Option ⌥ ⌘ C	Computer
Option ⌥ ⌘ H	Home
Option ⌥ ⌘ I	iDisk
Option ⌥ ⌘ F	Favorites > Go To Favorites
Option ⌥ ⌘ A	Applications
⌥ ⌘ ~	Go To Folder
⌥ ⌘ K	Connect To Server

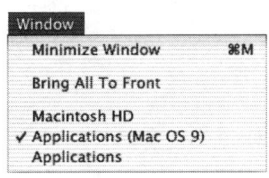

Window Menu

⌥ ⌘ M	Minimize Window

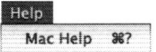

Help Menu

⌥ ⌘ ?	Mac Help

GO, WINDOW, & HELP MENUS

APPLE'S INTERNET TOOLS

Internet Tools

Although this book concentrates on the software that comes with Mac OS X, it wouldn't be complete without at least a brief mention of the services and software available from Apple on the Internet.

This appendix takes a look at three things:

◆ **iTools** is a group of five Internet-based features that help you share information with others.

◆ **iTunes** is "jukebox" software you can use to play MP3 files, convert audio CD tracks to MP3 format, and connect to Internet-based radio stations.

◆ **Tech Info Library** is where you can find technical documents to help you learn more about your computer or troubleshoot problems.

✔ Tip

■ The Internet is covered in detail in **Chapter 9**.

iTools

Apple's iTools is a group of Internet-based services you can use to exchange information with others and find Web sites for your family:

- ◆ **iCards** enables you to send greeting cards to anyone with an e-mail address.

- ◆ **mac.com** gives you an e-mail address ending with @mac.com.

- ◆ **HomePage** lets you create and publish a custom Web site hosted on Apple's Web server.

- ◆ **iDisk** gives you 20 MB of hard disk space on Apple's server for saving or sharing files.

- ◆ **KidSafe** enables you to find Web sites for children based on subject matter and grade level.

iTools is free. You must sign up to use all features except iCards.

The next two pages explain how to sign up for and log in to iTools.

✔ Tips

- ■ You can learn more about and sign up for iTools services at http://itools.mac.com/ (**Figure 1**).

- ■ iTools features are relatively easy to use, with step-by-step instructions and lots of online help.

Figure 1 This version of the iTools Home Page appears if you are not logged in to iTools.

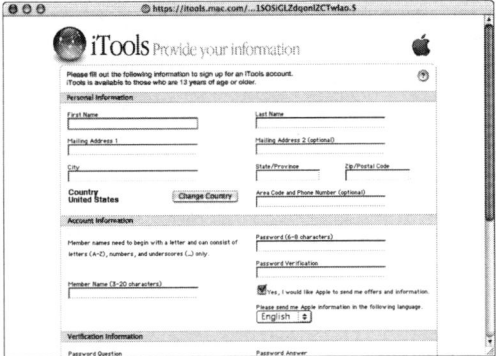

Figure 2 Fill in this form to sign up for an iTools account.

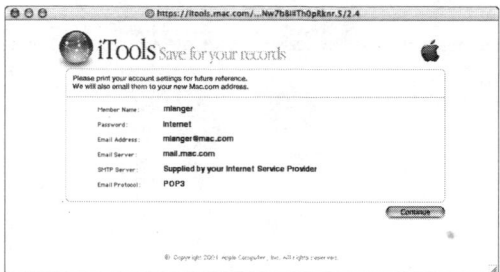

Figure 3 You'll need this information to log in to iTools and to set up your e-mail program to access your mac.com e-mail account.

Figure 4 You can use this handy form to send an iCard to friends to tell them about your new e-mail address.

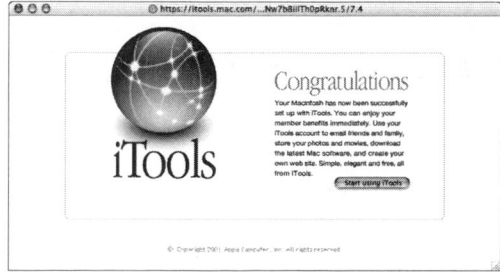

Figure 5 This window appears when the sign up process is complete.

To sign up for iTools

1. Launch your Web browser and use it to view http://itools.mac.com/ (**Figure 1**).

2. Click the Free Sign Up button.

3. Enter the requested information in the iTools Provide your information window that appears (**Figure 2**).

4. Click the Continue button at the bottom of the page.

5. Write down (or print) the information in the iTools Save for your records window that appears (**Figure 3**). It includes your member name and password, along with information you'll need to set up your e-mail software for using mac.com for e-mail.

6. Click Continue.

7. The iTools Announce your new e-mail address window appears next (**Figure 4**). You can use this window to send iCards to your friends to tell them about your mac.com e-mail address.

   ▲ To send an iCard with your mac.com e-mail address to friends, enter a friend's e-mail address in the Recipient's e-mail field and click Add to list. Repeat this process for each person you want to add to the list. Then click Send iCard.

   ▲ To skip sending an iCard with your mac.com e-mail address, click No Thanks.

8. A Congratulations window appears next. It tells you that you have been successfully set up for iTools. Click Start Using iTools.

SIGNING UP FOR iTOOLS

To log in to iTools

1. Launch your Web browser and use it to view http://itools.mac.com/ (**Figure 1**).

2. Click the I'm Already a Member link near the bottom of the page.

   or

   Click a link for any of the iTools members only features.

3. The iTools login window appears (**Figure 6**). Enter your User Name and Password in the appropriate fields, and click Enter.

   or

   If you do not have an account, click the Sign Up button and follow steps 3 through 8 on the previous page to sign up for iTools.

   The main iTools window appears (**Figure 7**) or the main window for the feature you clicked a link for appears (**Figure 8**).

To log out of iTools

Click the Logout button at the top of any iTools window (**Figure 7**).

✔ Tip

- You don't have to log out of iTools. The system will log you out automatically after a while. But if your computer is accessible to other people, you may want to log out to prevent others from accessing your e-mail messages and iDisk files.

Figure 6 The iTools log in window.

Figure 7 The iTools Home page looks like this when you're logged in.

Figure 8 The Email main window.

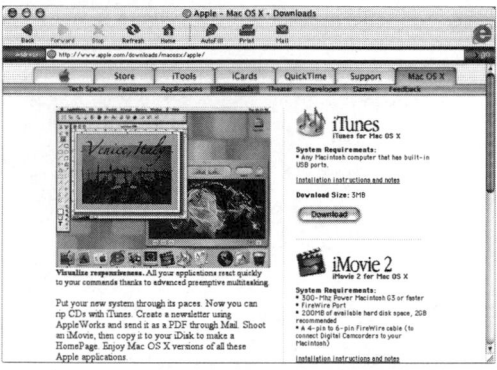

Figure 9 You can download the Mac OS X version of iTunes and other software from the Apple - Mac OS X - Downloads page.

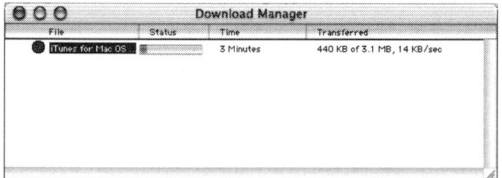

Figure 10 The Download Manager window shows download progress.

Figure 11
The iTunes for Mac OS X 1.1.smi file icon appears on the desktop when you download iTunes.

iTunes

iTunes is a computer-based "jukebox" that enables you to do several things:

◆ Play MP3 format audio files.

◆ Record music from audio CDs on your Mac as MP3 files.

◆ Create custom CDs of your favorite music.

◆ Listen to Internet-based radio stations.

The next few pages explains how you can get iTunes and use it to record and play MP3 music.

✔ Tips

■ MP3 is a standard format for audio files.

■ The Mac OS X version of iTunes did not support the creation or "burning" of CDs as this book went to press in April 2001. This feature will be added before the end of calendar year 2001.

To download & install iTunes

1. Launch your Web browser and use it to view http://www.apple.com/downloads/macosx/apple/ (**Figure 9**).

2. Click the Download button in the iTunes for Mac OS X area.

3. If a Security Notice dialog appears, click Send.

4. Wait while the software downloads. The Download Manager window shows download progress (**Figure 10**).

5. When the download is complete, quit the Web browser software.

6. Double-click the iTunes for Mac OS X 1.1.smi file icon that appears on the desktop (**Figure 11**).

7. If a Software License Agreement window appears, click Agree.

Continued on next page...

DOWNLOADING & INSTALLING iTUNES

Continued from previous page.

8. Wait while Disk Copy opens the iTunes for Mac OS X 1.1.smi file and displays the iTunes for Mac OS X window (**Figure 12**).

9. If necessary, open your hard disk window.

10. Drag the iTunes for Mac OS X folder onto the Applications folder icon (**Figure 13**) to copy it into the Applications folder.

✔ Tips

- When you download iTunes from Apple's Web site, it is download as a disk image file. Double-clicking it launches Disk Copy, which mounts the file as a disk (**Figure 14**). Disk Copy is covered in detail in the sequel to this book, *Mac OS X: Visual QuickPro Guide*.

- You can learn more about iTunes by reading the About iTunes for Mac OS X.rtf file in the iTunes for Mac OS X window (**Figure 12**).

- Copying files and folders is covered in **Chapter 3**.

- After installing iTunes, you can drag the iTunes for Mac OS X disk on your desktop to the Trash to unmount it and delete the iTunes for Mac OS X 1.1.smi file on your hard disk.

To launch iTunes

Open the iTunes icon in the iTunes for Mac OS X folder (**Figure 15**) in your Applications folder. One of two things happens:

- ◆ If this is the first time you're launching iTunes, it displays its iTunes Setup Assistant window (**Figure 16**). Follow the instructions in the next section to continue.

- ◆ If you have already configured iTunes, it displays its main window (**Figure 19**).

Figure 12
The iTunes for Mac OS X window.

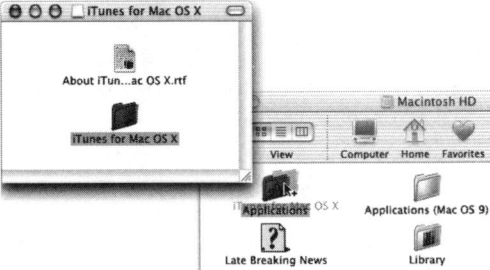

Figure 13 Drag the iTunes for Mac OS X folder onto the Applications folder icon in your hard disk window.

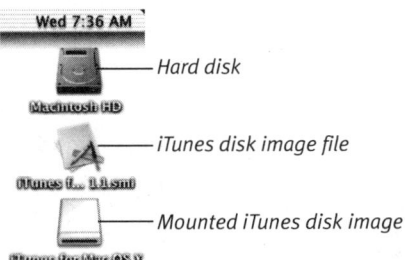

Figure 14 You'll see at least three icons on the desktop when you install iTunes.

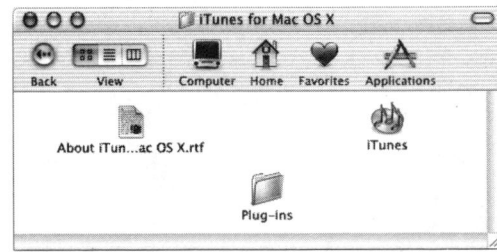

Figure 15 The iTunes for Mac OS X folder contains the iTunes application and some support files.

DOWNLOADING & INSTALLING ITUNES

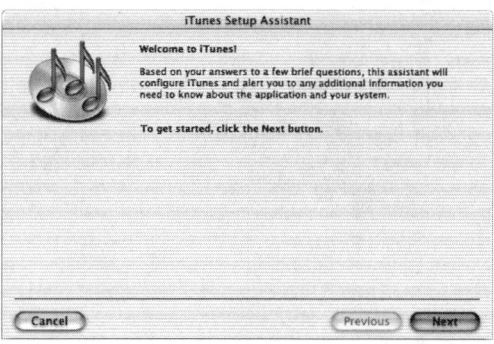

Figure 16 The Welcome to iTunes! window of the iTunes Setup Assistant gets the configuration process started.

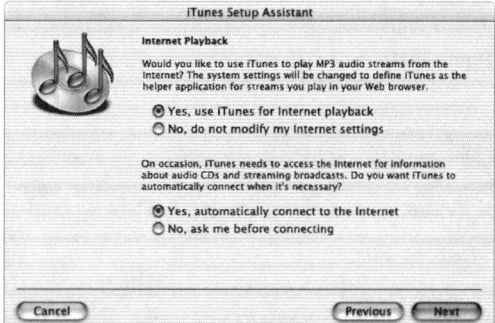

Figure 17 Use the Internet Playback window to set Internet playback and connection options.

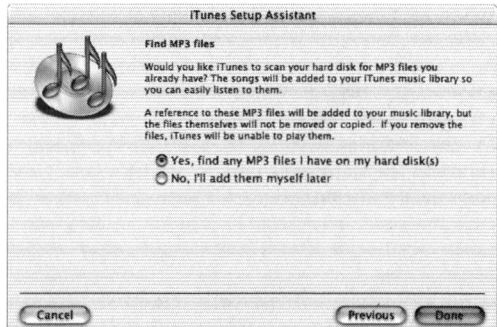

Figure 18 Use the Find MP3 files window to indicate whether you want iTunes to find MP3 files on your hard disk for you.

To configure iTunes

1. In the Welcome to iTunes! window of the iTunes Setup Assistant (**Figure 16**), click Next.

2. In the Internet Playback window (**Figure 17**), set options as desired:

   ▲ Select an Internet playback option. **Yes, use iTunes for Internet playback** instructs your computer to change your Web browser helper settings to use iTunes for all MP3 audio playback. **No, do not modify my Internet settings** does not change your Web browser's helper settings.

   ▲ Select an Internet connection option. **Yes, automatically connect to the Internet** tells iTunes that it's okay to connect to the Internet anytime it needs to. **No, ask me before connecting** tells iTunes to display a dialog that asks your permission before connecting to the Internet.

3. Click Next.

4. In the Find MP3 files window (**Figure 18**), select an option:

   ▲ **Yes, find any MP3 files I have on my hard disk(s)** tells iTunes to search your hard disk for MP3 files and add them to you music library.

   ▲ **No, I'll add them myself later** tells iTunes not to look for MP3 files.

5. Click Done.

   iTunes completes its configuration and displays the iTunes main window. If you instructed iTunes to find MP3 files and it found some, those files are displayed in the window (**Figure 19**).

CONFIGURING ITUNES

To add songs from an audio CD to the Library

1. Insert an audio CD in your CD drive. After a moment, the CD's name appears in the Source list and a list of the tracks on it appears in the Song list (**Figure 20**).

2. Turn on the check box beside each song you want to add to the Library. (They should already all be turned on.)

3. Click the Import button. iTunes begins importing the first song. The status area provides progress information (**Figure 21**). The song may play while it is imported.

✔ Tips

- Sometime during step 1, iTunes may ask your permission to connect to the Internet. It must do this to retrieve information about the songs on the CD.

- You can specify whether a song plays while it is imported by setting iTunes preferences. Choose iTunes > Preferences to get started.

- When iTunes is finished importing songs, it plays a sound. In most cases, iTunes will finish importing songs from a CD before it finishes playing them.

To add songs on disk to the Library

1. Choose File > Add to Library (**Figure 22**).

2. Use the Choose Object dialog that appears (**Figure 23**) to locate and select the MP3 file you want to add.

3. Click Choose.

4. A dialog like the one in **Figure 24** appears. It explains that although a reference to the file will be added to your library, the file will not be copied. Click OK.

   The song is added to the Library list.

ADDING SONGS TO iTUNES

Figure 19 iTunes main window.

Figure 20 iTunes displays the contents of an audio CD.

Figure 21 The status area tells you what's going on.

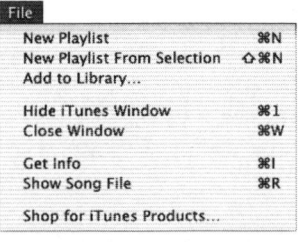

Figure 22
The File menu.

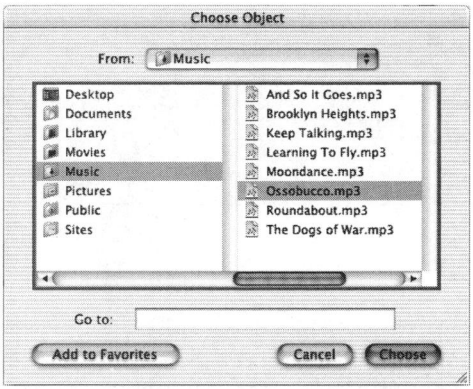

Figure 23 Use the Choose Object dialog to locate and select an MP3 file to add to the Library.

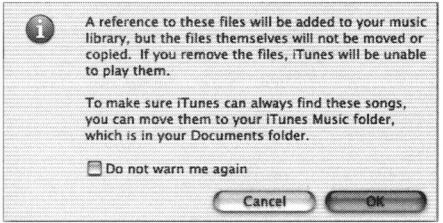

Figure 24 This dialog appears when you add a file.

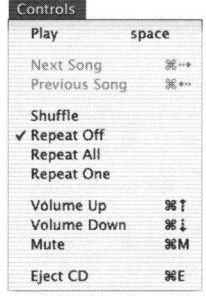

Figure 25
The Controls menu.

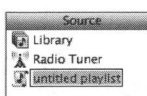

Figure 26
An untitled playlist appears in the Source list.

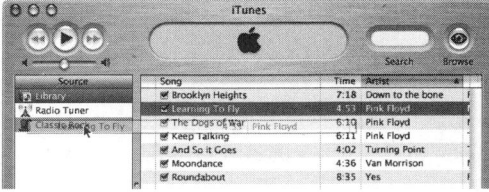

Figure 27 Drag a song from the Library list to the playlist.

To play MP3 files

1. If necessary, select the Library or playlist in the Source list that includes the song you want to play.

2. Select the song you want to play.

3. Click the Play button (**Figure 19**), choose Controls > Play (**Figure 25**), or press [Spacebar].

✔ Tip

■ When the song is finished playing, the next song in the list automatically begins playing.

To pause play

Click the Stop button, choose Controls > Pause, or press [Spacebar].

To create a playlist

1. Click the New Playlist button (**Figure 19**), choose File > New Playlist (**Figure 22**), or press [⌘ N].

2. A new untitled playlist appears in the Source list (**Figure 26**). Type a name for the list, and press [Enter].

3. If necessary, select Library in the source window to display all MP3 files.

4. Drag a song you want to include in the new playlist from the Song list to the new playlist name in the Source list (**Figure 27**).

5. Repeat step 4 for each song you want to add to the playlist.

6. When you're finished adding songs, click the playlist name. The songs appear in the list. You can play them by following the above instructions.

✔ Tip

■ You can change the order of songs in a playlist by dragging them up or down.

Apple's Tech Info Library

Apple's online Tech Info Library (TIL) offers a wealth of general and troubleshooting information for Macintosh computers and Apple software, including Mac OS X. Available 24/7, it's a great resource for learning more about your computer and solving problems.

To find information in the Tech Info Library

1. Use your Web browser software to visit the AppleCare Tech Info Library search page, http://til.info.apple.com/ (**Figure 28**).

2. Choose a specific topic from the pop-up menu in area 1. If you're not sure what to choose, leave it set to All Documents.

3. Enter a search phrase in the field in area 2. Check the examples below the field to get an idea of how a phrase should be constructed.

4. Select one of the radio buttons in area 2 to determine what should be searched:

   ▲ **Search Article for** searches article text.

   ▲ **Search Titles for** searches article titles.

   ▲ **Find Article #** searches for a specific article number. If you select this option, you must enter the correct article number in step 3.

5. Click the Search button in area 3.

6. If a Security Notice dialog appears, click Send.

7. Wait while the Tech Info Library's search engine searches for articles and builds a Web page full of results. **Figure 29** shows an example of results for the search phrase "Mac OS X and iDisk."

8. Click the link for an article that interests you. The article appears in the Web browser window.

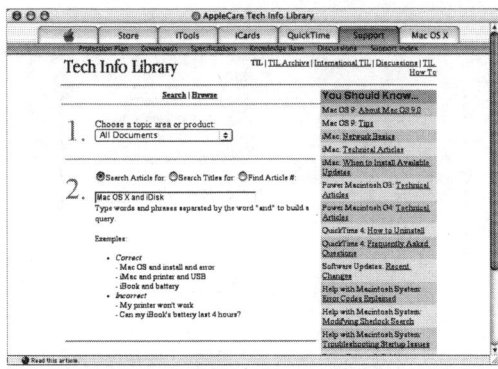

Figure 28 Start by entering a search phrase on the AppleCare Tech Info Library search page.

Figure 29 A list of articles that match your query appears.

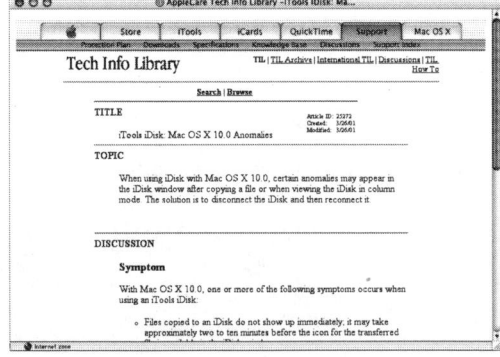

Figure 30 Clicking the name of an article displays it.

INDEX

Symbols

: (colon), in filenames, 62

... (ellipsis), in menu options, 6, 28

~ (tilde), in pathnames, 52

A

About window, 94

accented characters, 130

account information
  Mac OS X installer, 18
  Mail Preferences, 178

Activation option, Screen Savers pane, 211, 212

active application, 91

Add Folder command, 198

Add Page to Favorites command, 182

Add Printer button/command, 151, 152

Add To Favorites command, 82, 224

Address Book, 117–119
  adding categories to, 118
  adding contact records to, 118
  deleting contact records from, 119
  editing contact records in, 119
  icon for, 117
  including photos in, 118
  launching, 117
  and LDAP directories, 117, 119
  and Mail application, 117, 179
  purpose of, 115, 117

Address Card window, 118

administrator, system, 51

Adobe Acrobat, 123

Adobe Photoshop, 89

Adobe Systems, 150

Advanced Settings options, Print dialog, 159

alert sounds, 201, 213

aliases, 80–81
  creating, 81
  defined, 80
  and Favorites, 82
  naming, 80
  tips for working with, 80

Align Left/Right options, Text submenu, 140

alignment, paragraph, 140

America Online, 89

Analog option, Clock Preferences window, 122

Appearance options, General pane, 208

Apple
  Human Interface Guidelines, 94
  Internet tools, 227–236
  printers, 150
  privacy policy, 18
  Tech Info Library, 236
  Web sites, 126, 221, 236

Apple channel, Sherlock, 184, 193

Apple Help, 215, 217–219

Apple menu, *xii*, 45, 223

AppleTalk
  network connection, 168
  printers, 152, 153

AppleWorks, 89, 131

application icons, 32, 36

application menus
  consistency among, 94
  descriptions of specific, 94–106

application modal dialogs, 107

applications
  activating, 91
  consistency among, 94
  dialogs, 107–109
  examples of, 89
  getting information about specific, 94
  hiding/displaying, 95
  identifying open, 91
  installing new, 51
  launching, 92–93
  "lite" versions, 89
  locking, 87
  Mac OS X built-in, 115–116
  Mac OS X *vs.* Classic, *xiii*, 90, 110 (*See also* Classic applications)
  menus, 94–106
  quitting, 96
  setting preferences for, 95
  switching among, 91

Applications command, 225

Applications folders, 50, 53, 90, 115

Aqua interface, *x*

Arrange by Name command, 59

Arrow keys, 30

audio, streaming, 124, 126

audio CDs, recording and playing, 231–235

automatic indexing, 200

B

Back button, toolbar, 43

background, window, 55–56

Balloon Help, *xiii*, 215, 216

battery life, PowerBook/iBook, 46, 207

bold font, 139

bookmarks, 182
BootP, 171
Border pop-up menu, 156
Bring All to Front command, 39, 105
browser. *See* Web browser.
bullet character, for unsaved changes, 101, 104
burning CDs, 231
button view, *xi*
byte, 70

C

cable modem, 19, 20
"Calculate folder sizes" check box, 57, 60
Calculator, 115, 120
Cancel button, 109
case-sensitive option, Find panel, 144
CD-R disc, 70
CD-ROM disc, 70, 71, 187
CDs, burning, 231
Center option, Text submenu, 140
Channels menu, Sherlock, 184
character keys, 30
check boxes, dialog, 108, 109
check mark, in menu, 28
Check Spelling As You Type option, TextEdit, 145
Chess application, 121
Choose a Picture dialog, 55–56, 74, 75
Chooser, 151
Classic applications, 90, 96, 110–114
Classic environment
  applications written for, 90
  location of files for, 50
  requirements for, 1, 90
  setting computer to start automatically, 110
  starting/stopping, 110–111

Classic icon, 110
Clean Up command, 59
Clear command, 103
Clear key, 30
clicking, 26, 27
Clipboard, 142
clock, system, 203
Clock application, 115, 122, 205
Clock Preferences window, 122
Close All command, 38, 224
close button, 37
Close command, 99
Close Window command, 38, 87, 224
closing *vs.* quitting applications, 96
Cnet's Downloads.com, 199
colon (:), in filenames, 62
Color Controls options, Print dialog, 159
Color Management options, Print dialog, 159
Color Picker window, 55
color scheme, choosing, 208
ColorSync, 159
column-headings control, 37
column view, *xi*, 54
columns
  changing width of, 61
  displaying names of, 37
  moving, 61
  sorting, 37, 60
Command key, 30
commands, 28, 30–31, 223–225. *See also* specific commands.
Comments box, Info window, 86
Comments column, list view, 57
communications programs, 89
Communicator, Netscape, 177
companion Web site, 13, 14
company box, Mac OS Setup Assistant, 9
compatibility information, Mac OS, 4, 16

Compose button, 179
computer
  changing default name of, 11
  changing work state of, 45–47
  organization of hard disk, 50–51
  putting to sleep, 45, 46, 207
  sharing, 51, 214
  shutting down, 45, 47
  starting/restarting, 3, 7, 15, 45, 47
  waking, 46, 207
Computer command, 53, 225
Computer icon, 50
Computer Name and Password window, Mac OS Setup Assistant, 11
Conclusion window, Mac OS Setup Assistant, 13
Connect To Server command, 225
contact records, Address Book, 118–119
contextual menu, 28, 29
Control key, 30
control panel, *x*
Copies & Pages options, Print dialog, 155, 156
Copy command, 103, 142, 224
"Copy status" window, 67
copying, 64–67, 103, 142, 224
Create Your Account window, Mac OS X installer, 18
Custom Installation and Removal window, 5, 7
custom search criteria, Sherlock, 188–190
customization features, 74. *See also* Finder Preferences window.
Customize Toolbar command, 76, 77
customized installation
  Mac OS 9.1, 2, 5
  Mac OS X, 17
Cut command, 103, 142, 224

INDEX

D

databases, 89
date
  displaying relative, 57
  searching for files by, 188
  setting with Mac OS Setup
    Assistant, 10
  setting with Mac OS X
    installer, 23
Date & Time pane, System
    Preferences, 122, 201,
    203–205
Date Created/Modified
    columns, list view, 57
Del key, 30
Delay Until Repeat slider, 209
Delete command, 103
Delete Job command, 163
Delete key, 30, 103, 134, 137
DeskJet printers, 150
desktop
  customizing, 74
  illustration of, 25
  purpose of, 25
Desktop button, 113, 114
Desktop files, rebuilding, 8
Desktop Pictures folder, 75
Desktop Printer Utility, 151
Destination Disk pop-up menu, 3
.dfont file extension, 214
DHCP server, 20
dial-up connection, Internet, 19,
    165, 166
dialog sheets, 107
dialogs. *See also* specific dialogs.
  new features, *xii*
  purpose of, 107
  types of, 107
  using, 108–109
dictionary, spelling, 145
digital movies, 124. *See also*
    QuickTime Player.
Digital option, Clock
    Preferences window, 122
Digital Subscriber Line. *See* DSL.

dimmed/gray menu option, 28
direct connection, Internet,
    165, 166
disk. *See also* hard disk.
  checking available space on, 70
  ejecting, 72
  indexing, 186, 187, 198
  locked, 70
  mounting/unmounting, 68,
    70, 71, 72
  naming, 62
  opening/displaying contents
    of, 36, 37
  organization of, 50
  write-protected, 70
Disk Copy, 232
disk icons, 32, 37, 68
Disk Utility, 89
diskette, 70
Display menu, Preview, 123
DNS host, 20
Dock
  customizing, 78, 206
  displaying Clock in, 122
  identifying items in, 44
  location on desktop, 25
  and multitasking, 91
  opening items in, 36, 44
  purpose of, *xi*, 44
  and Trash icon, 32
Dock pane, System Preferences,
    201, 206
document icons, 32, 36
document modal dialogs, 107
documents
  creating, 92, 97
  entering/editing text in,
    134–137
  locking, 87
  modifying contents of, 103
  naming, 62
  opening, 93, 98–99, 148
  orphan, 92
  saving, 100–102, 114, 133,
    146–147

Documents folder, 50, 51
domain name, 20
Double-Click Speed slider, 210
double-clicking, 26, 27, 210
download location, Web
    browser, 174
Downloads.com, 199
drag and drop, opening
    document with, 93
dragging, 26, 27, 64
drawers, *xi*
drivers
  hard disk, 6
  printer, 150
DSL, 19, 20, 165, 171
Duplicate command, 67, 224
DVD disc, 70
dynamic IP address, 169
dynamic menu items, 38

E

e-mail. *See also* Mail application.
  creating and sending
    messages, 179–180
  directories, 195 (*See also*
    Address Book)
  forwarding messages, 180
  replying to messages, 180
  setting options for, 173, 174
  setting up account, 23, 178
Edit menu, 103, 141, 142, 224
Eject command, 72, 224
ejecting disk, 68, 72
ellipsis (...), in menu option, 6, 28
Email options, System
    Preferences, 174
Empty Trash command, 69, 223
End key, 30
Energy Saver pane, System
    Preferences, 45, 201, 207
Enter key, 30
Entertainment channel,
    Sherlock, 184, 193
entry fields, dialog, 108, 109
Epson printers, 150, 159

INDEX

Error Handling options, Print
  dialog, 158
errors, printing, 164
Esc key, 30
Export dialog, 129
extensions, system, *x*
external storage media, 70

F

Favorites, 182
  adding, 82, 101
  and aliases, 82
  purpose of, 82
  removing, 83
Favorites button, 112, 114
Favorites command, 225
Favorites submenu, 53, 82
fields, dialog entry, 108, 109
file download location, Web
  browser, 174
file management, 49–72
  and Arrange by Name
    command, 59
  and Clean Up command, 59
  and folders, 63
  and Go menu, 53
  and hierarchical filing system,
    50–51
  and icon names, 62
  and list views, 60–61
  moving and copying items,
    64–67
  and pathnames, 52
  and storage media, 70–72
  tasks associated with, 49
  and Trash, 68–69
  and window views, 54–58
File menu, 63, 97–102, 224
FileMaker Pro, 89
files
  entering pathnames for, 52
  naming, 62
  organizing and storing, 50–51
  saving, 146–147

searching for, 185–192
sharing, 12, 51
Files channel, Sherlock, 184, 198
filing system, hierarchical, 50
Find by Content feature,
  Sherlock, 186–187
Find command, 224
Find panel, 143, 144
Finder
  advanced techniques, 73–87
    aliases, 80–81
    Dock customization, 78
    Favorites, 82–83
    Info Window, 85–87
    outlines in list view, 79
    Preferences, 74–75
    recently used items, 84
    toolbar customization,
      76–77
  cleaning up and arranging
    icons with, 59
  and file management, 49
  icons used in, 32
  launching, 25
  menus, *xii*, 28–29, 223–225
  purpose of, 25, 49
  quitting, 25
  standard *vs.* Simple, 11
  windows, 37–42, 54
Finder menu, *xii*, 223
Finder Preferences window, 11, 74
Fix Alias dialog, 80, 87
floppy disk, 70, 71
Folder Background option, 55–56
folder icons, 32, 36, 37
folders. *See also* specific folders.
  adding to Sherlock Files
    channel, 198
  creating, 63, 100
  designating as Favorites, 101
  displaying disk space
    occupied by contents of, 57
  entering pathnames for, 52
  indexing, 187
  naming, 62, 63, 100

opening/displaying contents
  of, 36, 37, 79
organizing and storing, 50–51
purpose of, 63
searching contents of, 185–192
sorting, 60
spring-loaded, *xi*
Font menu, 130
Font panel, TextEdit, 138
font style, 139
fonts, *xi*, 138–139, 214
Fonts folder, 214
"Format for" pop-up menu, 154
formatting
  storage media, 70
  text, 138–140
Forward button, 180
FreeHand, 89
freeze, computer, 91
FTP, 177
function keys, 30

G

game, chess, 121
GB, 70
General pane, System
  Preferences, 201, 208
Geographic Location window,
  Mac OS Setup Assistant,
  10
Get Internet Ready window,
  Mac OS X installer, 19, 21
Get iTools window, Mac OS X
  installer, 22
Get Mail button, 180
GIF files, viewing, 123
gigabyte, 70
Global Icon option, 55
Global List option, 57
Global View Preferences check
  box, 56, 58
Go menu, *xii*, 52, 82, 225
Go To Favorites command, 225
Go To Folder command, 53, 225

graphic user interface, *ix*, 25, 26. *See also* desktop; Finder.
graphics programs, 89
gray/dimmed menu option, 28
grid, snapping icons to, 55, 59, 74
Guide Help, *xiii*, 215

H

hard disk
  defined, 70
  organization of, 50–51
  preventing update to driver, 6
  searching for files on, 185–192
Hayes modems, 170
Help command, 218
help features, 215–221
  alternatives to, 221
  Apple Help, 215, 217–219
  application-specific, 220
  Help Tags, 215, 216
Help key, 30
Help menu, 106, 225
Help Tags, *xiii*, 215, 216
Help Viewer application, *xiii*, 215, 217
Hewlett-Packard printers, 150, 157
HFS, 50
Hide Finder command, 223
Hide Status Bar command, 58
Hide Toolbar command, 224
Hide View Options command, 224
hierarchical filing system, 50
Highlight color controls, General pane, 208
Hold Job command, 163
Home command, 53, 225
home folder, 51, 53, 82, 214
Home icon, 51
Home key, 30
home page, Web browser, 174, 182
HomePage service, iTools, 228

Hot Corners option, Screen Saver pane, 211, 212
Human Interface Guidelines, Apple, 94

I

iBook, conserving battery life of, 46, 207
iCards, 228
Icon Arrangement option, 55, 74
Icon Size option, 57
Icon Size slider, 55, 74
icon view, 54, 55–56
icons, 32–36
  adding/removing from Dock, 78
  illustrations of, 32
  moving, 35, 64–67
  new look in Mac OS X, *xi*
  opening, 36
  purpose of, 32
  renaming, 62
  resizing, 55, 74, 75
  selecting/deselecting, 33–34
  types of, 32
iDisk command, 225
iDisk service, iTools, 228
image files, viewing, 123
image well, dialog, 108
ImageWriter printers, 150
Important Information window, installer, 4
Index Now command, 186
indexing options, Sherlock, 200
Info window, 85–87
  closing, 87
  information included in, 85
  opening, 86
  purpose of, 85
initializing, storage media, 70
Ink options, Print dialog, 158
insertion point, moving, 135
Install Software window, 5, 7

installation log file, 6
installer
  Mac OS 9.1, 1, 2–7
  Mac OS X, *x*, 1, 14–23
integrated software, 89
internal storage media, 70
Internet
  connection options, 19, 165, 166
  features, 173
  searching, 183, 193–196
  setting up Mac OS X to access, 19–21, 167–175
  software for connecting to, 89, 177 (*See also* specific programs)
Internet Access component, Mac OS 9.1, 13
Internet-based services, Apple, 227–236
Internet channel, Sherlock, 184, 193, 199
Internet Connect, 89, 166, 176
Internet Explorer. *See also* Web browser.
  compatibility considerations, 181
  purpose of, 89, 177
  and System Preferences, 174
  using, 181–182
Internet panel, System Preferences, 167, 173–175
Internet Protocol address, 152
Internet Service Provider. *See* ISP.
Internet Setup Assistant, 13
IP address, 20, 152, 169
ISP
  alternatives to, 165
  connecting/disconnecting, 176
  and e-mail account, 178
  and modem-connection setup, 169
italic font, 139
iTools, 22, 23, 173, 227, 228–230
iTunes, 227, 231–235

INDEX

J

jams, paper, 164
Jaz disk, 70, 71
JPEG files, viewing, 123
"jukebox" software, 227. *See also* iTunes.
Justify option, Text submenu, 140

K

KB, 70
Key Caps program, 115, 130
Key Repeat Rate slider, 209
keyboard
    setting repeat rate for, 209
    types of keys on, 30
keyboard equivalents, 28, 30–31, 223–225
Keyboard pane, System Preferences, 201, 209
KidSafe service, iTools, 228
kilobyte, 70
Kind column, list view, 57

L

Label column, list view, 57
LAN, 19, 20
language preference
    Mac OS 9.1, 9
    Mac OS X, 15
LaserJet printers, 150, 157
LaserWriter printers, 150
launching applications, 92–93
Layout Direction option, Print dialog, 156
Layout options, Print dialog, 156
LDAP directories, 117
LDAP Directory Search window, 119
Library folder, 214
License Agreement
    Mac OS 9.1, 4
    Mac OS X, 16
links, Web page, 181

list view
    purpose of, 54
    selecting columns for, 57
    setting options for, 57–58
    sorting column headings in, 37, 60
local area network, 19, 20
Local Network Introduction window, 11
Locked check box, Info window, 85, 87
locked items, 70, 87
log file, installation, 6
Log Out command, *x*, 223
LPR printers, 152, 153
Lucida Grande font, *xi*

M

Mac Help command, 225
Mac OS 9
    Applications folder, 50, 51
    Classic environment, 1, 50, 51, 90, 110–111
    compatibility information, 4
    creating System Folder for, 3
    installer, 1, 2–7
    Open dialog, 112–113
    Save As dialog, 114
    Software License Agreement, 4
    standard *vs.* customized installation, 2, 5
Mac OS 9.1: Visual QuickStart Guide, 13
Mac OS Setup Assistant, *x*, 1, 7, 8–13
Mac OS X
    applications, 90
    built-in applications and utilities, 115–116 (*See also* specific programs)
    compatibility information, 16
    customization options, 201
    customized installation, 17
    determining amount of hard disk space required for, 17
    installer, *x*, 1, 14–23

new features, *x–xiii*
    Software License Agreement, 16
Mac OS X: Visual QuickPro Guide, *x*, 51, 85, 116, 121, 159, 168, 201, 232
Macintosh user groups, 221
Macromedia FreeHand, 89
magazines, Macintosh, 221
magnetic media, 70
mail. *See* e-mail.
Mail application, 117, 177, 178
Mail icon, 177
Mail Preferences window, 178
Mailbox button, 180
Make Alias command, 81, 224
Make Default command, 153
MB, 70
media, storage. *See* storage media.
Media Type pop-up menu, Print dialog, 158
megabyte, 70
memory, 70. *See also* RAM.
Menu Bar Clock option, Date & Time pane, 203, 205
menus. *See also* specific menus.
    basic techniques for using, 29
    consistency across applications, 94
    controlling appearance of, 208
    gray/dimmed options on, 28
    keyboard equivalents for commands on, 223–225
    new features, *xii*
    "stickiness" of, *xii*, 29
    types of, 28
messages, e-mail, 178–180. *See also* e-mail; Mail application.
Microsoft Internet Explorer. *See also* Web browser.
    compatibility considerations, 181
    purpose of, 89, 177
    and System Preferences, 174
    using, 181–182

Microsoft Outlook Express, 175, 177
Microsoft PowerPoint, 89
Microsoft Word, 89, 92, 131, 143
minimize button, 37
Minimize Window command, 41, 225
Mode options, Print dialog, 158
modeless dialogs, 107
modem connection, Internet, 19, 165, 166, 168–170
modem sounds, turning on and off, 170
modifier keys, 30, 31, 38
mounting, disk, 68, 70, 71
mouse
    basic techniques for using, 26–27
    customizing, 26, 210
Mouse pane, System Preferences, 201, 210
mouse pointer, 25, 26
Move To Trash command, 68, 224
Movie menu, QuickTime Player, 125
movies, 124–125. *See also* QuickTime Player.
moving
    columns, 61
    icons, 35, 64
    windows, 40
MP3 files, recording and playing, 227, 231–235
multitasking, *x*, 91
music, recording and playing, 231–235
My Channel, Sherlock, 184

N

Name and Organization window, Mac OS Setup Assistant, 9
Name column, list view, 61

names
    for aliases, 81
    for computer, 11, 12
    for folders, 12, 62, 63, 100
    for icons, 62
navigation icons, toolbar, 43
Netscape Communicator, 177
network connection, Internet, 165, 166, 168, 171–172, 176
Network icon, 50
Network panel, System Preferences, 167, 168–172
Network Time option, Date & Time pane, 203, 204
networks, 11, 19, 51
New command, 97
New Finder Window command, 38, 224
New Folder command, 63, 224
New Folder dialog, 100
New Window command, 97
News channel, Sherlock, 184, 193
news reader, 173, 175

O

online services, software for connecting to, 89
Open command, 93, 98, 224
Open dialog, 98–99, 112–113
Open Movie command, 125
Open Search Criteria command, 197
Open URL command, QuickTime Player, 126
OpenType fonts, 214
optical media, 70
Option key, 30
organization box, Mac OS Setup Assistant, 9
Orientation option, Page Setup dialog, 154
orphan document, 92
OS 9. *See* Mac OS 9.

OS X. *See* Mac OS X.
.otf file extension, 214
outline, displaying contents of folder as, 79
Outlook Express, 175, 177
Output options, Print dialog, 157, 161

P

Page Attributes command, 154
Page Down key, 30
Page Setup command, 97
Page Setup dialog, 154
Page Up key, 30
PageMaker, 143
pages. *See* Web pages.
Pages per Sheet pop-up menu, 156
Pane menu, 202
Paper Feed options, Print dialog, 157
paper jams, 164
Paper Size pop-up menu, 154
paragraph alignment, 140
parent application, 92
password
    how Mac OS uses, 11
    importance of remembering, 18
    and Internet connections, 170, 171
Password Hint field, Mac OS X installer, 18
Paste command, 103, 142, 224
pathnames, 52
PDF files
    saving documents as, 157, 161
    viewing, 123
People channel, Sherlock, 184, 195
Personalize Your Settings window, Mac OS X installer, 18
personalized work environment, *x*
Photoshop, 89
PICT files, viewing, 123

picture, background, 55–56, 75

playlist, creating MP3, 235

plug-ins, Sherlock, 199

pointing, 26

pop-up menus, 28, 108. *See also* specific menus.

pop-up windows, *xi*

portable document format, 123

PostScript

    fonts, 214

    interpreter, 150

    printers, 150, 158

PostScript Errors options, Print dialog, 158

Power key, 45, 46, 47

PowerBook, conserving battery life of, 46, 207

PowerPoint, 89

PPP connection, 166, 168, 169, 176

PPPoE connection, 168, 171

preemptive multitasking, *x*, 91

preferences. *See* Finder Preferences window; System Preferences.

presentation programs, 89

pressing, 26, 27

preview area, dialog, 108

Preview area, Print dialog, 156

Preview button, Print dialog, 160

Preview program, 115, 123, 160

Print Center, 151–153, 162

Print command, 97

Print dialog, 155–161

    previewing document, 160

    printing document, 161

    purpose of, 155

    saving settings, 160

    selecting printer, 155

    setting options

        Advanced Settings, 159

        Color Management, 159

        Copies & Pages, 156

        Error Handling, 158

        Layout, 156

        Output, 157

        Paper Feed, 157

        Print Settings, 158

print jobs. *See* print queue; printing.

Print Preview command, 160

print queue

    canceling job from, 161, 163

    defined, 162

    sending job to, 161

    stopping/starting, 162–163

Print Settings options, Print dialog, 158

printer drivers, 150

Printer List window, 151

Printer pop-up menu, 155

Printer Queue window, 151, 162

printers

    adding, 152–153

    deleting, 153

    desktop, 151

    displaying list of, 151

    installing, 150

    PostScript *vs.* non-PostScript, 150

    selecting, 155

    setting default, 153

    setting options for, 155–161

    troubleshooting problems, 164

Printers menu, 151

printing, 149–164. *See also* Print Center; Print dialog.

    canceling job prior to, 161, 163

    holding/resuming specific job, 163

    overview of process, 149

    previewing document prior to, 160

    saving settings for, 160

    setting options for, 156–159

    setting page attributes prior to, 154

    stopping/starting print queue, 162–163

    troubleshooting problems, 164

privacy policy, Apple, 18

products, using Sherlock to search for, 196

programs. *See* applications.

protocol, Internet, 166

Proxies pane, Network panel, 172

proxy server, 20

pull-down menu, 28

pulse dialing, 170

push button, dialog, 108, 109

Q

QTV menu, 126

queue. *See* print queue.

Queue menu, 162

Quick Clicks, 217

QuickTime Player, 124–126

    controls, 125

    launching, 124

    opening content on Internet, 126

    purpose of, 115, 124

QuickTime TV, 126

QuickTime Web site, Apple, 126

Quit command, 96

Quit Preview command, 160

Quit TextEdit command, 133

quitting *vs.* closing applications, 96

R

radio buttons, dialog, 108, 109

RAM, 70, 91, 92, 96, 132

Recent button, 112

Recent Folders submenu, 53

recent items, opening, 84

Redo command, 103, 141

Reference channel, Sherlock, 184, 193

Regional Preferences window, 9

Register With Apple window, Mac OS X installer, 21

Registration Information window, Mac OS X installer, 18

relative dates, 57
Remote Access, 166
removable media
    descriptions of, 70
    ejecting, 32
    icons for, 32
repeat rate, setting keyboard, 209
Reply button, 180
resize control, 37
resizing
    columns, 61
    icons, 55, 74, 75
    windows, 37, 40, 41
Restart command, 3, 7, 15, 45, 47
Resume Job command, 163
Return key, 30, 134
Rich Text Format files, 146
router address, 20
RTF files, 146

S

Save As command, 100, 102,
    146, 147
Save As dialog, 114, 146
Save as PDF File check box,
    157, 161
Save command, 100–101, 146
Save dialog, 101
Save Location dialog, xii, 101,
    146, 147, 161, 197
Save Search Criteria
    command, 197
Saved Settings pop-up menu,
    Print dialog, 160
Scale field, Page Setup dialog, 154
Screen Saver pane, System
    Preferences, 201, 211–212
scroll bars, 37, 42, 108, 208
scrolling lists, dialog, 108, 109
search features
    Apple Help, 219
    Sherlock, 183, 185–196
    Tech Info Library, 236
search page, Web browser, 174
search-site files, 199

Select All command, 103, 224
Select Destination window, Mac
    OS X installer, 17
Select Language window, Mac
    OS X installer, 15
Select Time Zone window, Mac
    OS X installer, 23
Send button, 179
Set Up Mail window, Mac OS X
    installer, 23
Set Your Date and Time window,
    Mac OS X installer, 23
Settings pop-up menu, 154
Setup Assistant
    Internet, 13
    Mac OS, x, 1, 7, 8–13
Shared folder, 12, 50, 51
Shared Folder window, Mac OS
    Setup Assistant, 12
sheets, dialog, xii, 107
Sherlock, 183–200
    automatic-indexing
        options, 200
    channels, 184
    compared with Internet
        search engines, 193
    customizing, 198–200
    launching, 183
    plug-ins, 199
    purpose of, 183
    saving searches with, 197
    searching with
        for files, 185–192
        for people, 195
        for products, 196
        for Web pages, 193–194
Shift key, 30
Shopping channel, Sherlock,
    184, 196
shortcut keys, 31. See also
    keyboard equivalents.
Shortcuts button, 112, 114
Show Columns check box, 57
Show Info command, 86, 224
Show Original command, 81, 224
Show Queue command, 162

Show Status Bar command, 58
Show Toolbar command, 224
Show View Options command,
    55, 56, 57, 224
Shut Down command, 45, 47
Simple Finder, 11. See also
    Finder.
Size column, list view, 57
Sleep command, 45, 46
sleep mode, 46, 207
slider controls, dialog, 108
snap to grid option, for icons,
    55, 59, 74
Software License Agreement
    Mac OS 9.1, 4
    Mac OS X, 16
sorting columns, 37, 60
Sound pane, System Preferences,
    201, 213
sound volume, system, 201, 213
speakable items, 121
special character keys, 30, 130
spelling checker, 145
spooling, print, 161
spreadsheets, 89
spring-loaded folders, xi
Standard Installation,
    Mac OS 9.1, 2
standard state size, window, 41
static IP address, 169
Stationery Pad check box, 85
status bar, 58, 70
Stickies, 127–129
    closing, 129
    creating, 127
    formatting, 128
    icon, 127
    launching, 127
    printing, 128
    purpose of, 115
    saving, 129
sticky menus, xii, 29
Stop Job button, 164
Stop Queue command, 162
storage media, 70–72

INDEX

contrasted with memory, 70
formatting/initializing, 70
internal *vs.* external, 70
mounting/unmounting, 68, 70, 71, 72
types of, 70
streaming audio/video, 124, 126
StuffIt Expander, 89
StyleWriter printers, 150
Stylus printers, 150, 159
submenu, 28
subnet mask, 20
system extensions, *x*
system files, 50
System Folder, 3, 50
System Preferences, *xi,* 201–214
Date & Time pane, 203–205
Dock pane, 206
Energy Saver pane, 45, 207
General pane, 208
Internet panel, 167, 173–175
Keyboard pane, 209
Mouse pane, 210
Network panel, 167, 168–172
Screen Saver pane, 211–212
Sound pane, 213
System Preferences window, 201

T

tab control, dialog, 108
Tab key, 30
TCP/IP, 20, 166, 168–169
Tech Info Library, Apple, 236
technical support, 221, 236. *See also* help features.
telephone modem connection, Internet, 19, 165, 166, 168–170
text
aligning, 140
copying, 142
cutting, 142
entering and editing, 134–137

finding and replacing, 143–144
formatting, 138–140
pasting, 142
text-editing application. *See* TextEdit.
TextEdit, 131–148
contrasted with word-processing software, 131, 143
Copy, Cut, and Paste commands, 142
document window, 132
entering/editing text with, 134–137
find and replace features, 143–144
formatting text with, 138–140
launching, 132
opening and closing documents with, 148
purpose of, 131
quitting, 133
saving documents created with, 133, 146–147
selecting text in documents created with, 136
spelling checker, 145
undoing and redoing actions in, 141
TIFF files, viewing, 123
tilde (~) character, in pathnames, 52
time, setting
with Mac OS Setup Assistant, 10
with Mac OS X installer, 23
with System Preferences Date & Time pane, 203
Time and Date window, Mac OS Setup Assistant, 10
time zone, setting
with Mac OS X installer, 23
with System Preferences Date & Time pane, 203, 204
title bar, 37, 39

tone dialing, 170
toolbar
customizing, 76–77
hiding/displaying, 43, 224
purpose of, 43
trackball/trackpad, 26
Tracking Speed slider, 210
Trash
appearance of icon for, 32, 68, 72
dragging disk icon to, 72
emptying, 68
moving item to/from, 68–69
opening, 36
Trash warning dialog, 69
Trash window, 69
Tray Switching options, Print dialog, 158
troubleshooting, 164, 221, 227, 236
TrueType fonts, 214
.ttc file extension, 214
.ttf file extension, 214
TV button, QuickTime, 126
typeface, 138, 214

U

underline font, 139
Undo command, 103, 141, 224
uniform resource locator. *See* URL.
unmounting disk, 68, 72
URL, 181, 182
USB printers, 152, 153
Use Global View Preferences check box, 56, 58
"Use relative dates" check box, 57
user groups, 221
user state size, window, 41
Users folder, 50–51
utilities
Mac OS X built-in, 115–116
third-party, 89
Utilities folder, 115, 151

V

version, determining Mac OS, 3
Version column, list view, 57
video, streaming, 124, 126
view buttons, toolbar, 43, 54
View menu, 54, 224
views, 54–58
    changing, 54
    setting options for, 55–58
volume, system sound, 201, 213

W

waking computer, 46, 207
Web, 165, 181. *See also* Internet.
Web browser
    purpose of, 165
    setting default, 173, 174
    using, 181–182
Web options, System
        Preferences, 174–175

Web pages
    adding to Favorites, 182
    defined, 181
    using Sherlock to search,
        193–194
Web sites
    Apple, 221
    Apple QuickTime, 126
    Apple Tech Info Library, 236
    Apple User Group, 221
    companion site for this book,
        13, 14
Window menu, 39, 104–105, 225
windows, 37–42
    active *vs.* inactive, 39
    arranging icons in, 59
    and Bring All to Front
        command, 39, 105
    changing views for, 54
    closing, 38, 99, 104
    controlling appearance of, 208
    controls for manipulating, 37
    creating new, 97
    displaying contents of, 54–56

    minimizing, 41, 105
    moving, 40
    new features, *xi*
    opening, 38
    purpose of, 37
    resizing, 40, 41
    scrolling contents of, 42
    sorting contents of, 37, 60
    zooming, 41, 104
Word, Microsoft, 89, 92, 131, 143
word processors, 89, 131, 143
word wrap, 134, 135
work states, computer, 45
World Wide Web, 165, 181. *See
    also* Internet.
wrapping, text, 134, 135
write-protected disk, 70

Z

Zip disk, 70, 71
zoom button, 37, 41
Zoom Window command, 104

INDEX

New from Peachpit Press

VISUAL QUICKSTART **FREE TRIAL OFFER** ONLINE LIBRARY!

25 top Web and Graphics QuickStarts, just $49.95* a year!

25 Books!
a $450 value
for $49.95*

Our new **Visual QuickStart Online Library** offers you

- Easy access to the most current information on Web design and graphics via the Web—wherever you are, 24 hours a day, 7 days a week
- Powerful, advanced search features that enable you to find just the topics you want across multiple books, ranked by relevance
- Updates to new editions of the books as they become available
- Easy ways to bookmark, make notes, and send email alerts to colleagues
- Complete access to 25 bestselling books for only $49.95* (that's more than $450 worth of books for less than the price of three *Visual QuickStart Guides*!)

You'll find all your favorite *Visual QuickStart Guides*, as well as those you want to read next, including:

> **HTML 4 for the World Wide Web**
> **Photoshop for Macintosh and Windows**
> **Illustrator for Windows and Macintosh**
> **PageMill 3 for Macintosh and Windows**
> **Flash for Windows and Macintosh**

Free Trial Offer!

Check it out! We invite you to sample a FREE trial subscription to Peachpit's new Visual QuickStart Online Library for one week. Just go to **www.quickstartonline.com** and sign up for your free trial today! You'll have complete access to the Library for one week, absolutely free.

*Charter price of $49.95 is available for a limited time to early subscribers. Subscribe now to take advantage of this special low rate!

www.quickstartonline.com

Quick search... Quick find... QuickStart!

| Articles | Free Library | eBooks | Expert Q & A | Training | Career Center | Downloads | MyInformIT |

Login   Register   About InformIT

Topics
Operating Systems
Web Development
Programming
Networking
Certification
and more...

Expert Access

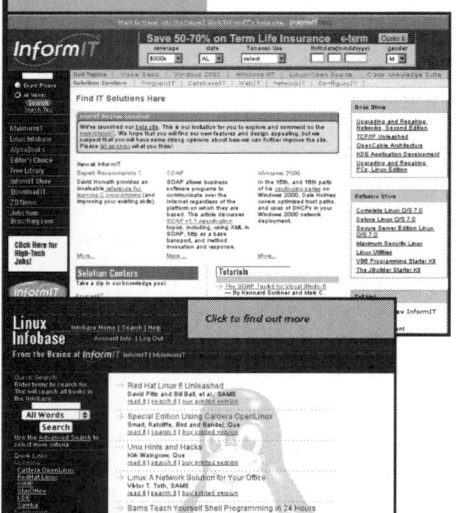

Free Content

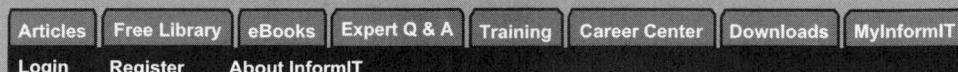

Solutions from experts you know and trust.

✓ Free, in-depth articles and supplements

✓ Master the skills you need, when you need them

✓ Choose from industry leading books, ebooks, and training products

✓ Get answers when you need them—from live experts or InformIT's comprehensive library

✓ Achieve industry certification and advance your career

Visit *InformIT* today

www.informit.com

InformIT is a trademark of Pearson plc /
Copyright © 2000 Pearson